THE TRADITIONS OF
EUROPEAN LITERATURE

From Homer to Dante

VOLUME I

Barrett Wendell

THE TRADITIONS
OF
EUROPEAN LITERATURE

From Homer to Dante

Volume I

THE TRADITIONS OF
GREECE AND ROME

FREDERICK UNGAR PUBLISHING CO.
New York

Republished 1964

First published 1920

Printed in the United States of America

Library of Congress Catalog Card No. 64-15702

NOTE

Separately to acknowledge my debts to the friends, colleagues, and assistants who have helped this book take form would at once demand undue space and perhaps now and then commit them to views other than their own. I cannot refrain, however, from expressing my gratitude to Mr. Charles Knowles Bolton, of the Boston Athenæum, for his constant and considerate kindness during the seasons when I have written there almost daily. The preparation of the Bibliographic Suggestions was originally undertaken by Dr. Frederic Schenck. After his untimely death it was taken up by Mr. Daniel Sargent. When Mr. Sargent was called to Europe, it was completed by Mr. Edward Motley Pickman, who has also made the Index. I cannot too heartily acknowledge my deep sense of what they have done for me; nor too gravely express the sorrow brought to all his friends by Frederic Schenck's death. If I felt sure that the book deserved such honour, it should be dedicated to his brave and happy memory.

B. W.

Portsmouth, New Hampshire
15 August, 1920.

CONTENTS

BOOK V

THE TRADITIONS OF THE MIDDLE AGES

THE TRADITIONS OF EUROPEAN LITERATURE

INTRODUCTION

Though this book is intended for general readers, it originated in lectures given at Harvard College between 1904 and 1917. Years of dealing with Harvard students had shown me not only that Americans now know little of the literary traditions of our ancestral Europe, but also that they are seldom aware even of the little they know. Beginning with no more clear purpose than to help these needs, I gradually came to see my object more definitely; it was at once to revive knowledge which was sinking beneath the level of consciousness, to indicate the gaps which each man must supply for himself, and to encourage in all the habit of so thinking things together instead of scrutinising them apart that each might gradually come habitually to see in perspective whatever he might know or learn about the traditions, historic and literary, which have accompanied our civilisation to the point where we are part of it.

This task is so obviously beyond the power of any modern scholar that it mercifully limits itself. Nobody can fully have mastered even all the languages involved, not to speak of the erudition in which centuries have enshrouded unnumbered facts concerning them and the matters

they set forth. All we can attempt is to take a
recognised point of view and to give account of
what thence remains visible. Our own point of
view is fixed by the accident that we are English-
speaking Americans of the Twentieth Century of
the Christian Era. The traditions of history and
literature consequently ours are evidently those
which, we need not ask why, have chanced among
ourselves to survive the times of their origin. The
test of such survival must soon become fairly
clear: it has little to do with their positive value
or their actual truth; it is whether they have so
endured that Englishmen and Americans of general culture may now hold them proper matters
of literary allusion. If so, we may rightly dwell
on them as much as may be; if not, whatever
their importance in other schemes than ours, we
may contentedly neglect them.

The moment we thus approach our subject,
one welcome condition of it appears. If only because human beings have so long been aware of
what we touch on, the matters before us would
have relative importance. So far as these matters
are literary, they prove on even slight scrutiny to
have positive importance. A pleasantly reassur-
ing fact in the history of human expression is that
the names and the works which have survived
have done so largely because, though each originally came to light in historical conditions as
distinct as those which surround us now, each
has proved, when its original surroundings have
faded, to appeal for one reason or another to
generations widely different from that which it
chanced to address in the flesh. It has thereby
proved itself more enduring than any contempo-

rary could confidently have asserted it; something in its substance, or in its form, or oftener in both, has such general human interest as to be independent of momentary limitation. Thus the classics, ancient and modern, have slowly revealed themselves as standards of perception; whoever comes to know them has a measure by which he can test or correct his impulsive judgment concerning new works of literature, or works presented to him for the first time. Even cursory glances at classics may therefore provide men with perhaps the most fundamental element of culture.

Just as the purpose of this book defined itself slowly, and consequently in the most natural way, so did the method. To treat any considerable subject intelligently, one must somehow arrange it under definite headings or—to use a convenient big word—categories. These categories may take any form; and in recent times they have often taken forms which, however agreeable to the habitual thought of their makers, turn out to be arbitrary or at least debatable; even poetry and prose, for example, are less easy to separate than you would guess until you try to draw a sharp line between them. Common sense is enough to assure us that the more nearly categories follow the habit of human thought, and thus agree with facts assumed by everybody, the more easily they can be remembered, the more firmly grasped, and the more confidently thought with. Among the few definite facts in human record are those of chronology. Though the groups of years which we call centuries are doubtless arbitrary, the centuries have two pervasive characteristics of their own: each is long enough to be at least as distinct from the others as human beings are in their successive generations; and whoever lives in any century not only inevitably knows the circumstances of his earthly surroundings, but is thought of and remembered by later times in more or less intimate connection with them. For such purpose as ours, therefore, the safest categories are the indisputable categories of the centuries.

The moment one begins thus to arrange the traditions of European literature, two or three facts about them clearly appear. In the first place, these traditions, originating in the primal European civilisation of Greece, and extending throughout the imperial dominion of Rome, remained for many centuries a common possession of all Europe. This phase of them may be held to culminate in the Divine Comedy of Dante—the earliest European masterpiece cf literature expressed in any other language than Greek or Latin. The point of view there assumed Dante states in his opening line,

> Nel mezzo del cammin di nostra vita,
> (Just midway in the journey of our life),

to be precisely that of the year 1300. In the second place, all subsequent traditions of European literature have been not universally European but specifically national, and set forth in extant modern languages, of which the most important are French, Italian, English, Spanish, and German. Thus our subject divides itself into two distinct parts, clearly different from each other.   From the Fifth Century before Christ to the Thirteenth of the Christian Era, we may properly consider it as on the whole single and complete; from 1300 to the present time, it is not only diverse, but in many aspects, divergent, and the literatures concerned are still in progressive, independent, and interacting existence. These two clearly separate phases of our subject may most conveniently be treated separately. In the third place, when we confine our attention to what chronologically belongs in the first phase, it proves to fall into fairly definite successive groups, each virtually at an end before its successor comes into existence.   Broadly speaking, the highly localised and specific traditions of Greece stop with the Second Century before Christ; those of Rome, less excellent if you like, but vastly more extensive, begin with the First Century before Christ, and persist in their antique purity no longer than the end of the Second Century of our Christian Era; those of what we vaguely name the Dark and the Middle Ages, sharply distinguished from the earlier by the intermingling with European traditions of the originally Asiatic traditions of Christianity, ensue—marking the long transition from antiquity to modernity. Yet throughout, each century sees the past in an increasingly remote perspective, each adding to our traditional heritage new traditions of its own.

The plan of our work, to the year 1300, accordingly defines itself.   Assuming the categories of the centuries as its general basis, and asking ourselves what of our traditions each century or group of centuries inherited from its past and what each added to its future, we can hardly help setting forth our subject in five successive parts or books: I. The Traditions of Greece; II. The Traditions of Rome; III. The Traditions of Christianity; IV. The Traditions of Christendom; and, V. The Traditions of the Middle Ages.

BOOK I

THE TRADITIONS OF GREECE

PART I

THE TRADITIONS OF SCIENCE

CHAPTER I

TO 500 BEFORE CHRIST

I

HISTORICAL TRADITIONS

Though few could readily define what the word
European means, when applied to a subject so
broad and so vague as traditions, almost everybody can feel with something like certainty its
general significance. The ruins of Egypt, for
example, and the sculpture and the painting
which have been found among them are not
European; no more is what travellers find in
India, ancient or modern; no more are the temples or the admirable fine art of China or of
Japan. The Book of the Dead is as alien to
Europe as are the hieroglyphics in which it is
written. So are Sanskrit hymns, and Confucian
precepts, and the story of the Forty-Seven Ronins.
So, indeed, when we come to scrutinise familiar
things, a candid mind must probably find even
the moods and the expressions recorded for us in
the Bible; otherwise we could hardly have that
sense of illumination cast by a few days in the
Near East on the scriptural stories which we half
thought we wholly understood. On the other
hand there are relics of long-past times which
any European or American must instantly feel
comparatively his own. The forms of Grecian
temples and of Roman arches or amphitheatres
still affect our architecture; we still make statues

after the manner which was first clearly defined
in Periclean Athens; we think in terms like those
idiomatic in Rome and in Greece, as distinguished
from those in which Egyptians thought or the
diverse peoples of Asia. Our religious history
has doubtless made the Old Testament vastly
more familiar to twelve or fifteen of our ancestral
centuries than we can ever again find the Odyssey.
Yet whoever will take the trouble to read, side
by side, the Book of Ruth and the story of Nau-
sicaa[1] will probably come to feel, perhaps with
surprise, that Ruth was written ages ago by some
one whose nature was far less like ours than was
the nature of the poet who ages ago set down the
story of the Phæacian girl, at play with her hand-
maids.   Though such reflections as these may not
carry us far towards the precision of definition,
they can hardly help even better serving our present purpose; for they will bring us to a point where,
without troubling ourselves about definitions, we
can clearly perceive that for us the word European
generally means something directly ancestral to
ourselves.

As soon as we come to this understanding, another fact must grow clear.   The first records of
such expression as we now call European are by
no means so general in character as that word
has become and must inevitably remain.   Rather
they are extremely local.   Centuries and centuries
ago there chanced to develop in the southeastern-
most region of Europe a civilisation and a language
not originally extensive, but clearly different from
any other which had hitherto existed.   Though
it hardly came to what we should now call fully

[1] Odyssey, VI.

developed political existence, though it was cen-
tred not in an organised state, but in many and
widely various cities most of which controlled no
great extent of the territory about them, and
though, indeed, it flourished quite as much on
the Asiatic as on the European shores of the
Ægean Sea, it gradually became something which
made those who possessed it think of themselves,
despite their incessant mutual conflicts, as distinct
from others. They were Greeks; all the rest of
the world—North, South, East, and West—was
barbarian, babbling in terms unintelligible to the
cultivated ear. Whatever Greece may be now,
there were ages between antiquity and these times
of ours when Greece was living Greece no more,
when the spirit and the heritage of its traditions
persisted, if at all, only in regions which to ancient
Greeks would have been vaguely and negligibly
barbarous. The course of time, however, has
proved the originally peculiar civilisation of Greece
and the traditions which it came to cherish historically ancestral, like nothing else, to every phase
of the development of Europe. Thither, most of
all, we must look to see whence, in almost everything but the body, we ourselves came.

So looking, one historical date soon shows itself truly as important as mere tradition has
made it seem to careless moods. In the year
500 before Christ, Greece already existed, and
already possessed traditions, both historical and
literary, which have never quite faded from European memory. At that time, the existence of
Greece, and with it the future, if not the existence,
of its traditions, was threatened by an Asiatic
power whose civilisation was what the Greeks

called barbarous and we should call alien. If the Persian wars of the first twenty years of the Fifth Century before Christ had overwhelmed Greece, as some three hundred years later Carthage was overwhelmed by Rome, there might doubtless have survived antique records of what Greece had been, but these would have survived in something other than the Europe which has ensued through twenty-five hundred years. The whole northern half of the Eastern Hemisphere might rather have developed under such conditions as we now think Asiatic. The relics of Greece, in such event, might at best have seemed remote, fragmentary, and broken, like those of Twelfth Century Provence through the seven centuries which now separate us from the Albigensian crusade. Both historically and in literature, nevertheless, something might probably have remained. We shall see our way most clearly through the periods which are to follow, if we begin by asking ourselves what that something would probably have been.

At least a little while ago, the Wonder Book of Hawthorne and his Tanglewood Tales were familiar in American nurseries, and with them the stories of Perseus, Andromeda and Medusa, of Midas, of Pandora, of Hercules and some of his labours, of Bellerophon, of Theseus and the Minotaur, of Cadmus, of Jason and the Golden Fleece, and more. Thus told, in staid New England terms, diluted from the voluptuous Latin of Ovid, they might well have seemed as odd to a Fifth Century Greek as we find old German pictures of the Garden of Eden, where Adam and Eve, with no clothes to speak of, have a stolid Nuremberg house to sleep in. But just as, unlike the Greeks, none of us would have the shadow of doubt as to who Adam and Eve were, so your Greek would have known, long before the Persian Wars, who the heroes were, and the worthies, and the monsters—man-bulls and winged horses—that Hawthorne has made or kept freshly familiar for us. This body of heroic legend is compactly and systematically summarised in the third chapter of the French History of Ancient Greece written as a school-book by Monsieur Charles Seignobos. Just as it stays ancestral to us, it was ancestral, and nationally ancestral, to historic Greece.

In the year 500 historic Greece was by no means confined to the region which has borne and bears its name. Its commercial energy had led to wide colonial expansion in every direction where the shipping of that period could regularly proceed. To confine ourselves to what subsequently became Europe, Sicily was virtually Greek, and Southern Italy. The city we now call Naples, for example, was already Neapolis—which is literally the Greek for Newtown, or Newton. Massillia existed— to this day called Marseilles—establishing a civilisation which was never to be wholly broken at the mouth of the Rhone. The temples of Paestum and of Girgenti still stand, ruinous and solitary, to show what the monuments were like in dozens of colonial cities once throbbing with Greek life. These colonial regions, however, bore to Greece itself some such relation as that of America, during its first four centuries, to the Europe from which its own civilisation has been so lately derived. Though they were not alien to Greece, like the antique and rigid civilisation of Egypt or of Assyria, or like the crescent empire of Persia they were something else and newer than the central origin from which all had sprung.

Apart from its community of language and of tradition, meanwhile, Greece had not developed into what we should now call national unity. It virtually consisted of a number of distinct cities, each controlling more or less adjacent territory, each tenacious of its own political and local traditions, and all disposed to incessant and intriguing quarrel. They had certain common grounds of meeting, such as the oracular Sanctuary of Delphi, or the templed plain of Olympia where they came together for some of their athletic contests. In general, however, each thought first of itself, and next of how to down its neighbours. Among them already two or three emerged to stay more memorable in tradition than the rest. Thebes had been the legendary home of Cadmus and of Œdipus. Sparta, whence the Trojan Paris had fled with Helen, the half-divine queen of Menelaus, stayed monarchic, military, more conservative, and more compactly powerful than any of the others. Athens, the city of Ægeus and of Theseus, and the principal shrine of the goddess Athene from whom its name was traditionally derived—though for centuries Europe was apt to call her rather by her Latin name of Minerva— loomed already to the front as the chief centre of Greek intelligence and Greek expression. It is from Athens, accordingly, or at least through Athens, that the Greek traditions mostly came which have remained the common possession of subsequent Europe. The word *acropolis*, for example, is the Greek name for *citadel*—a general term for that part of any Greek city which domi-

nated the rest of it and was most securely fortified.
To us, however, it chiefly means, as it meant to
the Athenians, their own local stronghold, still
grand with the ruin of their special shrine, the
Parthenon. So, whatever the actual history of the
Greeks before the year 500, we traditionally think
of it in something like Attic terms. Outlying antiquity—Egypt and Assyria, Babylon and Nineveh,
the shadowy legends of Crete—seems not only
remote, but alien. Sparta, still loyal to the already venerable polity of Lycurgus and generally
dominant to the southward, seems vaguely threatening to the institutions ancestral to ourselves.
The pitiless code of Draco, the shrewd wisdom
of Solon, the benevolent tyranny of Pisistratus,
weakening into the self-indulgence of Hippias
and Hipparchus overthrown by the liberty-loving
outbreak of Harmodius and Aristogiton, seem
comparatively our own. So does the restlessly
intelligent succession of incessant political experiment, tending further and further from the
restraints of monarchy and of aristocracy to the
untested license of democracy.

All this, no doubt, is now far away. Even now,
however, we are dimly aware of it. We are dimly
aware, as well, of other traditions existing along
with it—of the Seven Wise Men, for example,
and some of their precepts, such as "Know thyself" and "Nothing beyond measure." What
remains more distinct among the relics of that
olden time is the literature which had already
come into its Greek existence, and which persists
to this day. Of this the chief works, already immemorially antique, were the Iliad and the
Odyssey.

II

HOMER

By the beginning of the Fifth Century, the Iliad and the Odyssey were already, as they have always remained, traditionally ascribed to Homer. Who Homer was, too, when he lived, and where, had even then become matters of dispute. We need not trouble ourselves with the controversy. Whether he ever actually existed or not, whether the two great poems which bear his name are by the same hand,[1] on what lost ballads or court poems they may perhaps have been based, and all the other myriad and unprovable conjectures about them are not really our concern. Just as the Bible has existed and exists for Christendom, so Homer existed for historic Greece—remote, antique, perennial, and familiar. His language, like that of Scripture for us, was no longer such as men used in daily life, and indeed may have been not quite such as they had ever used; nevertheless, partly by reason of its own existence, it was permanently and superbly comprehensible. Above all the rhythmic sweep of it had fixed the hexameter as the primal idiom of heroic expression for antique Europe.

Few if any modern languages can be forced into this metrical form. If we may trust those who know most of the matter, indeed, no modern ear can quite unhesitatingly imagine how the hex-

[1] The late Samuel Butler, an ingenious Englishman just now rather admired, believed the Odyssey to have been written by a youngish woman of Trapani, in Sicily, where a public place has consequently been named for him.

ameter line sounded to the Greeks. It seems to
have depended on two circumstances both no
longer familiar—the fact that a long vowel was
dwelt on perceptibly longer than a short, and the
fact that the modification of sound later indicated
by Greek accents was not a stress, such as modern
European ears are used to, but a modulation of
the voice, raised or lowered a note or so above or
below the normal pitch. The nearest approach
to the consequent effect now to be heard anywhere is probably the traditional chanting of
Sanskrit hymns in certain Buddhist ceremonies
of China, and other Asiatic regions. The hexameter line may nevertheless be somehow pronounced in the stressed and emphatic accents
demanded by modern habit; and a couplet of
Coleridge—"The Homeric Hexameter Described
and Exemplified" [1]—beautifully tells what this
poetic line has come to be for us:

Strongly it bears us along in swelling and limitless billows,
Nothing before and nothing behind but the sky and the
    ocean.

Every line of Homer can still be read in this swift,
sustained manner.

This vehicle, of course, was not peculiar to
Homer, any more than the most idiomatic poetic
line in English—the line common to blank verse,
the sonnet, the heroic couplet, and other technical
forms—is peculiar to any one English poet.
Traditionally, however, the hexameter was most
familiar, and therefore most enduringly influential, in the Iliad and the Odyssey. Nothing could

[1] He translated this, I am told, from Schiller. Whether Schiller invented
it I have not inquired.

better have suited the swift, simple, noble mood of their sustained though excursive narrative. In substance they detail two long episodes from the legendary—and perhaps vaguely historic—story of the Trojan War. The outline of this story was familiar to all historic Greece, and stays so everywhere. Paris, one of the numerous princely sons of Priam, King of Troy,—or Ilium, as the Greeks called it,—was asked by three goddesses to award to one of them the prize of supreme beauty. After the artless manner of unsophisticated nature, each offered him a bribe—one wisdom, another power, and the third the love of women. He chose the third. As a result he incurred the displeasure of Hera, or Juno, the mistress of power, and of Athene, or Minerva, the mistress of wisdom; but under the protection of Aphrodite, or Venus, the mistress of love, he presently eloped from Sparta to Troy with Helen, the most beautiful of all women, and the wife of the Spartan King, Menelaus. Menelaus proceeded to collect his fellow Greek princes, who resented his treatment, and they all went to Troy, with a view of reclaiming Helen. The Trojans resisted their claims; the consequent war, in which the two offended goddesses favoured the Greek side, lasted ten years. In the end Troy fell; and Helen, duly captured, went back to Sparta, where she ended her days in peaceful conjugal respectability.

The two great poems of Homer, though they do not tell the whole story, assume or imply it throughout. The Iliad relates, in extreme detail, how Achilles, on the whole the most formidable Grecian warrior, displeased by deprival of an engaging Trojan captive, withdrew for a while from combat, to

the great disadvantage of the Greeks; and how at
last, enraged by the death in battle of his dearest
friend Patroclus, he resumed his arms and over-
came Hector, the eldest and most eminent of the
Trojan princes. All through the Iliad the war is
at its height. In the Odyssey the war is ended.
Troy has fallen, and the victorious Greek princes
have betaken themselves home. The course of
one of them, Odysseus, or Ulysses, King of Ithaca,
is long and perilous. At last he is landed, alone
and unrecognised, on the shores of his country,
where his faithful wife, Penelope, long supposed
widowed, has been beset by inconveniently im-
portunate suitors. These he presently does to
death, and resumes his sovereign and marital
rights. His journeyings have led him through all
manner of regions and adventures, legendary and
human. Just as the scene of the Iliad is fixed,
that of the Odyssey is shifting, wandering, panoramic; in the Iliad the heroic life of the Trojan
conflict is in its full flush, in the Odyssey it is
already an heroic memory.

Though to feel anything like the complete effect
of these poems, throbbing with life in every incident they dwell on, and inexhaustible in their implication of antecedents and surroundings, one
must read them through and often—though, indeed, their full glory begins to fade as soon as
one forgets the surgent splendour of their hexameter rhythm—three comparatively short passages
will give, even in translation, an impression of
what is to be found there. The first consists of
the beginning of the Iliad, to the fifty-second line,
pungent with the smoke of the pyres which con-
sume the Grecian dead, slain by pestilential shafts

from the clanging silver bow of Apollo. Here one instantly feels the supreme simplicity and swiftness of this pristine poetic method, its matchless freedom from self-consciousness, and its unsurpassed precision of imagination. Even though Homer sometimes nods, these qualities pervade his work from beginning to end.

The second is an episode in the Third Book of the Iliad, beginning with the line (121) where Iris comes to summon Helen, and ending with the mournfully tender lines (243-4) which tell how, unknown to her, Castor and Pollux, her brothers, lie deep in the life-bearing earth of their own dear country, Lacedæmon. There is a short armistice. Priam with Trojan elders about him looks down from the walls of his besieged city and sees the Grecian captains, for a little while at rest from war in what one feels to be breezy sunshine. He asks Helen who this warrior may be, and that; she tells him, knowing them all. And as you read you can hardly help imagining them still alive. Among them is Odysseus, not tall but broad-breasted, deep-voiced, and wily. No single passage more wonderfully summarises the freshness of conception which makes one feel these heroes as real to-day as they were when poetry first brought them into being, centuries before Athens was historic.

The third passage is much longer; but, as we shall see, it has chanced to have such direct influence on subsequent literature that, even for no other reason, it would be worth reading through. It is the Eleventh Book of the Odyssey, which contains only six hundred and forty lines. In the course of his wanderings, Odysseus is cast

alone on the coast of Phæecia. There received by
King Alcinous, he tells at great length what has
happened to him since Troy fell; and the adventure he describes in the Eleventh Book is very
distinct. Freed from the enchantments of Circe,
he is bidden consult the shade of the blind prophet
Tiresias as to how he may finally make his way
back to Ithaca. To do so he sails westward,
through seas unknown to men, until he reaches
the shadowy shores beneath which the dead lurk.
He makes sacrifice, filling a trench with the
blood of sheep; and the spirits swarm up to
drink it, and thus regain for an instant some
semblance of life. He sees Tiresias, and has his
counsel. He sees, too, countless shades from times
olden even to him; and mingled with them he
sees and talks with shades of those whom he has
known in life—his mother, and Agamemnon, and
Achilles, and more. Of all the heroes who a little
while ago were alive in the Trojan sunshine, he
alone is surely living here. Most of the rest are
already shadows, memories, no longer heroic
facts but immortally heroic traditions, merging
with the older traditions of their own antiquity.
Even for its contrast with the glowing actuality
of the Iliad, this book would stay wondrous. For
us, it has another significance as well. Without it,
we should never have had the Sixth Book of
Virgil's Æneid; and without that, no small part
of Dante's Divine Comedy would hardly have
taken the form in which it lives and moves.

Familiar to Fifth Century Greece as Scriptural
story to Christian Europe, or as the Bible to
Protestant England, the Iliad and the Odyssey
might probably have persisted even though the

Persian Wars had swept Greece from existence. If so, they would have been lasting records not of what Europe and European tradition have grown to be, but of the pristine mood from which, through the centuries, Europe and its traditions have developed. Between the fall of the Roman Empire and the period which we now call the Renaissance, there were hundreds of years when the Greek language was virtually unknown in Western Europe. There has never been a generation, however, to which the name of Homer was not familiar as the first and therefore the most enduring of Grecian poets, nor yet a generation to whom countless names which first spring to life in his poems would have been altogether strange. In later Europe, no doubt, Achilles and Agamemnon, Menelaus and Helen and Paris, Priam and Hecuba, Hector and Andromache, Odysseus and Penelope and Telemachus, Polyphemus, Circe, Calypso, and the Sirens—to go no further—may often have meant, and may often mean, little enough; they can never have meant, however, or mean so little as names altogether alien to our ancestral traditions—Seti, for example, of Egypt, Vishnu or Gautama of India, Jimmu Tenno of Japan. Since the Revival of Learning made Greek once more familiar, bringing back to knowledge the source whence these traditions were poured, two features of the Iliad and the Odyssey have grown increasingly clear.

The first is chiefly of historic interest. Whoever made them, and however they are made, they fixed, long before authentic history began, the epic idiom of Europe. What we mean by epic poetry is doubtless hard to define, but not to

feel. When heroic story is told in terms themselves heroic, the task is done; all that is left for us
is to listen. So far as we are concerned now, if we
have a shade of doubt as to what we mean, it is
enough to glance once more at that passage from
the Third Book of the Iliad; as Homer told his
story there, so Europe has instinctively tended to
tell heroic story ever since. In that passage,
however, we can instantly see at least two literary
devices, Homerically normal, which would hardly
have occurred to any poet of much later times.
One appears at the very beginning, where the
goddess Iris comes, in the form of Laodice, to
summon Helen to the wall of Troy: this antique
world is at once human and superhuman. Deities
and men still mingle together—as the Lord God
walked in Eden when Adam and Eve hid there.
The second device is more formal. When Helen
comes within earshot of the old men who cluster
about Priam, there is a famous simile to describe
the cracked utterance of senility: "Like grass-
hoppers that in a wood sit on a tree and utter
their lily-like voice"—a reedy chirp is what the
words mean—"even so sat the elders of the Trojans upon the tower." Because in Homer gods
and men appear together, and similes are elaborately stated, so you will find things in Virgil,
deliberately following literary conventions instinctively established ages before; and from
Virgil these devices have been copied or adapted,
again and again, at least till the days of Camoens
and those of Milton; and Fielding burlesqued
them in Tom Jones, under King George the
Second. When anything has once been excellently
done, nobody can again attempt the like without

some fettering consciousness of the masterpiece he would imitate or rival. One refreshing merit of Homer is that throughout his work you somehow feel what appears like blissful freedom from any inhibitory models. Despite the conventional fixity of his epithets, and other details which imply antecedent custom, he never seems consciously hampered by academically fixed types of expression; he rather seems eager only to make his words fit his meaning. Thereby he unwittingly creates a type of expression never thenceforth to be quite ignored.

The second feature of the Iliad and the Odyssey which is now as clear as their historic importance is perhaps the deepest and the surest proof of why they are great. Fully to feel it, you must come to know at least a little of them in the original Greek. To do something like this is not so hard as it might seem. They have been frequently translated; and each translation is of course a fresh effort to render their meaning and their spirit clearer to the unlearned than it has been before. The first enduring English translation is that of Chapman, made under Queen Elizabeth and James I; the most nearly popular is probably still that of Pope, made in George the First's time; as both of these are rhymed, it is well to compare with them a translation in that English form, blank verse, which English custom has now made our idiomatic vehicle of heroic poetry—Cowper's, or Bryant's, or Lord Derby's; and, to remind ourselves that none of these metrical versions has any metrical likeness to the hexameter, it is well, in addition, to glance at a prose translation—such as those in which Andrew Lang collaborated with Butcher and with Leaf and Myers. Take whatever passage you choose—the three on which we have already touched, or any of them, will serve. Read it in all four English versions, remembering that different as the versions may seem each stands for the same great original; and the composite effect will begin to give you a growing sense of what that original is like. Then, if you know your Greek alphabet, and have even a slight notion of hexameter rhythm, turn to the original lines; at least here and there, they will suddenly flash into the fulness of life which each separate version has attempted and variously failed to reproduce. Each time you thus recur to them, you will find in them a quality which will impress you the more the better you know them. No matter how familiar they may become, it is hardly possible to read them without a sense that they are always as new as if you had never read them before. Age cannot wither nor custom stale them.

Some such quality, no doubt, pervades all enduring literature, at least for those who love it; and most lovers of literature, having their special favourites, will now and again find it in works and men where it is not quite apparent to everybody. The more widely and certainly it is recognised anywhere, the more assured you may be that the work or the man thus appealing to humanity through the ages is great. To be so beyond dispute it must be sanctioned by the consent of the generations. Thus tested, two comparatively modern poets slowly but admirably emerge as somehow greater than the rest—the Italian Dante and the English Shakspere. In all antiquity, their only incontestable fellow is Homer; in European literature, as in the untortured region of the Divine Comedy[1] where, pagan and unredeemed, antique worthies forever long for that salvation which is hopelessly denied them, Homer stays first of poets still. Dante never knew him in the Greek. It is only since the Fourteenth Century that Greek has been brought back to European life. From the moment that it was, there has been increasing consent that here the tradition which Dante accepted was profoundly right. Great though other antique poets be, Homer—swiftly, simply, nobly primal—is greatest.

He has created, or at least brought into permanent being, many now traditional characters: Achilles, for example, and Hector, and Penelope, and Odysseus, to go no further. As we consider these, and those with whom they mingle, and the world about them all, one phase of their primality grows increasingly clear. They are full-grown men and women, who live amid conditions as normal to them as conditions of our own time are to us. The great difference between them and any such men and women as now cluster about us lies in the fact that, for all their years, sometimes running into age, they have qualities, hard to define but easy to feel, which resemble those of modern savages or modern children. Although their dignity is incontestably heroic, it resembles rather the dignity of babies, or of naked Islanders, or even of the higher animals, than that of civilised later Europe. Their passions and their reasoning are European, but not those of European maturity. Not children themselves, they combine

[1] Inferno, IV.

implicitly to set forth Europe in its world infancy. This is what Homer records.

Just how the work which traditionally bears his name was preserved is not certain. The form in which we now possess it is based on that sanctioned by the critical scholars of Alexandria, two or three centuries before Christ. By that time, it had long been reduced to writing; but whether writing was in literary existence when the poems were made has been disputed. Very probably they were for an indefinite period transmitted orally, through professional reciters, bards, or whatever you choose to call these antique protagonists of publishers and libraries. All this makes less difference than we should now be apt thoughtlessly to suppose. Printing has for centuries made literature and other forms of written language so increasingly copious that we instinctively assume them to be addressed primarily to the eye. Even lyric poetry, of which the soul is the sound, we rarely read aloud to ourselves. Throughout European antiquity, the case was different. In the Confessions of St. Augustine there is a casual passage which goes to the heart of the matter. Augustine was a highly cultivated man of the Fourth and Fifth Centuries of the Christian Era—a professor of rhetoric, or literature as we might now called it, at a period when not only the great literature of Greece but also that of Rome had long been complete. Writing about the habits of St. Ambrose in his study at Milan, he specially notes that "when he was reading, he drew his eyes along over the leaves, and his heart reached into the sense, but his voice and tongue were silent." [1] Even so

[1] St. Augustine: Confessions, VI, iii (ed. Loeb, 273).

late as when all pagan antiquity was virtually a
thing of the past, the notion that any page could
be read inaudibly was not instantly familiar to
an accomplished university man, concerned with
letters from his childhood.   Throughout the whole
course of antique literature in both Greece and
Rome, any written text was assumed to be of the
nature which we still recognise in a musical score;
its primary task was not to convey meaning, but
to indicate to the eye the sounds by which meaning might presently be conveyed to the ear.   A
manuscript was hardly more than a memorandum,
which should assure textual accuracy of utterance.
Some faint trace of this once universal practice
may still haunt our fancy when we read the pages
of plays, of sermons, or of public speeches.   So the
lines with which Andrew Lang closes the sonnet
prefatory to the translation in which he had his
part are hardly figurative;   he is almost literal
when, touching on those who turn back to Homer
even now, he says:

> They hear like ocean on a western beach
> The surge and thunder of the Odyssey.

III

THE LOST EPICS AND HESIOD

How remote Homer already seemed to Fifth
Century Greece is curiously implied in a tradition
related by Herodotus.[1]   Not very long after the
death of Lycurgus, who is supposed to have
flourished about the Ninth Century before Christ,

[1] I, 67–8.

the Spartans were informed by an oracle that if
they wished to get the better of the Tegeans,
in Arcadia, they must remove to Sparta the bones
of Orestes, son of Agamemnon. Where his bones
lay the Spartans did not know. A Spartan who
chanced to visit Tegea was surprised to find there
a smith working in iron—a detail which, although
iron occurs in Homer, implies the legend to have
come from a time when iron was a novelty, and
bronze the usual base metal. The smith happened
garrulously to mention that he had lately un-
earthed some gigantic bones, evidently from an age
more heroic in stature than his own. The Spartan,
finding the circumstances to fit certain obscure
parts of the oracular utterance, assumed the
bones to be those of Orestes, adroitly managed
to get hold of them, and brought them to Sparta.
Whereupon the Spartans became habitually victorious over the Tegeans; so they were as sure of
their Orestean relics as ever Venetians were of
St. Mark's.

Though this story, of course, throws no manner
of light on the question of when Homer made his
poems, it clearly places in an extremely distant
past the incidents and the characters he touches
on. In the Eleventh Book of the Odyssey, for
example (l. 461), the shade of Agamemnon refers
to Orestes as still probably living; he was too
young anyway to have gone to the Trojan War.
And Homer's instinctive objectivity seems on the
whole to set forth human life in terms of his
own day—much as the maker of Chevy Chase
does when compared with the conscious antiquari-
anism of Scott. Whatever else, the Trojan War as
Homer tells of it seems contemporary, and as

Herodotus alludes to it seems already almost as ancient as it seems to us.

During this indefinitely long interval, a considerable amount of other Greek literature had come into being, still more or less known by name. Little of it, however, has been preserved; and the chief importance of that little is that it confirms the supremacy of the Iliad and the Odyssey. To begin with, such masterpieces as these would in any event imply the existence of what may be called a school about them—just as the masterpieces of Shakspere, even if no other trace of the great period of English drama were left us, would imply that he was chiefly master of his art because his art was there to be mastered. On the lesser epics than Homer's we need hardly touch; some of them are said to have concerned other episodes of the Trojan War than those with which he dealt; another, or others, which dealt with the story of Thebes, have an accidental importance because they became sources of lasting tragedies during the Fifth Century at Athens. In any special treatment of Greek literature these would need attention. Here, concerned chiefly with the literary traditions of Europe, we need only mention that minor epics once existed.

We must linger longer, however, over the didactic poet whose name the Fifth Century had already come traditionally to group with Homer's. A familiar passage in Herodotus[1] mentions Hesiod and Homer as if they had been contemporaries, four hundred years or so before the words were written. Nothing could more distinctly indicate how completely traditional, as distinguished from

[1] II, 53.

historical, both of these names had already become by the Fifth Century. We have already
reminded ourselves that there is a reasonable
doubt as to whether such an individual as Homer
ever existed; if he did, nobody can ever be sure
exactly when he flourished. The one certainty
is that the poems attributed to him somehow
emerged from the depth of Grecian antiquity.
With Hesiod, the case is different. Though his
dates may be doubtful, we can hardly doubt either
that there once was such a man, or that he lived
pretty obscurely in the region of Mount Helicon,
or that the personal details which occasionally
appear in his work are on the whole genuine. An
almost inevitable inference is that, even though
the Homeric poems may have taken their final
form somewhere about Hesiod's time, they originated earlier. The surviving poems attributed
to Hesiod, indeed, are comparatively personal,
and therefore distinctly later in character. He is
now conjectured to have flourished during the
second half of the Eighth Century.

Compared with Homer, his work is not copious,
and certainly is not entertaining. It consists of
two didactic poems, called the Works and Days
and the Theogony, and of a fragment concerning the Shield of Hercules. All three are in
hexameter verse, and the purpose of the first two
is primarily instructive. A familiar passage in
the Theogony (26-28) may be taken to signify
that the Muses, generally occupied in making fic-
tions sound like truths, are equally disposed to
inspire poets who prefer to express truth directly.
The Theogony proceeds compactly to set forth
the genealogy of the gods, and such matters.

The Works and Days, in which there is more or less personal detail concerning legal disputes between Hesiod and his brother Perses, contains considerable ethical matter, sometimes epigrammatic in proverbial conciseness, and a good deal of precise advice about methods of agriculture. Perhaps the most familiar legend contained in this poem is the story of Pandora and the caskets, which occurs near the beginning. Neither this nor the much more extensive agricultural passages are in themselves impressively memorable. What makes the latter deserve our attention for a moment is hardly more than that they happened, centuries later, to inspire the Georgics of Virgil. In Augustan Rome, as in the Athens of Herodotus, Homer and Hesiod were the two first great poetic names of traditional Greek antiquity. Virgil tried to rival Homer in the Æneid, and to rival Hesiod in the Georgics. Whatever his success, there can be no doubt that the Æneid has never obscured the Iliad or the Odyssey, but that without the Georgics, held by many lovers of Virgil his highest technical achievement, the Works and Days might very likely have been virtually forgotten. Through the Georgics, Hesiod has had an evident influence on later literature; without them he would probably have had little. As surely as epic narrative makes permanent appeal to human beings, so didactic admonition—however admirable it may be—has the fatal fault of generally boring them.

There were other traditional names in the times of Herodotus besides those of Homer and Hesiod; among them was that of Æsop, often attached to fables even still, though none of the work origi-

nally attributed to him survives. For our present
purposes these lesser facts may generally be neglected. The true thing for us to remember is that
if the Persians had overcome Greece in the early
years of the Fifth Century there might always have
remained from what was by that time immemorial
Greek antiquity at least two still extant records,
in hexameter verse, of what Greece might have
been—the supreme epic poetry of Homer, and the
far less stirring didactic poetry of Hesiod.

IV

LYRIC POETRY

To Fifth Century Greece, Homer and Hesiod
were already traditional, prehistoric. They did
not comprise, however, all the literature which it
inherited and has transmitted to us. By the
year 500 another kind of poetry, some later
phases of which were then contemporary, had
produced masterpieces of its own, to this day
unsurpassed. The names of its chief masters remain familiar, but hardly their actual work; for
its excellence was of a kind completely beyond the
resources of translation, and since ancient times
general readers have seldom known enough to
enjoy the original Greek.

Though the name—lyric—by which we now
describe this later phase of early Greek poetry
is of Greek origin, and sounds Greek, it is said
never to have been used in its general sense by the
Greeks themselves. For them, so far as they applied it to poetry, it stayed literal, referring only
to such verse as was sung to the actual accom-

paniment of the lyre. This very fact may well remind us of something now generally forgotten. Originally poetry was not what we now conceive it formally to be—only a modulated, rhythmic arrangement of language; even in its epic form, it was almost certainly sung or chanted, rather than merely recited, and at least often the movement of it was probably sustained by the notes of some simple accompanying musical instrument. The Greek instrument most familiar in tradition was the lyre—a small portable harp, carried by the left arm and played by the right hand. To this day the most usual symbol of music is a conventional drawing or image of what it is supposed to have looked like. Now, most probably, even the narrative material finally collected in such epic poems as the Iliad and the Odyssey first came into existence as more or less distinct episodes, regularly sung and sometimes improvised. When these first took the form which has proved permanent, they may very likely still have been sung. The fact that their narrative meaning provides interest enough to hold the attention has had a good deal to do with their subsidence into something now thought of as wholly apart from music.

All the while, however, both in days before the full splendour of the epic hexameter was developed and in later days, as well, there must probably have been, as there always is everywhere, actual song. Until pretty lately, too, if we measure time by the centuries, actual song had a quality which the extremely elaborate development of modern music has tended not only to obscure but even to suppress. At present, the music of any song first attracts the attention, and lingers longest in memory. Originally, and we may generally believe for ages, the music of any song was so comparatively elementary that attention was attracted rather by the words, and the words might well be remembered when the music was partly if not wholly forgotten. Thus the words of a song were bound to do for those who listened no small part of the office now done by music alone. In this fact lies the true secret of that phase of poetry and indeed of that quality throughout poetry to which modern custom has given the name of lyric. Definitions of this term have been numberless, various and confusing. But any one can understand, or at least can feel, what the term broadly means: when any arrangement of words in poetry excites you to such emotion as nowadays would most normally be excited by music, pure and alone, you have heard the lyric note.

There is general agreement that the great lyric period of poetry in Greece, coming later than the epic, extended from somewhere in the Seventh Century to somewhere in the Fifth, and that on the whole it was at its height in the Sixth. For two or three reasons, however, the relics of it which have survived, mostly in small fragments, though they must always be traditionally important, can never touch us anything like so closely or so certainly as the epic poetry which preceded them does, or the dramatic which followed them. In the first place, the Greek music to which they were sung has almost, if not quite, perished; scholars may conjecture what it was like, but nobody can surely know. Our Greek lyrics, indeed, are little more than the words of "Auld Lang Syne" might

be, or of the "Marseillaise," if the tunes of them
had been altogether lost. In the second place, no
one now knows quite how the Greek words were
originally pronounced and modulated; scholars
can somehow manage to read the lyric metres just
as they can read hexameter lines, in rhythmically
consistent ways. At best, however, this must
be like French after the school of Stratford-atte-
Bowe. In the third place, even such approach
to the lyric original as may thus be made must
mostly, if not utterly, disappear when one attempts translation. Try, if you like, to see what
becomes of any song of Shakspere's—such as
"Full fathom five thy father lies"[1]—when turned
into French, or German, or Italian. Something
like the literal meaning of it, which is its body,
may perhaps be left; but little vestige of the lyric
music which is the soul that gives it being. Lyric
translation must at best be parody. However
exquisite, its beauty can never quite reproduce
that which it tries to render in terms other than
those of which the final excellence is that they are
just what they are. One might as well hopefully
attempt to keep a plucked flower in dewy freshness.

Tradition, accordingly, has preserved for us
not so much the Greek lyrics themselves as certain facts about them—the names of the poets
who made them, for example, and some of the
technical forms which these poets invented or preferred. Of these technical forms the most nearly
enduring is thought to have been perhaps the
earliest. The elegiac couplet, which in form is
closely related to the hexameter line, may almost

[1] Tempest, I, ii, 396.

be used now. Coleridge at once described and exemplified it thus:[1]

> In the hexameter rises the fountain's silvery column,
> In the pentameter aye falling in melody back.

Later than ancient times, however, have known elegiac verse not so much in the original Greek as in its secondary form, the Latin. It happened to be the favourite measure of Ovid, who has more than once been the most widely popular of Latin poets. Two other forms of Greek lyric verse have stayed to some degree familiar—the Alcaic stanza or strophe, frequently employed by Alcæus, and the Sapphic, believed to have been invented by Sappho. Both occur again and again in the Odes of Horace, which for centuries have been known to every English schoolboy. How little either adapts itself to modern use, however, may be seen at a glance when we turn to Alcaics by so masterly a poet as Tennyson,[2] or to English Sapphics by so consummate a master of rhythm as Swinburne.[3] At least in form, these lyric utterances were made for ears perhaps finer than ours but, better or worse, other than ours have come to be.

When we turn from the form of Greek lyrics to their substance we shall find similar conditions. Beyond question, the lyric poets of Greece were

---

[1] Again, I believe, he translated from Schiller.

[2] *e. g.*: O Mighty mouthed inventor of harmonies,
     O skilled to sing of Time or Eternity,
       God-gifted organ-voice of England,
         Milton, a name to resound for ages—

[3] *e. g.*: All the night sleep came not upon my eyelids,
     Shed not dew, nor shook nor unclosed a feather,
       Yet with lips close and with eyes of iron
         Stood and beheld me.

known, admired, studied, and reverently imitated by the lyric poets of Rome; beyond question, the considerable body of Latin lyric verse still in existence is full of allusion to things Greek; of the original Greek, however, amazingly little is left us. Compare, if you will, the admirable pages concerning Sappho[1] in Professor Mackail's Lectures on Greek Poetry with the one hundred and seventy fragments or mentions of her work collected and translated by Mr. Henry Thornton Wharton, and stated to comprise every authentic trace of her now extant. The marvel is how from such crumbled ruin, Mackail has managed to rescue anything at all.

For our present purpose, accordingly, we must be content to remember that Greek lyric poetry excellently existed by the beginning of the Fifth Century, that the names of some of its masters— Alcæus, for example, Sappho, Anacreon, and Pindar—have never faded from tradition, and that, as the contrast of the last of these names with the three others may well remind us, it had already taken two pretty distinct forms.

These forms correspond with what must have been true throughout the history of vocal music. Song, the moment we stop to think, must evidently proceed either from a single voice or from more than one. Song written for a single voice must generally, or at least most fitly, express or pretend to express the mood of an individual singer; song written for more than one or for many voices, however harmonised or not, must more fitly concern not individual emotion but collective, setting forth not the mood of any single singer but that

[1] 92–112.

which for the while may be taken as common to the congregations or the choirs, the ogling chorus girls or the convivial roysterers, who sing it together. On the whole, the lyrics of Alcæus, of Sappho, and of Anacreon—to go no further—are written as if to express individual emotion; without exception the surviving odes of Pindar are written to express collective emotion, and collective emotion of a kind so different from any now usual that, even for no other reason, they would be hard for us to understand.

As conventionally named, they celebrate athletic victories in one or another of four great periodical contests of the Greeks—the Olympian, the Pythian, the Nemean, and the Isthmian games. Though thus remotely similar in purpose to the joyous and dancing doggerel with which American undergraduates have been accustomed to rejoice over the result of an intercollegiate football game, they are in many respects much more nearly like processional hymns of the Church. To come anywhere near sympathy with them, we must somehow try to fuse, in grave yet enthusiastic harmony, two states of feeling now habitually and discordantly separate—that of sport and that of religion or something like it. Some such fusion, though now unusual, may still exist: not very long ago a celebrated football captain, equally eminent in the Young Men's Christian Association, was said often to prepare himself for the fray by prayer; he never went so far, however, as to establish the custom of crowning his triumphs by choral services of thanksgiving; and his preliminary state of mind was generally thought exceptional. In Pindar's time something as near

it as Greek things can ever be to modern seems to
have been normal.

At least, we can be fairly sure that these odes,
like the lost odes which Pindar and others wrote
for occasions of patriotic or civic celebration,
were intended for what we may call serious performance. They were not only sung; they were
sung processionally in elaborate movements which
had many characteristics of solemn, rhythmic
dance. The nearest approach to such rendering
now extant may possibly be found in the slow ritual
perambulation of certain religious solemnities.
Yet the sombre sense of eternal reward or punish-
ment which pervades Christian tradition gives to
our religious functions a reverent intensity completely foreign to the religious conditions of Greek
antiquity, when religion was at once more legendary and more conjectural than it became in Christian Europe. A better modern parallel for the
Odes of Pindar, indeed, may perhaps be found in
a phase of fine art never fully developed until the
Nineteenth Century—the music-drama of Richard
Wagner. Here, as all who have heard and seen
it will remember, powerful dramatic poetry—
usually serious and symbolic in purpose—is set
to peculiarly and subtly appropriate music, and
is performed with a precision of arrangement,
movement, and gesture where the slightest divergence from the canon would more or less disturb the triple artistic harmony.

This comparison has for us the advantage of
bringing to mind how much of Pindar has long
been irrevocably lost. It is not hard to imagine
that the tradition of how a music-drama of Wagner's was originally performed might in time dis-

appear, and the very fact that we have already
almost forgotten the precise instruments for which
John Sebastian Bach wrote, or even Mozart,
should remind us that the music of Wagner, as
we know it now, might well fade from human
knowledge until it vanished from human memory.
All the while, the poetic text of Tannhäuser, of
Tristan and Isolde, or of Parsifal might survive
virtually intact. If so, it would probably be
recognised and admired as highly developed
poetic literature; but little vestige would remain
of the multiplex power exhibited by its full original rendering. With the Odes of Pindar this has
actually been the case for ages. Their music is
forgotten, and so is their ritual movement or
dance or whatever you please to call the visible
phase of their performance; all we have left are
words originally meant to be sung with music
and with processional movements peculiar to
themselves.

If only for this reason Pindar would at best be
rather a tradition nowadays than a fully living
literary fact. Another reason lies in his frequent
obscurity, remarked even when his work was almost new. Neither of them can quite eclipse the
swift and fiery flash of his utterance, nor yet the
sustained splendour of sonorous phrase for which
he was held matchless. These great qualities,
however, defy translation. So, as we have seen,
do the purpose and the mood of the poems in
which they are preserved. Accordingly the influence of Pindar on literature—an influence by no
means at an end—has been of a curiously, and perhaps uniquely, accidental character. To understand it, you must glance at one or two of his

Odes in the original Greek. There is no sort of need that you should know even the Greek alphabet. Any eye can soon, if not instantly, observe that they are generally written in groups of three rather long stanzas. The first, called the Strophe, consists of lines evidently and to all appearances arbitrarily varying in length—in an instance at which the volume chances to open, for example, one line contains nineteen syllables and the next eight. The second stanza, called the Antistrophe, is equally irregular to the eye; but when you compare it with the strophe you will find the apparent irregularities of each precisely to correspond; irregular in themselves, they formally coincide with each other. The third stanza, called the Epode, you will find as irregular as either of the others, but not a bit like them. You may be tempted to infer that Pindar has thrown regularity to the winds. But glance at the next group of three stanzas: you will find the metrical structure of strophe and antistrophe to correspond with that of those in the first group, and that of the two epodes similarly to agree with each other. What at first looks like almost wanton irregularity thus proves to be elaborately regular. The cause of the apparent irregularity, meanwhile, is probably the nature of the music and of the rhythmic postures, or dances, for which the lines were written.

At least in English literature, the fundamental regularities of Pindaric structure have long been neglected or forgotten. The apparent irregularities of it, on the other hand, have been remembered, and have had a sort of fascination for many poets by no means inconsiderable. Artlessly reproducing the looks of it, they have produced memorable works of poetic art. The so-called Pindaric Odes of Cowley, for example, were sometimes held in the Seventeenth Century to be even more admirable poetry than the minor poems of his contemporary Milton; and Nineteenth Century imitations of them have given our literature such masterpieces as Wordsworth's Ode on the Intimations of Immortality; as Coleridge's Dejection; and in America as the Commemoration Ode, in which Lowell recorded the noblest spirit of our Northern States during the Civil War. Such free structure as you will find in all these is traditionally called Pindaric; though its only real likeness to Pindar is visual, and though it is bound together by the device of rhyme, never used by the ancients, it could not have come into existence without the grand precedent of the choral Odes of Pindaric Greece.

The names we have touched on by no means comprise the lyric poetry of Greece. In the conventional canon long accepted there were nine lyric poets; and there were countless lyric poems from other hands than theirs. For our present purpose, however, it is enough to remember that by the beginning of the Fifth Century Greece already possessed not only epic poetry and didactic but lyric, too, and that though the influence of this has been chiefly secondary it has been permanent. For one modern who can in the least appreciate the extant lyrics of Greece, there are hundreds and thousands who can still, if they choose, make something out of the extant lyrics of Rome, and these were deliberately based on Grecian models. Even if the Persians had prevailed in the Fifth

Century, therefore, at least some trace of the Greek lyric might probably have remained.

One fact about it we have not remarked, a fact equally true of Hesiod and of Homer. When and where the Homeric poems were made, nobody can ever be quite sure, but everybody agrees that they were not originally made at Athens. Hesiod was almost certainly of a stock which had emigrated from Asia Minor to Bœotia and lived in the regions dominated by Thebes. Though the lyric poets were apt to wander over the Grecian world, and at one time some of them did their best work in Sparta, they were generally from the eastern shores of the Ægean Sea: Sappho came from Lesbos, and so did Alcæus, if we may believe the stories of them; Anacreon was of Teos in Asia Minor. Pindar, a true Greek, was of Bœotia like Hesiod before him; so late as the time of Alexander the Great, his house was preserved at Thebes as a sort of literary shrine. And so on. Whatever else, early Athens was not yet what Fifth Century Athens was to be—the virtual centre of Greek expression, in all its phases.

CHAPTER II

THE FIFTH CENTURY BEFORE CHRIST

I

HISTORICAL TRADITIONS

If our purpose were to study and to summarise the facts of history, we should have to dwell on the Fifth Century long. Our immediate concern, however, we can hardly too often remind ourselves, is only with traditions which have so lingered in literature as to become part of the habitual thought of Europe. Tendencies, events, truths of great importance may often not thus have survived; if so we may neglect them. Things in themselves less weighty, or even legendary, may sometimes be more noteworthy for us. Our true business, when considering any century, is only to ask ourselves what traditions were in existence when it ended which did not exist when it began. In the case of the Fifth Century—the supreme period of "the glory that was Greece"[1]—tradition chances to be fairly harmonious with history.

When the century began, the principal historical fact from the Greek point of view was the recent and rapid growth of the Asiatic power of Persia. Under Cyrus Persia had conquered Lydia and brought to ruin the once dazzling fortune of the Lydian king, Crœsus. Incidentally, we may well

[1] Poe: To Helen.

remind ourselves that legendary anecdote, preserved in literature, has made Crœsus traditional
both as a type of wealth and prosperity—a fact
which has some sort of historical sanction—and
as a contemporary of the Athenian Solon, which is
at best doubtful. The conquest of Lydia had
brought under Persian domination virtually all
the Greek regions of Asia Minor, thus concen-
trating the national life of the Greeks, so far as
this may ever be thought of as politically united,
in Greece itself and its colonies to the westward,
such as Southern Italy and Sicily. Under Cambyses the Persians had invaded and conquered
Phœnicia and Egypt. Under the first Darius,
who was on the Persian throne in the year 500,
it had already made incursions into European
regions to the north of Greece. Such expansion of
an Asiatic power clearly threatened the existence
of Greece, and with it that of subsequent Europe.
Had it prevailed, the civilisation of the whole
European world might probably have taken on a
character such as we now think of as Oriental.
Broadly speaking, something like what happened
when the Turks possessed themselves of the regions
where European traditions originated might have
happened to begin with.

Instead, our historical traditions are on the
whole true in remembering the Fifth Century as
comprising three periods which together not only
directed the future traditions of Europe, but to a
considerable degree controlled their course. The
first is that when the Greeks, forced by circumstances into something like political union, held
back and defeated the Persian invaders, thereby
securing a European independence of Asia; the

second is that when the civilisation of Athens was at its highest and most powerful, to such degree that the Athenians dreamed of what we should now call imperial domination throughout the regions where Greek civilisation prevailed; the third is that when the internal dissensions of Greece, culminating in the Peloponnesian War, fatally broke Greek union, or perhaps rather proved the Greeks so incapable of long-united action that they must ultimately submit to some imperial control other than their own.

Broadly speaking, the historical traditions of the first of these periods are based on events which happened during the second ten years of the Fifth Century. It was in the year 490 that the seemingly overwhelming forces of Darius, already on Attic soil and with strong naval support, were defeated by the Greeks, under the Athenian general Miltiades, on the Plain of Marathon, little more than twenty miles from Athens across country. This defeat resulted in the withdrawal of the Persian invaders for a period of some ten years. In 480, they returned under Xerxes, the son of Darius, after preparations as elaborate as those of Spain to overwhelm the England of Queen Elizabeth, or those of Germany to destroy France in 1914. At the narrow pass of Thermopylæ, the Persian tens of thousands were held in check by the Spartan king, Leonidas, with only three hundred men; all but one of these devoted defenders of Greece fell on the spot, and the sole survivor, deeming life in such circumstances a disgrace, had the happiness to fall a year later in victorious battle. Sweeping on, the Persians occupied and virtually destroyed the city of Athens. The

Athenian fleet, however, remained intact. Under the command of Themistocles, it decoyed the far more numerous Persian navy into the narrow strait of Salamis, and there, almost within sight of Athens, so crushingly defeated the invading enemy that they withdrew in consternation. A year or so later the Greek victory at Platæa, in Bœotia, completed the liberation of Greece, and of Europe, from the danger of Asiatic dominion.

The fleeting period of Athenian ascendency ensued. In historic fact, and in detail, it is at once dissentious and confusing. For one thing, Themistocles, the victor of Salamis, was compelled to fly from his country, and ended his days as an unpatriotically confidential guest of the Persians. What has survived in tradition, however, is clear, inspiring, and on the whole true. The increasingly democratic and turbulent government of Athens was for years under the virtual control of its most eminent citizen, Pericles, whose name is now generally given to the age he dominated. Athens was fortified as never before; and at the same time was enriched with works of fine art such as never had existed previously and have never been surpassed. What we possess of them now are only fragments or ruins. Every art flourished. As we have already reminded ourselves, to be sure, little trace of Greek music survives; and with painting, unless we count as painting the exquisitely drawn figures on vases and other pottery, the case is the same. But the remains of the Parthenon, to go no further, are still so nearly preserved as to demonstrate the wondrous approach to perfection of Grecian architecture; given a structural and artistic purpose, none before and none afterwards was ever so nearly attained. Sculpture, too, was at its height —freed from the cramping limitations of archaic convention and not yet trembling into the restlessness or subsiding into the literalness which too anxiously copy the changes of human movement and the details of facial expression. The Elgin Marbles, stripped from the Parthenon but kept safer in the British Museum than they could have been anywhere else, are so instinct with life that when you think of them you hardly remember them actually to be little more than vestiges of what they were when they were made. With them, as with the temple they adorned for twenty centuries, tradition associates the name of Phidias. With the name of Pericles tradition remembers that of his mistress Aspasia. And while all these names were those of living humanity, there came into existence, as we shall see, at least two considerable phases of European literary art—the drama and history.

These phases of Greek expression persisted through the third, and disintegrating, period of Fifth Century Greece. On the details of this period, so far as they concern considerations so general as ours, we shall touch when before long we consider the work of its contemporary historian Thucydides. Here we need only remind ourselves that in the year 431 the incessant dissensions of the Greeks broke into war between Athens and Sparta, each with their adherents. Two years later Pericles died. Various constitutional and political confusions at Athens ensued. With one or two intervals of truce, the war lasted for twenty-five years. The military power of Athens was finally broken by the defeat of an imprudent expedition against enemies in Sicily, particularly at Syracuse. And when the Fifth Century ended, the greatness of Athenian empire was already a memory.

II

ÆSCHYLUS

If the Persians had prevailed in 490, the surviving literature of Greece would have consisted, as we have seen, only of epic, didactic, and lyric poetry. Its last developed form would have been the choral ode of which the greatest and for modern times the only surviving master was Pindar. Pindar's work, to be sure, was mostly done after the year 500, when he was probably little more than twenty years old; he is said to have died after the middle of the Fifth Century. In general, however, he only carried to its highest excellence a kind of poetry which had existed before him.

A new kind of poetry to which we now come, nowhere near its full development when the Fifth Century began and virtually complete when it ended, is not only the highest literary achievement of this noble period of antique fine art, but makes such inherent human appeal that, though it has taken various forms, it has never ceased to exist. In our Twentieth Century of the Christian Era, indeed, the most widely vital phase of literary expression throughout the European world is probably the drama. It is rarely poetic nowadays; it is often and generally vulgar; but it is so pervasively alive that if a great poet should anywhere arise, he might well find it at this moment his best means of commanding human attention.

This very fact is apt to bewilder untrained readers who turn to the primal drama of Fifth Century Greece. At that period the theatre was not, as it is now, principally a place of amusement; it had, indeed, a character for which we can hardly find a better name than religious. Though its actual origins are known only by allusions or references, there seems little reason to doubt that they were closely associated with festival ceremonies in honour of the god Dionysus—later much confused in tradition with the Roman Bacchus. Among other things, he was the presiding deity of the vineyard season, and of the process of generation as well. In both aspects he lent himself to celebrations not only of a seriously symbolic nature, but also of a gayety often extremely ribald. The serious phase of his worship seems immemorially to have taken the form of choral odes, touching with more or less elaboration on this or that of his exploits. They were generally in what is called dithyrambic verse, which appears to have had all the apparent irregularity of Pindar's and none of the regularity involved in his balance of strophe and antistrophe, epode with epode. The ribald phase meanwhile seems immemorially to have permitted, at least in speech and gesture, reckless license. From the serious phase, Greek tragedy is thought to have developed; and from the ribald, Greek comedy. This divergence of origin is very likely one chief reason why, even to this day, critics have so often been disposed to discuss tragedy and comedy as distinct and separate kinds of literature.

Though no error could be greater than to suppose the Odes of Pindar to be themselves the origin of Greek tragedy, they may accordingly help us to understand how this later form of literature originated. Pindar carries the traditional choral ode of his own antiquity to its highest and final literary form. From the same origin, another line of development led to the other kind of expression, which first survives in the tragedies of his contemporary Æschylus, said to have been only two or three years the younger and to have died ten or fifteen years before him. The dithyrambic odes which celebrated episodes in the career of Dionysus frequently concerned his various relations with human beings. The moment the monotony of their unmixed choruses was varied by the interpolation of what we might now call a solo by one of the company, generally supposed to have been the leader, the performance would evidently take on a freshly animated aspect. To introduce a second speaker, originally perhaps the tragic poet himself, who should converse with the soloist, would evidently enhance this animation. The step to impersonation on the part of the new speaker is obvious. Thus tragedy is thought to have come into existence; and by the Fifth Century it had so far developed as not only to have traditional names of its own, such as that of Thespis—actors have been called "Thespians" ever since,—but also to concern itself with pretty much any accepted divine or heroic story, whether directly connected with Dionysus or not. So far as Greek tragedies have survived, indeed, they do not extremely emphasise him.

Æschylus, an Athenian some twenty-five years

old in 500, is said to have begun his work as a
tragic poet at about that time, to have fought both
at Marathon and at Salamis, to have brought his
art to a point previously unapproached and in
some respects never surpassed, and to have main-
tained his full power until his death, which occurred
in Sicily a little before the middle of the Century.
In all he is thought to have written at least ninety
dramas; mentions or fragments of more than
seventy exist; but in complete form we possess
only seven—selected in antiquity as masterpieces,
and used then and thereafter for classical texts,
much as modern schools or colleges might use a
few selected plays of Shakspere.

The plays of Shakspere, as everybody knows,
were written for something similar to modern performances in regular playhouses; and if successful
were occasionally and perhaps often repeated.
The tragedies of Æschylus, on the other hand,
were written for something more like ritual presentation on single occasions of solemn festivity;
they appear, generally, to have been offered in
competition with other poets for a poetic prize,
such as was annually awarded at Athens; and the
conditions of their performance in the vast open-
air theatres of the Greeks were wholly different
from anything to which modern times have been
accustomed. For one thing, by the Fifth Century,
tragic actors wore megaphonic masks, and height-
ened their stature with high-soled boots or buskins.
These devices, which survive even now, like the
lyre, in the guise of conventional theatrical symbols or ornaments, imply that the chief feature of
ancient dramatic art was not action but elocution.
Facial expression, indeed, was out of the question.

The condition of a Greek performance which is strangest to us, however, and therefore the most perplexing as we read a Greek drama now, is the constant presence and the frequent dominance of the chorus. We can come nearest to understanding such dramatic works, perhaps, if we consider them as a phase of expression in which the character and the action now assumed to be the basis of the drama have not yet completely emerged from the choral ode of earlier times, and must therefore have had, to enhance their inherent power, the full freshness of æsthetic novelty.

Another phase of their novelty is almost as foreign to us nowadays. At least for two or three hundred years, a new play has often if not generally concerned a new subject. A considerable part of its preliminary interest has consequently lain in the fact that the audience does not know exactly what is going to happen. In the Greek theatre, on the other hand, the subjects of tragedy were always familiar; the interest of the audience was excited not so much by what happened as by the manner in which what must of course happen was presented. Of the seven surviving tragedies of Æschylus, for example, one—unique in dealing with an historical subject—concerns the defeat of the Persians, and incidentally contains a wonderful description of the battle of Salamis, where the poet had personally taken part; two— Prometheus Bound and the Suppliants—concern prehistoric legends; one—the Seven against Thebes—concerns the Theban story of Laius, Œdipus, and their descendants, which was then almost as familiar, in now lost epic form, as the Trojan story of Homer has remained; and a con-

secutive group of three—Agamemnon, the Libation Pourers (Choephori), and the Eumenides—
relate, in magnificent succession, one tremendous
episode of the Trojan story itself—that fatal
misery of the house of Atreus on part of which,
as we have already seen, the shade of Agamemnon
touches in the Eleventh Book of the Odyssey.
The central figure of the three is Orestes, doomed
by ancestral crime to matricidal expiation, itself
freshly criminal. Every one of these seven stories
was perfectly well known to all who came to see
and hear how Æschylus would set them forth;
and the same was probably true of all his many
tragedies now long lost.

In view of all this, it is amazing that within a
few years an open-air performance of the Agamemnon, with conjecturally restored music and
choral movement, proved absorbingly impressive
to American audiences, hardly any of whom knew
a word of Greek, or had much notion of the story.
Perplexed though they may have been, they could
not help feeling the colossal power of this primal
dramatic poetry; and whoever was among them
must always feel, when turning to the printed
text, that at best the text alone, unacted and un-
declaimed, is only a libretto. Even thus, however,
and even in translation, it remains grandly poetic.
The time you may give to Mrs. Browning's version of Prometheus Bound, or to Robert Browning's version of the Agamemnon—which, if
possible, should be compared with the freer but
clearer version by Edward Fitzgerald—will nowise be wasted. All three of these versions are
memorable English poems; and they all render
in English something of the spirit which keeps

alive to this day the first fully developed tragic poetry of Europe.

The essence of tragedy is to be found in an eternal conflict which nothing can ever long disguise. Human beings come into this world amid environments utterly beyond their control; no man can choose his parentage, or his country, or his century, or his station. If by chance men grow to maturity, such conditions as these must always to no small degree control them—both physically and morally; certain deeds may be in their power, more must always stay hopelessly beyond it, and even what they can do must inevitably be conditioned if only by their sense of principle, or duty. However virtuous, they cannot escape the past. Neither can they avoid the future. If there be such a thing as the present, it can never be more than a ceaselessly shifting point of division between these unfathomable depths. And in the depths of the future only one fact looms certain: human life must swiftly end, generation after generation, in human death. Yet on what men do while their fleeting earthly existence remains conscious must depend the irrevocable heritage to be borne by their posterity; just as nothing can modify what has been, so nothing can modify what shall have been when men have done it. For a little while they feel as if they were free to do what they will; so, perhaps, if we grant that they are creatures of their past, they may be; even if they be, their freedom can last no longer than they cast their shadows in the sunshine. At best, life is a struggle, during the little while when each man lives, between his individual being and the implacable environments of the past which is behind him and the future which must soon bring his earthly existence to a close. Fate you may call these surroundings of us all, or whatever else you will. Nothing can avert them, or even long obscure them. In the ceaseless conflict between each man and the uncontrollable force which must always surround him the essence of tragedy lies.

If we may trust those who know Æschylus best, no poet in all European record has ever more deeply felt, or more stupendously set forth, this ultimate tragic truth. What is more, you need go no further than the English versions of his work on which we have already touched, to make sure that he is essentially aware of both its terms— of environment and of individual consciousness. Pretty clearly, however, and perhaps partly because he is the first great master of that species of poetry which he brought into enduring European literature, he may well perplex modern readers by the intensity with which he dwells on the fact of environment, as distinguished from the fact of individual existence. Though he thus gains in grandeur, he inevitably makes less intimate and instant appeal to human sympathy. In his Agamemnon, for example, whether you have the fortune to have seen it acted or like most of us must confine yourself to its printed pages, you can hardly help so deeply feeling the sweep of fate that you half forget the men and the women, Agamemnon himself and Ægisthus, Clytemnestra and Cassandra, whom this fate sweeps on towards their doom. At best, you remember how the sacrifice of Iphigenia, years before, had stirred her mother Clytemnestra to depths which could not

dream of stillness until with adultery and murder
she had wrought expiatory vengeance on the husband and father who had done the deed; and you
feel, in turn, how nothing less than the expiatory
vengeance of Orestes, years later, which plunges
him, as the murderer of his mother, into new and
deeper crime, can atone for the doing to death
of his father Agamemnon.   What manner of man
Agamemnon felt himself to be you care little in
comparison, or what manner of woman Clytemnestra.   Partly, no doubt, this is by reason of the
constant dominance, throughout the drama, of the
chorus; partly, however, and to no small degree,
it comes from the mood of the poet who tells the
story.   Others have told more wondrously what
the subtleties of human nature are; he tells best of
all what the environment must forever be wherein
for its little while human nature has struggled and
must struggle until humanity shall come to an
end.

As we have already reminded ourselves, the
tragedy of Agamemnon, though itself complete,
does not stand solitary in the work of Æschylus.
It is the first of a group of three distinct but
consecutive tragedies, originally made for consecutive performance, and together setting forth
a story too extensive to be comprised in any single
one.   Though no other group of three plays happens to survive from Fifth Century Greece, such
groups, at least when the Century began, were
the usual form in which tragic poetry was written.
They are commonly called Trilogies.   Among the
extant works of Æschylus, to go no further, the
Seven against Thebes is known to have been the
third drama of a trilogy in which it was preceded

by one concerning Laius and another concerning
Œdipus; the Prometheus Bound was the first or
the second drama of a trilogy, too, where it was
followed by a drama called Prometheus Unbound—
though whether the third of the series, which was
named Prometheus the Fire Bearer, began or ended
it has been more or less disputed. Originally, we
are told, such tragic trilogies were regularly followed by a fourth drama, of distinctly different
character, where the chorus was composed of
Satyrs, and the subject, whether connected with
the trilogy or not, was treated in a spirit of broad
and ribald burlesque. The only extant example
of such comic afterpiece, however, chances to be
a dreary drama of Euripides called the Cyclops;
it concerns the adventure of Odysseus with Polyphemus, it is animated—if at all—only by the
buffoonery of conventional drunkenness, and those
who know it in Greek generally pronounce it as
empty in the original as it is when translated.[1]
We therefore have no means of knowing what
an Æschylean tetralogy—as the full group was
called, of three tragic dramas followed by a comic
—may originally have been like. Without the
trilogy of which Orestes is the central figure, we
should be equally in the dark concerning the three
tragic dramas, taken by themselves.

Of this remaining trilogy, the first part—the
Agamemnon—is the most interesting, perhaps the
most powerful, and certainly the only one which
has been translated into anything like English

[1] It is fair to add that Shelley translated the Cyclops and that many of
his devotees agree with him that the play is delightfully funny. Somehow,
though, you must worship Shelley very religiously if you would share his
notions of fun.

poetry; it is consequently more positively memorable than either of the dramas which follow it. For our present purpose, however, the second play of the series—the Choephori, or the Libation Pourers, as the title is usually translated—is in one respect more interesting to novices who desire any definite impression of Æschylus. The most nearly satisfactory English translation is probably that of Doctor Plumptre—pedestrian and uninspired, but nevertheless literate. Similar in general treatment to the Agamemnon, it deals with the story of Orestes and his sister Electra—the children of Agamemnon and Clytemnestra. Electra has remained at Argos, with her mother, who has married Ægisthus; but Electra has never for an instant forgotten her pious duty to the memory of her murdered father. Orestes has long disappeared; no one knows whether he is alive or dead. At length, he secretly returns, pays due filial honour to the tomb of Agamemnon, makes himself known to Electra, and with her aid avenges their father by taking the lives both of their mother and of her husband, who had been first the adulterous paramour of Clytemnestra and later accomplice in Clytemnestra's crime. Whereupon, the Furies swarm about Orestes, avenging his mother, and driving him into renewed and maddened exile. Give yourself up to the story, and you can hardly fail somehow to feel the imaginative power with which Æschylus has told it; yet you can hardly fail, either, to feel that his whole way of telling it is almost an obstacle to any modern mind. We are used now to dramas where the incidents and the characters are presented as if they were visibly and audibly before

us; compared with any such method, that of
Æschylus seems almost ritual—more nearly like
the solemn recital of some Scriptural story in an
elaborate religious ceremony. To get the full
effect you must probably read, and ponder on, the
whole short drama; the Greek has in all only one
thousand and seventy-four lines. If you lack
time or patience for such reading, you may find
something of the effect in the portion between the
first speech of Electra[1] and her full acknowledg-
ment that Orestes may be close at hand;[2] her
exchange of speeches with the chorus, for example,
resembles a responsive chant, like that of the
Anglican Psalter.

The reason why this drama may interest us
more than the others in the trilogy is accidental.
A drama on the same subject by Sophocles happens to have been preserved; and so has one by
Euripides. This opportunity for observing how
the three great tragic dramatists of the Fifth Century dealt, each characteristically, with the same
story is unique. What in each case is something
less than the best work of its author, therefore
becomes, for our present purpose, his most certainly distinct.

III

SOPHOCLES

The surviving work of Sophocles, the second
great tragic poet of the Fifth Century, includes,
like that of Æschylus, only seven dramas, selected
and preserved for educational purposes, and

[1] Line 83; Plumptre, line 86. [2] Line 210; Plumptre, line 203.

supplemented by fragments of others, often very short, which have happened to be quoted by later authors of classic antiquity. The subjects of his seven extant dramas resemble those of the extant dramas of his great predecessor. One, the Maidens of Trachis, concerns prehistoric legend—the story of Heracles, or Hercules as Roman and later times have often called him, unwittingly done to death by his wife Dejanira with the poisoned robe of the slaughtered centaur Nessus. Three, and on the whole the most memorable, concern—though not as a formal trilogy—the Theban story: Œdipus the King, Œdipus at Colonus, and Antigone. The remaining three—Philoctetes, Ajax, and Electra—concern separate episodes in the story of Troy. All these subjects, and all those of his numerous dramas which have not been preserved, were perfectly familiar, like the subjects treated by Æschylus, to the audiences for whom he wrote. What appealed to their interest was not the story of any of these tragic poems; it was the manner in which this story was presented by the poet.

Though the life of Sophocles overlapped that of Æschylus for some forty years, and though for twelve or fifteen of these years they were artistic rivals, the younger tragic poet really belonged to a later generation. At the time of the battle of Marathon, where Æschylus fought, Sophocles was no more than five years old; on the occasion of the battle of Salamis, where again Æschylus fought, Sophocles—who was somewhere about fifteen years old and is said to have been remarkably handsome—was called upon, if we may trust tradition, only to take part in a choral ode, cele-

brating the Grecian victory. It was eleven or
twelve years later, in 468, that he is first reported
to have won the prize for tragic poetry. The
power thus attested he retained, seemingly un-
diminished, throughout his long life. He is said
to have lived to the age of ninety, dying only a
year or two before the fall of Athens at the close
of the Peloponnesian War. His full maturity accordingly came when Athens was at the very
height of Periclean power; and, though he saw this
power bent, he did not survive till the moment
when it was broken. By chance, perhaps the
most impressive portrait-statue of all European
antiquity makes his aspect now almost as familiar
as his name. It is not of his time, nor even itself
an original work of art; it is thought to be a mar-
ble copy of a bronze statue set up at Athens some
fifty or sixty years after he died. Taken only as
it stands now, however, in the Lateran Museum at
Rome, it seems incomparable. He looks, as somebody has said, like one who has risen in response
to the applause which is his due; and throughout twenty-five centuries this applause has never
ceased.

Yet any modern reader who should approach
his work by itself, particularly in translation—
and no English translation of it has such literary
merit as has been attained in translations from
Æschylus and from Euripides—may well find it
perplexing, at least to begin with. It was made
for presentation under the same conditions which
surrounded the tragedies of Æschylus; as in them,
a considerable, even though clearly a smaller,
part of its utterance is assigned to the chorus, and
its formal methods are widely different from any

to which we are now used. We have utterly lost
both the music and the rhythmic motions which
were originally part of it. Taken by themselves,
therefore, we may well find the texts of Sophocles
perplexing, archaically strange. The moment we
compare them with the work of Æschylus, however, they take on another aspect. To discuss
whether this aspect is higher or lower, better or
worse, would be fruitless, and perhaps imperti-
nent. There can be no doubt of two things—
Sophocles is clearly different from Æschylus, and
at least a considerable part of the difference is
due to the fact that he treats his subjects with
something far more like human sympathy. This
difference is analogous to that between the earlier
sculpture of Greece and the Phidian sculpture
of Periclean Athens; something like it may be
observed in the development of widely different
phases of European art—such as Italian painting,
or the English drama under Queen Elizabeth and
King James the First. If one may generalise,
when a great school of expression dealing with any
kind of human affairs has gathered new creative
energy, it begins by breaking the bonds of outworn convention and proceeds to closer and closer
imitation of actuality, until the sense of actuality
—or perhaps a sense of the new conventions which
have incidentally come into being—freshly limits
and finally smothers its imaginative impulse.
There is hardly anywhere a clearer instance of
what this generalisation means, at least in its
earlier phase, than you may find when you consider the work of Sophocles not alone but in its
relation to that of the poet, a generation older, who
had virtually created the tragic poetry of Europe.

The real, permanent relation between Æschylus and Sophocles is implied in what, even now, is generally said or written about them by those who know and love them best. You may have read much concerning Æschylus without finding your attention particularly directed to the personages in his dramas; what his admirers dwell on is rather his dramas as they stand complete—setting forth with unsurpassed grandeur of both conception and diction how the sweep of irrevocable fate whirls to doom the conscious beings who for a little while raise their heads above the surface of the relentless stream of life. The moment you turn to what is said or written about Sophocles, you will grow aware of a difference: at least before long, your attention will be called, even though you hardly know quite how, to the grandly generalised yet human beings to whom his imagination has given individual life. In the sense in which men discuss a character of Shakspere's, there is hardly such a thing as a character among the personages of Æschylus; but you will find the Antigone of Sophocles, for example, or his Œdipus, almost as distinct and as inexhaustible to those who love his work as Hamlet is or Lady Macbeth to those who love their Shakspere. Something similar is implied in the effect of his dramas when performed before modern audiences. As we have already reminded ourselves, a performance of the Agamemnon of Æschylus, in open American air, with restored music and choral procession, was deeply and absorbingly impressive. Even those who felt its splendour most profoundly, however, can hardly imagine how this tragic thing could be pent within the walls and the roof of such a theatre as we are now used to. The Œdipus of Sophocles, on the other hand, literally translated into both English and French, has occasionally been acted, with tremendous effect, on our regular stage. Those who saw Mounet-Sully play the part, with all the modernities of lights and scenery about him, had little sense of strangeness in the drama; what they felt was rather its power and his as he embodied an antique but human character. The tragedy of Sophocles, in short, proved capable of translation not only into a living language but even into the theatrical terms of the present day. Though, like the text of Æschylus, the text of Sophocles is only a libretto, such as that of a Wagner music drama might be if both the music and the original methods of acting were completely lost, the text of Sophocles, alone and unsupported, proves to this day not only enduringly poetic, but also dramatically practicable.

The most memorable characters in the extant work of Sophocles are Œdipus and Antigone; his most powerful dramas are certainly those which bear their names. By comparing either of these with the Prometheus Bound or with the Agamemnon of Æschylus, you may most impressively come to feel the characteristics of each great tragic poet when at his best. As we have already reminded ourselves, however, the accident that the Electra of Sophocles deals with the subject with which Æschylus deals in the Choephori, or Libation Pourers, makes a comparison between these somewhat secondary tragedies more definite and therefore perhaps more suitable for our immediate purpose.[1] Fully to feel the difference,

[1] *Cf.* p. 61.

you should read both of them through—no great
task, for the Electra of Sophocles has only 1510
lines, which added to the 1074 lines of the Choephori make no more than 2584 lines in all. A
mere comparison of the opening scenes, however,
will go far to define the contrast. In both plays,
Orestes presently appears, secretly returning to
pay filial honours to the tomb of his father, Agamemnon; in both he is accompanied by his friend
Pylades, who speaks in neither. In the Choephori, however, Orestes proceeds at once to per-
form his ceremonial duty, almost as a priest might
do reverence before an altar; his conduct is not
human but ritual. In the Electra of Sophocles,
on the other hand, there comes in with him a nameless attendant—called a pedagogue in the Greek
—whose prologue-like opening speech states to
him and incidentally to the audience where they
are and what is the general situation; and his
own answer to this speech, before the voice of
Electra is heard behind the scene, sets forth what
in every sense of the term we may call a plot;
here, in short, there is nothing ritual at all.

A similar contrast you will find by comparing the
passages in the two plays concerning the way in
which the return of Orestes comes to the knowledge of Electra. We have already touched on
the ritual treatment of this matter by Æschylus;
in the Choephori, Electra goes straight to her
father's tomb, and there discovers the tress of
hair which Orestes has ceremonially deposited
upon it. In the Electra of Sophocles, on the other
hand,[1] her sister, Chrysothemis, comes joyously
in, with the tress of hair which she has found on

[1] Lines 871-933; Plumptre, lines 871-932.

the tomb and believes to have been cut from the
head of Orestes, and Electra for a long time cannot be persuaded that it is his. An even sharper
contrast may be found by comparing the passages
about the death of Clytemnestra: in Æschylus,[1]
after what amounts to a solemn responsive duet,
she is led off to slaughter; in Sophocles,[2] having
been induced to suppose Orestes dead, she is behind the scene, contentedly preparing for his
formal funeral, and you hear her cries of despair
when he reveals himself and strikes her down.
Electra, in this case, who at that period of the
action has long disappeared from the Choephori,
stays in the centre of the theatre, listening to the
sounds of horror, and so rejoiced that the murder
of her father is avenged as for the while to forget
how this vengeance could have been achieved
only by the murder of her mother. These comparisons, as we ponder on them, may well make
us feel almost as if the tragedy of Sophocles were
conceived and set forth in modern terms.

To correct such impression, we need only return to this tragedy by itself. The moment we
forget Æschylus, Sophocles must appear to us
almost as remote as the older poet. Though in
Sophocles the chorus is decidedly less prominent
than in Æschylus, the chorus even in Sophocles
might well impress any uninitiated reader of these
days as the most conspicuous and perplexing
feature of his dramatic method. Accepting this,
too, a modern reader might well feel his sense and
his presentation of the sweep of fate—of the environment which must always and forever relent-

---

[1] Lines 902–929; Plumptre, lines 890–917.
[2] Lines 1398–1421; Plumptre, lines 1398–1421.

lessly surround humanity—to be the dominant note of his work; and his sense of the other factor in tragedy, of the humanity which fate besets during our little while of anxious life, to be at best rudimentary. The truth is, however, that beyond any other tragic poet in the literature of Europe Sophocles was profoundly and equally aware of both terms in that tremendous conflict between humanity and its environment wherein the essence of tragedy lies; and therefore that the distinguishing feature of his poetic genius may be found in the balance with which he keeps himself from laying undue stress on either term of the conflict.

Some such balance those who know him best discern even in the detail of his poetry. Above and beyond all else, he has the serene poise of mastery. Thus, more than the elder tragic poet whose work began earlier than his, and more than the younger tragic poet who was the contemporary of his later days, he seems in the end to embody the most deeply characteristic spirit of his time. His long life began only a few years after the Fifth Century began, and ended only a few years before it ended. His maturity came literally in the full Age of Pericles at the very time when the Parthenon was built, and when Phidias made sculpture at once ideal and real. The words Periclean, Phidian, and Sophoclean mean, in different ways, the same thing; and there is no fourth to match them.

Though, as we have seen, Sophocles wrote on almost to the end of the Century, his quality as a tragic poet was fully developed by the year 450. Æschylus was then dead. Even if the Fifth Cen-

tury had no other claim to place in the traditions
of European literature, the first half of the Century
would therefore be enduringly memorable for
having added to the traditions of epic, didactic,
and lyric poetry which it inherited a fourth tradition which it created. During these fifty years
Æschylus brought tragic poetry into lasting existence; and Sophocles brought it well within the
range of human sympathy.

IV

HERODOTUS

At just about the time when tragic poetry had
thus developed its most beautiful balance, another kind of literature, widely different in both
form and purpose, first took permanent shape.
Its purpose was not to celebrate legend or to express imaginative emotion but intelligently to record facts—to tell as truthfully as might be how
the Greek world where the writers lived had originated and was behaving. Its form was accordingly free from the shackles of metre, and far
more nearly resembled the language used in daily
life; we have long called this form prose. Neither
purpose nor form was a novelty; both had existed
perhaps immemorially. Until this period, however, neither had so highly developed as to produce a literary masterpiece; or, if by chance either
had, no such masterpiece has been preserved.
The work of the first two surviving Greek historians, on the other hand, has qualities which
have hardly been surpassed. For narrative skill
and sustained interest Herodotus remains endur-

ingly excellent; for thoughtful and animated statement of contemporary fact, no writer has excelled
Thucydides; and together they give us a marvellous impression of how the Fifth Century began
and how it ended.

Both of them were contemporary with a considerable part of the career of Sophocles, and both
might have seen or known Euripides, too, the
third and last great writer of Greek tragedy.
Thucydides was also contemporary with much of
the career of Aristophanes, our only surviving
writer of Greek comedy. For reasons of chronology, therefore, as well as for the more obvious
reason that on general principles a given kind of
literature may conveniently be treated all at once,
it may now seem volatile to distract attention
from the later course of Fifth Century drama to
that of history as written in the Fifth Century.
Two considerations, however, justify this inter-
ruption: quite to understand the change in the
drama, we shall be the better for reminding ourselves afresh of the historical circumstances which
surrounded it; and any reader who has cared to
turn, as he reads, to the texts we have touched on,
may well have found his task by this time something of a strain. Poetry is not only harder to
read than prose, but lends itself much less readily
to translation. Just here, prose gives us what
Herodotus often and deliberately gave those whom
he addressed—a welcome chance to take breath.

In so doing, though, we must freshly remember
one feature which all antique prose had in common with antique poetry, and which modern prose
and even modern poetry has considerably if not
altogether lost. Nowadays we read print with

little sense that the words before us were originally symbols representing vocal sounds. At least until the time of St. Augustine, on the other hand, as we have already remarked,[1] few thought of a written page as anything else than a memorandum from which somebody might read aloud. The moment, consequently, that you compare any translation of Greek prose with the original text, you must begin to feel how much of the original has been lost. In the original, it is hard to prevent the voice from laying stress on the word which has most meaning; in almost any modern version, it is almost as hard not to throw your emphasis on words more or less insignificant. Ancient words were always addressed to the ear; modern words are generally addressed to the eye. Granting this, however, there can be no doubt that the substance of voiceless prose is far less hard to grasp than that of voiceless verse; for the primary purpose of prose is not to stir or to edify but to inform.

Herodotus has so long been called the father of history that we are apt to forget his perhaps deeper claim to respect: so far as surviving European literature goes, he is also the father of prose, almost as distinctly as Homer is the father of poetry. Though both had predecessors, both so eclipsed their predecessors as to make them, from our point of view, virtually invisible. In an auroral past, however, antique to Greece itself, Homer stays primally and almost legendarily impersonal; Herodotus, in the full light of a recorded century, is distinctly individual. A gentleman of Halicarnassus, in Asia Minor, he was born

[1] *Cf.* p. 27.

about half-way between the battles of Marathon and of Salamis. His birthplace, though Greek by origin and tradition, was under Persian dominion; his general situation may therefore be likened to that of a good French Alsatian born between 1870 and 1914. His natural sympathy was with one side of a great conflict; his youthful surroundings went far to make him familiar with the manners and customs of the other. He had the best of Greek education; among the writers we have touched on he quotes Homer, Hesiod, Alcæus, Sappho, Pindar, and Æschylus—and he quotes many more now known only by name, or from fragments. When he was about twenty years old, political troubles at Halicarnassus, which resulted in the execution of at least one of his kinsmen, appear to have driven him from his native city, never to return there. The details of his wanderings and of his travels are not clearly determined; it is certain, however, that he was for a while resident at Athens, when the power of Pericles was flourishing, that at one time or another he journeyed not only over the whole Greek world but into outlying regions like Scythia and Egypt, that the merit of his historical work was fully recognised, and that because the constitution of Athens forbade him as foreign-born to attain full rights of citizenship there he became a citizen of Thurii, an Athenian colony in Southern Italy, where he died at somewhere about the age of sixty.

His general sympathies, at least as his work reveals them, were nevertheless enthusiastically Athenian. The opening paragraph of his History, virtually a compact preface, states his purpose to set forth the great and marvellous deeds of both

Greeks and Barbarians,—a term by which he really means the Persians and the peoples who came under Persian dominion,—and the causes which brought them to war. Another way of putting this would be to say that in the full light of Fifth Century Athens he set himself the task of telling how the Greece of which Athens was the momentary leader had grown into its independent national consciousness.

Evidently, this Greece was surrounded by regions which it called barbarous; evidently, too, both Greece and its Barbary had emerged from an antiquity already as immemorial as any antiquity is now. Something of these circumstances, as they concerned both space and time, had been recorded by earlier geographers or chroniclers; and so had the principal facts of Grecian topography and story. This material, however, of which Herodotus apparently made full use, had never attained the dignity of enduring literature. He supplemented it by wide travel and extensive personal inquiry. He deliberately put it into a form which he meant to be permanent; and, for want of satisfactory prose models, he carefully imitated the methods of Homer, to the point of breaking by frequent episode what might otherwise have been the tedium of narrative too long sustained. There was never more conscientious artist than this Father of History and of Prose, devoted to the celebration of how Greece came to her victory over Persia, and fortunate enough to do his work before time had swiftly shown how short the life of politically independent Greece was to be.

As his history has come down to us, it is divided into nine books, each conveniently named for one

of the Muses. Professor Bury[1] points out that
this division, though made by Alexandrian editors
under the Ptolemies, really indicates the structure
of the work, and also that the whole work might
have been further grouped in three triads, each
consisting of three Books. There are reasons to
think that the last three Books, which deal with
the reign of Xerxes, and the final defeat of the
Persians—bringing into literature the names of
Thermopylæ, Salamis, and Platæa,—were written
first; and that the other six—the first three concerning the reigns of Cyrus and of Cambyses, and
the second three concerning that of Darius and
culminating with the Greek victory at Marathon,
were added as a colossal and magnificent introduction. However this may be, the nine Books, as
we have them, are composed together with remarkable artistic skill, leading us excursively but
surely from legendary antiquity, and often through
remote regions, to that climax of Greek warfare
when, as we can now see, what for the while appeared only the defeat of Persians finally assured
the existence of the spirit and the civilisation
which, in contrast with the Asiatic, has now for
twenty-five centuries been European. The story
they tell is that of the manner in which our whole
Western world was born.

Herodotus is by no means a philosophic historian. All he surely does is to collect facts as
well as he can, and to set them forth in fluent and
pleasant narrative style. He is more nearly critical, however, than you might at first think. An
amusing example of his method and his limitation
occurs in his account of Egypt. Cambyses, the

[1] The Ancient Greek Historians (Harvard Lectures), 1909. p. 38.

successor of Cyrus on the Persian throne, added this already immemorially antique dominion to those of the Persian crown. Egypt accordingly coming within the range of Herodotus, he devoted the whole Second Book of his History to an account, descriptive and historical, of this perennially fascinating region; and until modern ingenuity deciphered hieroglyphic inscriptions and otherwise discovered the actual facts of Egyptian history through tens of centuries, Egyptian tradition as known to Europeans was mostly based on Herodotus. Many of his names, indeed, still familiarly persist—Cheops, for example, Mycerinus, and Rhampsinit; it is not very long since his name of Sesostris was generally replaced by the true one of Rameses; and so on. He was not content to learn his Egypt from record or report, or such works as the geography of Hecatæus, now no longer in existence, which he is thought to have availed himself of in a manner such as modern prejudice would hold plagiaristic. He travelled to Egypt, he saw all he could there, and he made every inquiry in his power. Among other things, of course, he visited the pyramids, already, though not yet ruinous, more than three thousand years old; and he gives a probably correct account of how they were built. Naturally, however, he was unable to read hieroglyphic inscriptions; so he unsuspiciously accepted, and set down, the statement of his local guide—an evident pleasantry, most likely provoked by vexatious questioning—that the inscription on the pyramid of Cheops, which was probably the "cartouched" name of that half-legendary monarch, recorded how much had been spent for the radishes, leeks, and onions consumed

by the workmen who had built this artificial moun-
tain;[1] and he proceeds to conjecture how much
more must have been spent for tools, clothing,
and solidly nutritious food. It is fair to add that
he was not often caught so napping; the quiet
good sense of his comment on the preposterous
story is far more characteristic. His implication,
too, that these luckless labourers had no wages
seems to be true.

Even though he cannot be accepted as a final
authority on history, accordingly, he may be confidently regarded as an honest story-teller, who
not only tells us most of what we know about such
memorable facts as Marathon, Thermopylæ, and
Salamis, and such memorable personages as Darius
and Xerxes, Miltiades, Leonidas, and Themistocles,
but also, in his matchless episodic digressions, collects an incomparable treasury of legend, tradition,
and anecdote. He can never cease to be interesting; and there are few clearer contrasts between
the mood of Europe and that of Asia than you will
find by comparing his narrative with that in the
Books of Genesis and Exodus. His Egypt, for
example, though resembling that of Joseph, and
of Moses, and of their Pharaohs, is in many aspects much more like ours.

The substance of his work lends itself far more
readily to translation than can ever be the case
with poetry, or with prose whose purpose is more
or less poetic. In Rawlinson's English version—
on the whole our best—he stays thoroughly readable. Almost the only device which has become
quite strange nowadays is one which may be due
partly to his study of Homer as a narrative model,

[1] II, 125.

and partly to the fact that his work was written to be read aloud. Instead of telling what eminent men thought and purposed, he deliberately puts declamatory speeches into their mouths, more or less like those uttered by Homeric heroes; a casual example may be found in what Miltiades says to Callimachus shortly before the battle of Marathon.[1] This convention was followed by most of the ancient historians, Greek or Latin; and a trace of it survives even in the imaginary eloquence attributed to John Adams by Daniel Webster when called on, in 1826, to eulogise the lately dead second President of the United States. These formal declamations, however, leave undisturbed the narrative and anecdote which surround them. So long as men like good stories well told, they will not tire of Herodotus.

Not long after the middle of the Fifth Century, accordingly, Greek literature already had both poetry—epic, didactic, lyric, and dramatic—and admirable narrative prose. To this point, also, the course of Greek literature, like that of plastic art in Greece, had shown little symptom of decline. Each new phase of it had created an unprecedented type which has endured.

V

THUCYDIDES

By the middle of the Fifth Century Thucydides, the second of the great Greek historians, was certainly alive, and may have been some twenty years old. If so, he was only twelve or fifteen

[1] VI, 109.

years younger than Herodotus; in any event, he was no younger than an eldest son of his predecessor might have been, and was old enough to have remembered the effect produced at Athens by the history of Herodotus when it was a novelty. Although his own work is therefore almost contemporary with this, it nevertheless impresses one almost as if produced in a different epoch.

To some extent, the difference may be due to circumstance. Thucydides, a man of the highest rank in Thrace, where he possessed considerable property, was also closely related to eminent families at Athens, was an Athenian citizen, at one time during the Peloponnesian War held an important military command, and by reason of defeat was condemned to long banishment, which he seems mostly to have passed on his Thracian estates. He was thus both a full contemporary of the historical period he has recorded, and to some extent a participant in its action; while Herodotus was neither. As a matter of literary tradition, however, the difference probably goes deeper. For one thing, the history of Herodotus, held by some to have been written for public reading, has evident histrionic qualities; that of Thucydides, though doubtless intended to be read aloud, can hardly have been written with any view to public performance, which would indeed have been somewhat beneath his dignity. Again, the history of Herodotus, setting forth the great deeds which freed Greece and Europe from the danger of Asiatic dominion, ends at a time when he was less than ten years old; that of Thucydides, recording the progress of a civil war ultimately fatal to Greek independence, begins at a time when he can hardly have been less than twenty-five and perhaps may have been forty. Between the end of Herodotus and the beginning of Thucydides there is accordingly a historical gap of just about half a century; and this half century included almost all of the Age of Pericles—a period of which there is no important historian. Herodotus writes its magnificent prologue, Thucydides its fatal epilogue; neither tells its story. Yet each wrote in the full maturity of middle life. The contrast between the periods each dealt with would in any case have gone far to make their work different. Whoever celebrates an heroic past can never be quite like one who notes down the occurrences of a disintegrating and baffling present.

Almost as a matter of course, therefore, both the method and the proportions of the history of Thucydides contrast strongly with those we have glanced at in the history of Herodotus. Two-thirds of the older historian's work consists of his colossal and almost epic introduction to the still almost epic three books in which he finally records the already well-past defeat of the forces of Xerxes. If we may trust the opening paragraph of Thucydides, he perceived when the Peloponnesian War broke out, in the year 431, that this was to be the most critical incident in the history of Greek independence, and accordingly determined to record whatever happened as soon as possible after it had occurred. The first of his eight Books he devotes to a summary introduction; the other seven record the annual progress of the war until the twenty-first of its twenty-seven years. His work, never finished, breaks off abruptly. His temper throughout may be called philosophical; that is, he states his facts not so much for their own sake as for the reason that when duly recorded they will give the future data to think with. Except in his numerous speeches, however, which Professor Bury believes frequently to express his personal opinions,[1] he seldom philosophises directly; at least apparently he preserves the character of a dispassionate observer, content that conclusions be drawn, when the time comes, by others. Very likely, as some recent critics think, he was deliberately partisan, stating this fact or that in such manner as would induce readers to take his view of it, and occasionally suppressing matters inconveniently favourable to other opinions than his. However this may be, he manages throughout to appear unbiassed. Fair or not, he has hardly been surpassed in what looks like judicial fairness. He professes, probably with truth, to have collected and sifted his material scrupulously. He writes more like a judge, summing up evidence, than like an advocate emphasising facts to support his side of the case; so his prose, as he tells what men were, and what they did and what happened to them, has a literary quality almost Shaksperean. He often seems an almost final model for those who would provide others with a firm and solid basis for historical generalisation.

The moment you try thus to use him, however, you will grow aware of his limitations. History as we now conceive it, at least when we want to philosophise, is perhaps the most intricately complicated subject with which would-be philosophers can possibly deal. Superficially a matter of delib-

[1] *Op. cit.*, chap. IV.

erate politics, strategy, and tactics, more or less
conditioned by chance, it has other phases—economic, social, cultural, whatever else—so fundamental that wise men may well come to think it
really a manifestation of natural force, hardly if at
all more manageable by men than geology is or as-
tronomy. To generalise about it at all, if we
come anywhere near this opinion, we need immeasurably more data than have yet been collected, and very likely more than ever can be.
And all that Thucydides gives us, despite his unsurpassed power of statement, is an account of
how individuals behaved in attempting to control political or military affairs when at any moment accident might interfere with their best-laid
plans. You may read him through and through
with no perception that the half-century of Greek
history which came between the close of Herodotus, in 479, and the beginning of his own work,
in 431, had any economic or social aspect, or that
the Age of Pericles had produced a single work of
art or of literature. He tells you of politics, of
soldiering, of such freaks of chance as the plague
at Athens, and of public characters so far as their
conduct was public. Here he virtually stops.

This very limitation, on the other hand, con-
centrates his astonishing intensity—a quality the
more remarkable when we remember that, so far
as record goes, he had no model for just the kind
of history which he attempted. His omissions,
indeed, are probably deliberate. The task he had
set himself was not to write a general account of
his times, but rather to make the most careful
study he could of a war actually in progress when
he wrote. Whatever had no direct or apparent

bearing on this was therefore not within his scope; whatever concerned it, he set forth as firmly as he could. Though he lacks the charm of Herodotus, accordingly, his unsurpassed force and his apparent truthfulness make Herodotus in comparison seem pleasantly old-fashioned. Though Thucydides be the harder to read, he rewards every effort which he demands. To appreciate him, as to appreciate any great master, you must read him through. Characteristic passages, however, will give an impression of his qualities. His account of the last days and his summary of the character of Themistocles,[1] for example, shows how he can deal with matters already past—such as Herodotus dealt with throughout. His almost dramatic funeral oration,[2] put into the mouth of Pericles eulogising the first Athenians who fell in the war, at once implies the character and the bland idealism of Pericles and illustrates how Thucydides developed the already conventional use of speeches in what he meant to be authentic history; the method is something like that of Shakspere, when with frankly dramatic purpose he wrote the funeral speeches of Brutus and of Antony over the body of Julius Cæsar. The passage describing the plague at Athens[3] reveals at least two phases of Thucydidean mastery: coming directly after the funeral oration of Pericles, it so contrasts with this as both ironically and dramatically to emphasise how slightly idealism can foresee the chances of reality, and how relentless these chances must be; taken by itself it is one of the

---

[1] I, 135–138. The most readable English translation is Jowett's; but any will do.
[2] II, 35–46.   [3] II, 47–52.

three tremendous accounts of pestilence in European literature—the other two are Boccaccio's introduction to the Decameron and Defoe's description of the Plague at London. Finally, if you will take the time to read the Sixth and Seventh Books, which deal with the fatal expedition to Sicily, you will not waste a moment; should this task prove, as it probably may, too arduous, you will find the grim end of the story[1] incomparable for precision, clearness, and sheer narrative power. It has often been held the greatest masterpiece of military history ever achieved.

Whatever else, when with memories of Herodotus hovering in the background you ponder on the effect of Thucydides, you can hardly help feeling how he once for all sets forth, for enduring tradition, the fate of the glory that was Greece. When Sophocles was born this was dawning as if it might blaze forever; before Sophocles died, it was forever clouded. The memory of it stays so gleaming that we are apt to forget its fragility; it was at its best for less than a single long human lifetime. Somehow, too, Thucydides implicitly tells us why. His Greece, no doubt, is not primal; its intelligence is not only fully mature but often seems unsurpassed. In one aspect, however, this intelligence remains primitive or at least youthful, hardly ever imagining any more than children imagine, or than the restless spirit of reform imagines which throughout the ages persists childish, that intelligence cannot control events and remake the Golden Age unresisted and unfailing. Such a quality needs, for anything like endurance, the saving grace, which Greece lacked, of instinctive

[1] VII, 70–87.

common sense, recognising among other unwelcome facts that the most nearly sure means of
historic and social growth must be sought in com-
promise. Nothing else can long avert conquest
or anarchy; any government of men can persist
only so long as the men in power stay strong
enough to impose their will on those who dis-
agree; there is more hope for peoples who consent
humbly to submit themselves to the unintelligent
but colossally sensible government of law—usually
right in decisions, however blundering in the reasons given for them. The very excellence of Greek
intelligence during the Fifth Century, despite the
admirable self-control of its expression, was therefore a fatal cause of anarchic political weakness.
Here, on the whole, were men who still fancied
each for himself that he could have his own way.

When we compare this impression with that
produced by the men who live in Herodotus, and
then recall that produced by the Homeric heroes,
we shall find the three tending,—at least in comparison with any impression produced by later
Europe,—despite their evident differences, to group
themselves together. The characters of Thucydides, and those of Herodotus too, are no longer
like those of Homer, full-grown men at once European and yet somehow temperamentally in a state
variously resembling that of modern infancy;[1] at
the same time, for all their maturity of unbalanced
intelligence, they have not yet grown to what modern minds would instantly recognise as complete
maturity of character. Their racial inexperience
keeps them still youthful, if only in their blind-
ness to such limitations of human independence

[1] *Cf.* p. 26.

as wise experience has long been compelled sadly
to recognise. Achilles, for example, Miltiades,
and Alcibiades, when we compare them as a group
even with Romans, and still more when we compare them with Europeans of modern times,
merge together, grown men yet still juvenile; and
their composite embodies not only Greece but the
swift and beautiful childhood of Europe.

All three of the masters who have given us each
his own part of this triple composite, deal with
what has traditionally been accepted as history;
and none of them, so far as we know, had precise
models for the aspect in which he presented it.
Surely, though, Homer set forth in matchless
hexameters the splendid legends of heroic antiquity,
Herodotus in always fluent and limpid prose heroically celebrated a national past still within the
bounds of human memory, and Thucydides, struggling with a language not yet quite tamed to the
severity of his purpose, philosophically recognised
and did all he could to help explain the troublous
perplexity of contemporary circumstance.   Taken
alone, the history of Thucydides is a masterpiece
of classic grandeur; compared with Herodotus,
it seems by very reason of its intense concentration to have lost something of that serene exten-
siveness of view which marks Herodotus, the father
of prose, as belonging to the Age of Pericles,
Phidias, and Sophocles.   When we compare both
of them together with Homer, we can hardly help
feeling more deeply still that the course of Greek
expression is tending toward the limitation of
imaginative freedom by an inexorable sense of
fact.   In Thucydides the development of history
in Greece,—with which we have interrupted our

glance at the development of dramatic poetry, the other great form of literature developed there during the Fifth Century,—has clearly taken a shape still original but no longer surgingly crescent.

It was amidst such things as he records, and to a great extent while he was recording them, that the work of Euripides was at its highest, and that the work of Aristophanes began. When we turn now to them, completing our glance at dramatic poetry, we shall find their relation to Æschylus and Sophocles variously analogous to the relation we have already tried to define between the work of Thucydides and that of Herodotus. For all their imaginative power, they too are comparatively hampered by increasingly insistent perception of fact.

VI

EURIPIDES

Though Euripides, traditionally said to have been born at Salamis on the very day of the battle which saved Greece, can hardly have been much more than fifteen years younger than Sophocles, the contrast between them is much greater than that between Sophocles and Æschylus, who were far less nearly of an age. Euripides, even in his own day, was recognised as an innovator, welcome to those who liked a new phase of art, and by no means so to those who preferred the maintenance of artistic tradition. As a tragic poet, to be sure, he was throughout compelled to observe certain of the conditions imposed on tragedy by the circumstances of its development: his subjects had to be heroic and considerably religious in character, the unavoidable chorus forbade his methods to approach what we should now consider anything like direct portrayal of life, and the use of masks and stilted buskins prevented freedom of expression or of action. Compared with any such dramas as make instant appeal nowadays, his must therefore seem almost ritually formal, and dependent for stage effect rather on elocution than on representation either of human beings or of human conduct. Compared with those of his great predecessors, however, they take on another aspect, almost modern. He is said to have died in the year 406, a few months before Sophocles—both happily spared knowledge of the final collapse of Athenian power, two years later. For a full half century they had been rivals—one magnificently sustaining the old tradition of tragedy, the other and the more popular sturdily asserting a new.

A fortunate chance enables us to see pretty distinctly what this new tradition was, in comparison with that sanctioned by custom. Among the surviving dramas of Euripides is one concerning Electra, a subject also dealt with, as we have already seen,[1] by both Æschylus and Sophocles. When compared with the Choephori, or Libation Pourers, of Æschylus, the Electra of Sophocles seems, as we reminded ourselves, like things we are used to. Compared with the Electra of Euripides, however, it appears uncompromisingly antique. The Electra of Euripides, accordingly, though not the most powerful of his nineteen surviving works, becomes for our purposes the most

[1] *Cf.* pp. 60, 67.

distinctly characteristic.[1] What is more, as it contains only 1,359 lines, all three of the dramas now before us are comprised in 3,943 lines, about as many as are in Hamlet; so to read through all three is no great task. Euripides opens his in a manner substantially and doubly new to us. A peasant —called in Greek "Autourgos," or a man who does his own work—enters, and devotes a soliloquy of fifty-three lines to a precise statement of the situation with which the action begins. Though evidently a minor character in the drama, he thus makes his first appearance as the speaker of what amounts to a formal prologue, much as the Richard III of Shakspere does in the chronicle-history which bears that sovereign's name. Some such prologue generally occurs, until the device begins to seem mechanical, throughout the extant tragedies of Euripides. The substance of the Peasant's prologue is even more characteristic than this newly conventional use of it. The general situation is the same as that with which the dramas of Æschylus and of Sophocles open: Agamemnon has been murdered by Clytemnestra, who has married her paramour Ægisthus; Orestes has disappeared; and Electra remains pretty desperate in Argos. Both Æschylus and Sophocles, however, represent her as still of acknowledged princely rank. Euripides, on the other hand, sets forth how, by way of avoiding trouble concerning succession to the throne, Ægisthus and Clytemnestra have compelled her to marry the Peasant,

[1] Gilbert Murray's translation is the most literate. All his translations of Euripides are noteworthy English poems. On the whole, too, they appear quite as like the original as the careful but rather more diffuse versions of A. S. Way, which are printed with the Greek text in the Loeb Classical Library.

an incidentally loyal creature who states that he has secretly refrained from asserting his marital rights; and when, after the prologue ends, she makes her appearance, she enters with a water-jar, doing something like menial work. In comparison with the classical dignity of her other presentations, accordingly, the situation is either astonishingly more human or, if you prefer, senti-mentalised to a degree which may conveniently be described by the sadly abused word romantic. Anyhow it appears much more nearly real; and indeed when new may well have appeared almost altogether so.

A similar contrast appears when you compare the two treatments of how Electra recognises Orestes.[1] We have already compared the presen-tation of this incident by Sophocles with that by Æschylus.[2] In Euripides, an old man enters—comparatively an almost comic character—who has been a servant of Agamemnon, and deeply resents the social degradation of Electra. He tells her how he has just found on her father's tomb the new-cut lock of hair which figures in both of the other versions. Orestes, still un-recognised, enters while they are discussing this, to which Electra attaches no importance; and the old man presently recognises Orestes, mostly by reason of a scar on his brow—a traditional dra-matic trick until the absent strawberry mark on the left arm which brings about fraternal reunion of Box and Cox. Here, in comparison with either

[1] Lines 487–584. In Gilbert Murray's admirable version the lines are not numbered; the passage begins on p. 30, of the single-volume edition, and ends on p. 37.
[2] *Cf.* p. 67.

of the other treatments, is at once something like
what we should now think dramatic action and a
rather meretricious theatrical device. You will
find a similar contrast in the passages describing
the murder of Clytemnestra,[1] set forth by Euripides
at considerable length;[2] he makes Electra lure her
mother into the Peasant's hut, where Orestes is
awaiting them to wreak his atoning vengeance in
Electra's presence. Nowhere near so grandly
classic as the heroine of Æschylus and of Sophocles, the Electra of Euripides is much more like a
human being.

Here we come to what seems the fundamental
fact in the dramas of Euripides. Tragic though
they stay, and in many ways limited or controlled
by the conditions and the traditions of the Greek
theatre, they strongly emphasise the human factor in tragedy, comparatively neglected by Æschylus,[3] and brought by Sophocles into no more
prominence than is needed to balance it with the
other factor of tragic conflict[4]—fate, environment,
whatever you will.[5] Whether this nearer approach
to human sympathy makes Euripides greater or
less than his predecessors has been often and
fruitlessly disputed. There can hardly be a doubt
that his comparative popularity, from his own
time onward, is due to the appeal he thus makes
to human nature, the one fact which poets, readers, and spectators must always and inevitably
have in common. Here, at least, generation after
generation have found something addressed to
themselves, something which they can understand
instinctively and without deliberate imaginative

[1] Cf. p. 68.   [2] Lines 998–1157; Murray, pages 64–73.
[3] Cf. p. 57.   [4] Cf. p. 69.   [5] Cf. p. 56.

effort. It has been summarised in a quatrain of
Mrs. Browning, not itself remarkable yet somehow
haunting the memory.[1] In the previous stanza
she has four commonplace lines about "Æschylus,
the thunderous," and four still more commonplace
about "Sophocles, the royal." Then come those
which linger:

> Our Euripides, the human,
>   With his droppings of warm tears,
> And his touches of things common,
>   Till they rose to touch the spheres.

To return to the Electra of Euripides, you will
find that it ends with a stage device for which
there is no precedent in the dramas of Sophocles or
of Æschylus. At the end of the Choephori, to be
sure, the Furies reveal themselves to Orestes, beginning the merited tortures with which the third
drama of the Trilogy is concerned.[2] In the Electra of Sophocles, there is no divine interposition.
In the Electra of Euripides, on the other hand,
the demigods Castor and Pollux—on earth brothers
of Clytemnestra and Helen—suddenly appear in
the air; and Castor, who speaks for both, brings
the troubles of Electra to an end by arranging
her marriage with Pylades, the bosom-friend of
Orestes, and only afterwards pronounces the con-
science-smitten doom of Orestes himself.[3] It seems
probable that these god-like apparitions were represented by actors mechanically lifted off their
feet. At all events, such interventions frequently
occur in the dramas of Euripides, where divine
visitants are apt to solve the complications of the

[1] Wine of Cyprus, XII.   [2] Lines 1046–1074; Plumptre, 1038–1064.
[3] Lines 1233–1359; Murray, pp. 78-83.

plot; and the device has given rise to the term *Deus ex machina*[1] (the God in the machine) commonly used from Roman times to describe any personage introduced from nowhere to unravel narrative or dramatic intricacies which have got inconveniently snarled. Whatever their dignity, these interjected deities have little other artistic purpose than to save poets and writers the trouble of inventing solutions more logical. And, though their function may thus partake of the godlike quality of mercy, they are hardly impressive enough to excite any deeply religious or even earnest emotion. At least comparatively, these gods of Euripides are pretty thinly theatrical. They are not such deities as any one could ever quite have believed in. Here is one simple reason why those who disapproved of Euripides found him, among other objections, irreligious.

A less obvious practice of his points the same way. Though, as a matter of necessity, he retains the chorus, he uses it at once more freely, more separately, and perhaps more negligently than Sophocles; and, as we have seen, it looms larger still in Æschylus. The dramas of Æschylus, indeed, represent a phase of tragic poetry not quite fully emerged from its origin in choral odes.[2] Those of Euripides represent a phase where the choral ode is subsiding into the background, and tending towards something little more essential than lyric interludes, analogous to the music played between the acts of modern plays in Amer-

---

[1] The term, usually supposed to be originally Latin, is said first to occur, and only allusively, in the Hermotimus of Lucian (86), a Greek dialogue of the Second Century A. D.

[2] *Cf.* p. 54.

ican theatres. It is tending, as well, towards philosophic comment on lines of thought which the action may have started. To enter into the philosophic opinions of Euripides would lead us now too far afield; but chapters and books have been written about them, and doubtless more will be. Whoever thus independently preaches must be prepared to have his orthodoxy scrutinised.

Of one thing, meanwhile, there can be no doubt. Compared with either of his predecessors Euripides was popular, and has remained so. The familiar lines of Milton's sonnet, "When the Assault was Intended to the City," remind us how, at least in tradition,

Sad Electra's poet had the power
To save the Athenian walls from ruin bare.

There was a similar tradition that Athenian captives in the quarries of Syracuse owed privileges, and perhaps their lives, to the chance that they could recite Euripidean lines. Again, only seven dramas of Æschylus have been preserved, and only seven of Sophocles. Of Euripides, on the other hand, who is said to have written more than ninety, we still possess nineteen: and his influence on the drama in later languages than Greek has been preponderant—on Seneca in Latin, for example, on the Samson Agonistes of Milton, on Racine in French, on Alfieri in Italian.

Milton, as we have just seen, thought of him as the author of Electra, and the preface to Gilbert Murray's translation of this drama pronounces its heroine the most profoundly studied of all those left us by Fifth Century Greece. By themselves, however, certain other works of Euripides are per-

haps more positively memorable. The surgent
splendour of the Bacchæ makes many hold it his
masterpiece; the tenderness and pathos of the
Alcestis combine with its happy ending in appeal
to general modern feeling; the Medea has a sav-
age intensity befitting the half-barbarous and
half-divine origin of its passionate, wronged, and
merciless heroine; the Hippolytus, with its para-
doxical contrast between the accursed lust of
Phædra and the fantastic purity of her husband's
son, is perhaps melodramatic—whatever that
abused term may mean—but none the less absorbing. The character of the Nurse there, too, though
not the detail of her speeches, reminds one of that
masterpiece of dramatic realism, the Nurse in
Shakspere's Romeo and Juliet; and Racine's
Phèdre, which is based on the Hippolytus, more
nearly holds the stage than any other tragedy of
Seventeenth Century France. Considering his inevitable limitations of subject, scope, and method,
at the same time, Euripides very adroitly avoids
monotony. Throughout his dramas, nevertheless,
you will find the characteristics we have perhaps
tediously dwelt on when we compared his version
of the story of Electra with those of Æschylus and
of Sophocles. Greater or lesser than his great
predecessors, he is less grand and far more nearly
human. Compared with them, he takes a long
step towards reality, bringing heroic personages
down towards the level of this earth where we
live and move and have our being.

They are no longer like Periclean, Phidian,
Sophoclean ideals; in their veins runs something
like the blood of life. Thus, not altogether fantastically, we may group them with the virtually

contemporary historical personages and incidents of Thucydides, as compared with those of Herodotus, a little earlier in fact and measurelessly so in spirit. Though the surge of Greek invention which we have admired from Homer's time onwards persist throughout this later period of the Fifth Century, it is at last near the period where, if not yet ebbing, you begin to feel that it cannot rise much higher.

Of other tragic poets who flourished in these years only the names are left us. We need hardly regret the loss of their works, nor even much lament the loss of far more work by Æschylus, Sophocles, and Euripides than survives; for the fragments of it preserved by grammarians and critics are at best no better than the tragedies we still possess. These, thirty-three in all, are enough to define both the nature and the course of this great phase of European literature, unknown when the Fifth Century began and complete, in its primal form, when the Century ended. Had these hundred years added nothing else to literary tradition, they would stay memorable for their tragic poetry. As we have seen, besides, they also added to European literature the great tradition of historical prose. Thus doubly memorable, they would still have— even if neither of these monuments had been preserved—another claim to lasting memory. For towards the end of them there came into permanent existence another form of literature, in its kind unsurpassed.

VII

ARISTOPHANES

As we reminded ourselves when we first touched on dramatic poetry,[1] this phase of literature originated in choral odes or something like them made for the festivals of the god Dionysus; and the worship of this deity had two distinct phases. One, of solemn character, developed into tragedy, the other, concerned with obvious aspects of his conduct as the god of generation, was ribald to a degree which would now seem inconceivably remote from any European ideas of religion—and indeed would make the wildest grotesques of mediæval sculpture appear, in comparison, devoutly austere. This developed into comedy, which appears to have existed and flourished throughout the growth of tragedy. The very extravagance of its license may perhaps be one reason why it was later in taking permanent form; so far as words and conduct went, it seems to have been bridled only by the limits of invention imposed by nature on those who made it; within the limits of conventional dramatic conditions, they were permitted, not only every imaginable violation of general decorum and decency, but also the wildest range of personal abuse and of what Americans would nowadays call topical allusion. So long as their audience laughed, their work was well done; and few human emotions are at once more genuine and more transitory than such as excite laughter. For centuries the rude

[1] *Cf.* p. 51.

but persistent bases of it have now been condemned as obscene—a word which literally means
that they should be kept out of sight; and
the personal or topical bases of it fade out of sight
by themselves as, year by year, the men, the
politics, and the manners concerned are swiftly
forgotten. So old fun is apt either to make men
pruriently snicker and whisper, or else to be life-
less as corked champagne. Fun must sparkle,
and the very essence of effervescence lies in momentary freshness. To laugh healthily, you must
laugh loud.

It is perhaps more surprising, therefore, that
Greek comedy survives at all than that the eleven
examples of it still in existence are all by one man,
and that his literary career began with the last
quarter of the Fifth Century. Of the life of Aristophanes little is known. He was Athenian; he
was probably born after 450; his first appearance
as a comic poet, though precocious, seems to have
occurred well after the Peloponnesian War broke
out; and he lived for some fifteen or twenty years
after the Century ended. His extant comedies
imply that his sympathies were conservative or
even reactionary, at a period when the state of
things he cared for was swiftly bound nowhere;
the Symposium, or Banquet, of Plato, represents
him in good company. That is about the whole
story.

His work is at once hard to understand and
harder to translate. To appreciate anything like
its full meaning you must know every traceable detail of the political and social conditions
momentarily existing when each comedy was
written; you must guess what others, now beyond

recovery, may perhaps have been; and you must admit insoluble the problems occasionally presented by personal or topical allusions. When you try to render into another language what despite these difficulties you have discovered, you will find any modern language to fail. It could hardly manage the fundamental need of expressing serious purpose in terms of unbridled license and broad burlesque, reduced to a metrical form of exquisitely varied exactitude. When it strives to combine with this the need of animating the lines with incessant, unexpected fun, both witty and humorous, and of sweetening the whole with passages, mostly choral, unsurpassed for lyric beauty, the task becomes superhuman; and yet until the task is accomplished in a style of seemingly spontaneous, idiomatic ease, you can hardly even approach Aristophanic effect. There is no need to say that nobody has done so. The double wonder is that Aristophanes remains so fascinating to all who care for him in the Greek as to keep them incessantly attempting the impossible with a courage which he would have been the first to laugh at, and that after all they have managed to give English readers even a shadowy notion of what he was.

Fortunately for us here and now, the Comedy of Aristophanes which most instantly concerns the traditions of literature has been translated into English better than any other. Gilbert Murray's version of the Frogs is licentious, to be sure, only in its dainty avoidance of Aristophanic license; and its lyric beauties never reach the point of haunting charm. On the other hand, it is clear, swift, idiomatic, easy to read, and so faithful to the fun of the original that when read aloud it will often excite spontaneous laughter. The subject of the Frogs is the state of dramatic literature in the year 405. The death of Euripides the year before, shortly followed by that of Sophocles, had left the tragic poetry of the Greeks, as we can now see, virtually complete. There were plenty of tragic poets, and there were to be a great many more, but none to vie through the ages with the three great Fifth Century masters. This truth instantly impresses the divinely prescient god Dionysus, who bereft on earth of tragic artificers able duly to celebrate his festivals, feels impelled to bring back one of them from the shades. He appears in broadly comic conventional character, disguised as Heracles,—one of whose feats was the recovery of Alcestis from the dead,—and very much and reasonably afraid of the discomforts and misadventures he may have to undergo; among other things this Aristophanic deity is the most abject imaginable coward. Charon compels him to earn his passage across the Styx by taking a very inexpert hand at the oars; on the way he is scared and chaffed by a ghostly chorus of Stygian frogs, to whom the name of the comedy is due. All of which, despite Gilbert Murray's skill, may perhaps seem a little dull in Twentieth Century English. When we fairly get to the Shades, however, things wake up. For a good many years, it seems, there had been no question that in this mildly dismal eternity Æschylus was entitled to all the honours due the greatest of tragic poets; when Euripides followed beyond the grave, he proceeded to claim these dignities for himself. Æschylus violently disputes the claim, and the last half of the Frogs[1] is devoted to their quarrel. They appeal to Pluto, abusing each other with incessant quotations or parodies of their own verses. After much fluctuation, Pluto decides in favour of Æschylus, who takes the occasion to pronounce Sophocles, and not Euripides, second to himself. The comedy ends with his start back to Athens—which implies that, whatever happens to Euripides, the tragedies of Æschylus are not going to be shelved. There could be no broader burlesque; and certain passages—particularly that where Æschylus caps line after line of Euripidean prologue with two ridiculous words which fit both sense and metre,[2] yet state that Ægyptus, Dionysus, Cadmus, Pelops, and other divine or heroic beings have lost the Greek equivalent for their cakes of soap—are durably laughable. Incidentally, this buoyant popular criticism of almost contemporary poetry keeps the tragic poets astonishingly alive. It is not in the least judicial; it does not even pretend to be fair; but it contagiously expresses the mood which, from those days to ours, has resented the vulgarising of fine art, and has been impulsively disposed to regard changes as probably for the worse. The most wonderful thing about it is that, if you will let it recall you to the poets it concerns, you will find yourself appreciating and enjoying them decidedly more than when you read them first.

Most of our Aristophanic comedies concern matters either political or social, and therefore cannot be understood without considerable study of the conditions amid which they were written;

---

[1] Lines 755-1533; Murray (1908), pp. 58-108.
[2] Lines 1198-1248; Murray, pp. 88-91.

all have animation, to be sure, and passages so generalised both as fun and as poetry that you can hardly fail to find plenty of reason why they are· excellent; most, however, need a good deal of annotation, except for the initiated, and sometimes even for them. With one, however, this is less the case, if indeed it be comparatively the case at all. The Clouds, originally produced some twenty years before the Frogs, ridicules the influence of new-fangled philosophy on good old beliefs and manners, much as crusty Victorian churchmen did their best now and again, over their port, to laugh down evolution or the higher criticism; and the central figure of the comedy is a fantastic caricature of Socrates, who is traditionally said rather to have enjoyed this exhibition of himself on the popular stage. Beyond question, the Socrates of the Clouds, though his mask probably resembled the grotesque features of the real man and his costume the odd untidiness for which the real man was noted, has little more than a name in common with the character whom Benjamin Franklin thought worthy to place in the self-admonishing maxim "Imitate Jesus and Socrates." Dr. Henry Jackson's matchless article on him in the Encyclopædia Britannica[1] tells the true story incomparably for such purposes as ours. For more than one reason, nevertheless, the Socrates of the Clouds is worth our attention; no other account of this remarkable man is anywhere near so early, none other indeed is fully contemporary, and no other so clearly reminds us that Fifth Century Athens was the city where that life was lived which will live forever in the faithful

[1] Ninth edition; reprinted, with little change, in the Eleventh.

reminiscences of Xenophon and the idealised dialogues of Plato. These works themselves belong not to the Fifth Century but to the Fourth. The man they concern, however, passed all his years but the very last in the Fifth. To think of the Fifth without remembering that he was there would be almost as incomplete as to think of it without remembering Pericles or Phidias. Were any easily accessible English version of the Clouds half so readable as Gilbert Murray's translation of the Frogs, we should dwell on this comedy longer; for next to the Frogs it is the most important contribution of Aristophanes to the traditions of European literature.

Aristophanes, as we have seen, lived and wrote for some years after the Fifth Century ended. On the whole, however, his true place is in the last quarter of it. When his work began, the Century had already added to its inheritance of epic, didactic, and lyric poetry its own contributions of tragic poetry and of history; to these Aristophanes added the primal enduring example of comic poetry. No other hundred years of Europe has been quite so splendidly creative, even in literature alone. Though essentially European, however, that literature still remained, and complacently supposed itself nationally Greek and locally Athenian. Athens held everything else provincial or barbarous.

CHAPTER III

THE FOURTH CENTURY BEFORE CHRIST

I

HISTORICAL TRADITIONS

Again we come to a Century where, if our purpose were historical, Greece might detain and perplex us long. Concerned, however, only with facts which the Fourth Century brought into such traditional existence that they have remained matters of general literary allusion, we can summarise them pretty simply.

When the Fourth Century began, we have already seen, the imperial power of Athens was broken. Athens remained, however, an important centre of trade and of culture. The Age of Pericles, which has never faded from tradition, was still well within the limits of human memory. There were times, for nearly fifty years, when something like imperial recovery may have seemed more than possible. On the whole, however, the most significant circumstance in completely Greek perspective, seems the most nearly familiar name in military tradition from the first half of the Century. Just who Epaminondas was and what he did is perhaps generally forgotten; so indeed may also be the names of his living victory at Leuctra, and of what he believed his dying victory at Mantinea; but hardly, if he is remembered at all, the

fact that he was not of Athens but of Thebes.
There had been a while when Spartan power
looked dominant; Theban power suppressed that;
and Theban power virtually ended when Epaminondas fell. For our purposes it is enough to remember that almost to the middle of the Century
the history of Greece proper is in a state of kaleido-
scopic confusion.

To the northward of Greece, meanwhile, the
power of Macedon was rapidly assuming a form
more portentous than any previously known in
Europe. This region, from the Athenian point
of view, was semi-barbarous; but its culture and
its fashion were Greek, much as those of Prussia
were French under Frederick the Great. Its government was a monarchy, increasing in organisation and in strength; its best-remembered military
device, the phalanx, was more formidable than
anything previously known. In 359, a youth
named Philip became king. For twenty years
his authority increased, while that of the dis-
cordant Grecian states diminished. In 338 his
victory at Chæronea made him military master
of Greece; the next year he was formally acknowledged as commander-in-chief of the Greeks; and
what might have ensued if he had not been assassinated in 336, when only forty-seven years old,
nobody knows.

It could not have been more wondrous than what
came to pass. The next thirteen years comprise
the imperial career of Alexander, who succeeded
to his father's throne at the age of twenty, and
whose death at thirty-three prevented the consoli-
dation of an empire European in origin, unprecedented in extent, and professedly Greek in cul-

ture. He began by reducing Greece itself to subjection, incidentally destroying Thebes but sparing the house of Pindar. Then he swept over Asia Minor, and down through Syria; and Egypt submitted to him, and he founded at the mouth of the Nile the great seaport, Alexandria, which still bears his name. Then he turned his attention to Persia itself, where he completely overthrew the power of Darius III, and took possession of Babylon, of Susa, of Persepolis, and of Ecbatana. Then he pressed eastward even to India, where troubles with his troops prevented him from pushing on to the Ganges. Forced temporarily to withdraw, he went down the Indus, and so westward across burning deserts. He got as far as Babylon, where he died of a sudden fever in the year 323. There had never before been so triumphant a short life as his; and there has been none since. His military genius was of the highest. Wherever he went he founded cities on Greek principles, and introduced Greek forms of art. His name survives to this day in India—transmuted into Sikanda, or some such form; you can long trace Greek influence in Indian sculpture. And so on. No wonder his head was turned; in Egypt he is said to have declared himself the son not of Philip but of Zeus; in the Orient he assumed something like the character of its native sovereigns, requiring his courtiers and generals to prostrate themselves at his feet. There were times when he drank hard; in an outburst of fury, towards the end of a feast, he killed with his own hand his loyal friend Clitus; the excesses described in Dryden's Alexander's Feast are not far from literal truth. Yet if need were he could bear without complaint the hardships of a common soldier. Though he did not live to accomplish what he had begun, his Century stays traditionally his, and the tradition of him has never been forgotten or even much dimmed. To this day, for example, the most classic form of French verse is called Alexandrine because it is based on that in which a French poem purporting to describe the exploits of Alexander was written in the Twelfth Century, some sixteen hundred years after Alexander was dead and gone.

From the confusion with which the Fourth Century began, accordingly, there emerges in the mid-century this tremendously distinct fact of Macedonian empire, when Europe, reversing the earlier Persian story, possessed herself of the Levant, of Egypt, and of southwestern Asia. And though no longer purely Greek, the Europe which did so cherished and spread the cultural traditions of Greece.

On the death of Alexander, however, something like the old confusion ensued. Greece itself relapsed into internal quarrels and warfares. The Hellenised Orient was disputed among the generals of Alexander, several of whom established separate independent monarchies. In actual history all this is important. In tradition it has mostly faded. The single clearly surviving fact is what happened in Egypt. Here, one of the generals, Ptolemy by name, founded with its capital at Alexandria a Grecian dynasty destined to hold the throne until its last sovereign descendant, Cleopatra, took her life rather than surrender herself to be exhibited in triumph by the Roman conqueror who was soon to be Augustus Cæsar.

Yet, somehow, Athens held her course as the direct heir of Periclean culture. In sculpture the Fourth Century gave us the work of Praxiteles; and when you compare the Hermes of Olympia with the Elgin marbles, and feel the difference, you will be at pains to choose which you would keep if you must lose one. In literature, too, though the great period of Greek poetry was complete, the Century produced new masterpieces of prose.

II

XENOPHON

Though probably the least important Fourth Century writer on whom we shall touch, and indeed less so than any other Greek within our present scope, Xenophon is among the most widely familiar. His admitted lack of that indefinable quality called genius has combined with a not very strongly founded opinion that his prose is unusually good to make him at once comparatively easy to read, and suitable for those who are trying to learn the Greek language. So his work has been much used in schoolbooks, even to this day. The circumstance, with its dismal consequences of grammatical analysis, deprives him, to be sure, of anything like popularity—which he once and deservedly enjoyed; at the same time, it almost cruelly saves him from oblivion, at once giving him an eminence rather above his merit, and fixing in schoolboy minds the notion that all the trouble they are put to when trying to penetrate the mysteries of elementary Greek will lead them only into vistas of tolerably animated polite common-place.

He was by birth an Athenian gentleman, at a time not unlike our own, when persons of his condition, who once enjoyed perhaps more consideration than they deserve, are condemned by democratic enthusiasm to be rather impotent objects of popular distrust. In the year 400 he appears to have been somewhere between twenty-five and thirty years old, and had already had his two most noteworthy experiences: friendship with Socrates, and a considerable part in the celebrated retreat of ten thousand Greek mercenaries from what promised to be annihilating defeat in Persia. The confusion of Athenian politics led to his exile. For some years he lived a life of literary leisure under the more congenial and aristocratic dominion of Sparta. He is thought to have died before the middle of the Century.

His writings are rather more copious than we generally remember. The most carefully studied, the Cyropædia, pretends to be an idealised life of the great Persian, Cyrus, and introduces a good deal of matter concerning education; it was early included in the Loeb Classical Library. He wrote, too, a number of treatises or pamphlets about constitutional matters, about horsemanship both military and civil, about hunting, and about other things. For our purposes, none of these is remarkable. Other works of his, however, touch on three distinct matters, all worth our attention. The first is his Hellenica, an actual history. Xenophon took up the history of Greece at the point where Thucydides left it, and carried on the turbulent story until the death of Epaminondas.

His later sympathies were Spartan; he had nothing like the power of Thucydides, nor yet the advantage of creating what amounted to a new form of historical expression. So this history bears to the book which it attempts to continue a relation like that of Smollett's chapters on the history of England to the more impressive work of Hume. It has a certain value, partly for want of an immediate rival; but it is manifestly inferior. Had Xenophon done no more than this and his lesser works, he would hardly have risen above our present horizon.

His most familiar work, on the other hand, commonly supposed by schoolboys to be all he wrote, has two claims to our attention: it clearly records with considerable spirit a distinct episode in military history, and the general character of this episode so contrasts with the historical matters treated by Herodotus and by Thucydides as to make it strongly typical of the last two or three years of the Fifth Century. Herodotus almost epically celebrates the national victories with which that Century began; Thucydides superbly collects the story of the virtually civil wars in which the fruits of those victories were lost; Xenophon circumstantially tells what happened to a large body of Greek mercenaries, shortly after the Peloponnesian War came to an end. At just about this time Artaxerxes II succeeded to the throne of Persia; after the good old Oriental fashion his brother Cyrus attempted to supplant him, and accordingly hired a considerable force of Greek soldiers, no longer needed for hostilities among the Greeks. In the expedition Xenophon took part. The name, Anabasis, by which his

account of it is commonly called, properly applies
only to the first of his eight Books; for it means
something like "advance," and seven of the Books
are devoted to what happened to the Greeks after
Cyrus had been defeated and killed at Cunaxa, not
very far from Babylon. They made their way
across hostile country to the Black Sea. Xenophon's narrative of how they did so, and incidentally of the part he played in the retreat,—
as he always writes of himself not in the first person but in the third, he can commend himself un-
blushingly,—is said by the few who have been
allowed to read it without stopping for grammatical
excursions to be clear and interesting. Certainly
we possess no earlier record of a distinct military
operation so detailed, so apparently precise, and
so nearly animated. When we stop to think, however, there can be no doubt that he rather over-
emphasises what was at best a technically creditable tactical episode, important mostly to the few
thousand Greeks who thereby managed to escape
annihilation, and that these, at the moment, were
only soldiers of fortune, prepared to fight for the
highest bidder. Remember the mood of Herodotus, and Marathon, and Thermopylæ, and Salamis;
compare with these the mood of an autobiographer
whose great achievement is that he kept his skin,
and the skins of others, intact; and you will
ironically feel the difference between the beginning and the end of the great Fifth Century.

The remaining work of Xenophon, though less
generally known, is on the whole his most memorable. As a youth he had come under the influence
of Socrates, whom he appears to have known well.
Socrates at the age of seventy was condemned to

death by a majority vote of a fantastically democratic popular court, on the grounds of irreligion
and of corrupting the young; refusing more than
one means to avoid his penalty, he drank the
poisonous draught commanded by Athenian law,
and slept in peace. The account of his end by
Plato,[1] accepted as historical, is among the noblest passages of world-literature. Xenophon,
who loved and respected his memory, defended it
in a long, somewhat rambling series of recollec-
tions, now generally known by its Latin name,
Memorabilia. They come half-way between the
extravagant caricatures of Aristophanes, and the
idealised dialogues of Plato, and thus, when compared with either of them, have an appearance
of literal fidelity. Though this may be delusive,
—for one thing, Socrates is frequently presented
as speaking, and of course nobody could remember his exact words after an interval of years,—it
may be at least traditionally accepted; and it
makes the Memorabilia substantially interesting
beyond almost anything else on which we have
touched. Even in Dakyns's clear and fluent English version, to be sure, you will hardly have
patience to read them through. Open them at
random, though, as you might open a volume of
recent memoirs or letters, and you will have an
instant sense that what your eye lights on is not
only true but living. The oftener you do so, the
oftener you will be disposed to do so again. In
the end you will feel them to justify the loving
summary of the character of Socrates with which
they end.[2] Their definite and simple task is accomplished. Thus, in the perspective of European

[1] Phædo, 114–118.   [2] IV, viii, ii.

literature Xenophon takes his place as the first
enduring writer of anecdotic biography.

At least two of his minor works give other
glimpses of Socrates. The Economist, a longish
treatise on the Science of the Household, takes the
form of a dialogue between Socrates and one Cri-
tobulus; and the Symposium, or Banquet, introduces Socrates in a convivial company whose conduct and speech are occasionally such as unpleas-
antly to recall Macaulay's[1] celebrated comparison
of the morals of Plato with those of Sir George
Etherege. Negligible in themselves, at least for
students so cursory as we are now, these dialogues
have the interest of showing what Xenophon
could do when measured with Plato. For the
method of both and the substance of one—the
Symposium—are to be found in celebrated works
of that justly celebrated philosopher. The comparison is perhaps unkind to Xenophon. Without
it his portrait-sketches of Socrates might appear
stronger than they do now. With it, one feels
him, for all his loyalty and for all the fidelity of
his purpose, fatally free from insight. He implies what Socrates looked like and how he behaved; he tells you what kind of things Socrates
said, and how these affected the great variety of
Athenians to whom, through fifty years or more,
Socrates incessantly said them; but somehow
Xenophon keeps hopelessly outside of the character
he is attempting to portray. He does enough to
make Socrates both real and memorable, but hardly enough to make Socrates immortal. Doubtless,
the Socrates of Plato is variously idealised; very
probably the Socrates and the Athens of Xeno-

[1] Early in his essay on the Comic Dramatists of the Restoration.

phon—incidentally full of such social amenity as
one instinctively feels must have existed at a
period which produced the fine art of Fifth Century
Greece—are very like facts. These facts, too,
would be priceless if we had nothing else to balance
the extravagances of Aristophanes. As they stand,
however, they sink into little more than record of
how the last quarter of the Fifth Century was remembered by a cultivated Athenian gentleman,
condemned by circumstance to a life of literary
leisure during much of the first half of the Fourth.

Had this been the chief literature of the Fourth
Century, accordingly, we should have had from
that period only evidence of how the great phase
of literature brought into permanent being by
Herodotus, and brought nearer earth by Thucydides, was politely declining. Happily for everybody, this very period has given us literature as
priceless as any from the great Century it followed.

III

PLATO

Philosophy, which literally means love of wisdom, is as old as humanity. You can hardly
imagine men without desire for knowledge, without
aspiration toward truth. Such desire and aspiration they have always expressed, sometimes in the
crude form of aphorisms and proverbs, sometimes
in recurrently futile effort to think into order the
dazzling confusion of perception. By the Fifth
Century, both phases of expression were immemorial in Greece; and if our concern were with
philosophy we might already have mentioned

them, touching on such names as Thales, who is said to have flourished in the Seventh Century, and Pythagoras, whose traditionally more familiar name is usually placed in the Sixth. When Athens was at her height in the Fifth, there seems to have been considerable philosophical activity, along with the fine art and the literature on which we have dwelt. This, indeed, is what the Clouds of Aristophanes satirises and attacks. The old order was changing and with it the old faiths; compared with the gods of Æschylus, those of Euripides are feebly divine. In such conditions, as in our own times, you will generally find anywhere numerous more or less honest purveyors of new truth, beautifully systematic at first sight, but apt soon to prove filmy and flimsy.

When the Fourth Century began, this kind of thing, even though permanently traceable, had not yet developed into lasting literature. From Homer down, no doubt, there was much detached aphorism scattered through Greek poetry and Greek tradition; this, however, was either incidental to the poems—epic, lyric, or dramatic— where it occurred, or else took the form of separate and fragmentary sayings, such as "Know thyself." By the Fifth Century, too, there were philosophic poets, of whom the most eminent was probably the Sicilian Empedocles. One reason why their hexametric statements of doctrine do not quite rise to the level of world-literature may very likely be that, so far as they have been preserved, they survive only in few and broken fragments. A more substantial reason why Fifth Century philosophy produced no literary masterpiece is pretty clear that, as a matter of principle, Socrates, by far the most important Athenian thinker of that period, never wrote a line. Neither did he ever have anything like a school, or centre of systematic teaching; the fact that Aristophanes represents him as the head of a regular establishment for instruction was itself, when the Clouds appeared, an incisive thrust of satire, implying that Socrates was really what he had all his life professed himself and persistently tried not to be. There can be no doubt that his eccentric and often vexatious habit, throughout his career, was to mingle with men in public places, to pretend to seek the wisdom they believed themselves to possess, to ply them with ingenious questions until they were driven into mazes of contradiction, and then to proceed to speculate about the rays of truth which might begin dimly to illuminate the darkness of an ignorance which he professed himself to share with them. He was often stimulating, generally salutary, and seldom negligible; his purpose, though now and again disguised by irony and humour, was honest and high; his conduct, granting the accepted morals of his time, was blameless to the point of saintliness; but he was frequently irritating, and hardly ever conclusive. All this clearly appears in the Memorabilia of Xenophon, one of the younger men whom he most deeply influenced; but nothing, as we have already seen, can make Xenophon of more than secondary literary importance. So the Socrates of world-literature is hardly more Xenophon's than he is that of Aristophanes; he is the Socrates set forth in the Dialogues of Plato.

Like Xenophon, Plato was a gentleman of Athens, who could remember the last fifteen or

twenty years of the Fifth Century and who wrote
during the first half of the Fourth. Like Xenophon,
he was deeply influenced by Socrates. Unlike
Xenophon, he took as little part as possible in
public affairs, and he was himself a man of the
highest intellectual and literary power. Even if he
had written nothing, indeed, Plato might still be
traditionally remembered as one who never ceased
to think forward with the impulse given him by
Socrates, and whose comparatively systematic
teaching has made the name of the place where he
habitually taught—the Academy, which seems to
have been a kind of public park, very near Athens
—a general European name for institutions of
learning or of instruction. And even if he had
never taught, his writings would stay memorable,
not only for the portrait-sketches of Socrates on
which they seem originally to have been based,
nor yet only for the uncodified philosophic system
or tendency which they increasingly developed, but
also for the artistic skill and beauty of their literary form.

It was perhaps the lifelong colloquial habit of
Socrates which first led Plato to set forth the
character and the doctrines of his master in dialogues; thus, whatever else, he could best represent that unique, inspired, grotesque figure, incessantly mingling and talking with all sorts and
conditions of men. Besides this particular advantage, the form of dialogue has two or three
general conveniences: it is animated, it allows
considerable variety, and above all it never quite
commits a writer to the opinions thereby put
into the mouths of other human beings. Yet, as
these speakers, however distinctly characterised,

are really his own creatures, he can use them when he likes as vehicles for himself, with a freedom both artistic and intellectual hardly to be enjoyed otherwise. Given the form, it has never been better used than by Plato, who first established it in the enduring literature of Europe. Quite apart from what he has to say, the manner in which he says it is admirable.

To go no further, the first page or so of the Republic gives a glimpse of daily Athenian life almost as lastingly fresh as are the heroic incidents of the Iliad ; the beginning and the end of the Symposium, or Banquet, take one into the heart of antique, and to us exotic, conviviality; and the two dialogues concerning the last days of Socrates, the Crito and the Phædo, are masterpieces of narrative told through the speeches of clearly individualised characters. Throughout, indeed, the Dialogues of Plato exhale the atmosphere of social Athens and the politeness which kept its most vagrant excesses within the limits of classic decorum. Not long ago a reader who accidentally opened Jowett's translation, with no knowledge of Greek, no disposition to philosophic speculation, and a general impression that time-honoured masterpieces are tiresome, was surprised to find how, if you skip the passages which bore you, the Dialogues can still impress you, carelessly turning the pages, as not only interesting but often amusing, like animated and witty conversational books of one's own time. Thus to dwell on the mere surface of works inexhaustible for depth may perhaps appear inadvertent. By itself, however, that surface has had permanent effect on European literary tradition. Though

no later writer of dialogues has surpassed, and
indeed none has quite equalled, the primal animation of Plato, you will find his method and
the semblance of his devices imitated through the
centuries, much as the drama of Rome, of France,
and of Italy has imitated the methods and devices of Euripides. Except for Plato's dialogues,
Romans might never have used the form; and,
confining ourselves to English, we might be at
pains otherwise to see why Dryden should have
chosen it when discussing dramatic criticism, Addison when writing about medals, or Mr. Alexander H. Stephens when, a few years after the
American Civil War, he wrote two large volumes
justifying the constitutional principles of the
Southern Confederacy. Masterpieces of any art
are tyrants that die hard.

Though the order in which Plato's Dialogues
were written can never be certainly known, one
fact about them seems generally admitted. He
began by an effort to set forth, for all future time,
the character and the general teachings of Socrates, who without such record might soon fade
into little more than a name. As his work proceeded he tended increasingly to think for himself,
and to use the characters in the dialogues as
vehicles for speculative opinions of his own. At
last his Socrates became pretty shadowy; and the
longest of the dialogues, the Laws, — which is
generally thought his latest, — drops Socrates
altogether, consisting of a political discussion
between an Athenian, a Cretan, and a Lacedæ-
monian. Even here, however, Plato never expresses himself directly; throughout, he sets forth
what he has to say after the Socratic manner.

Men meet, and fall to talking about whatever subject he chooses them to deal with; they question one another politely and adroitly; incidentally they express a considerable variety of more or less tenable opinion. Their desire is by inquiry to ascertain or at least to approach truth. They never arrive, however, at anything much more conclusive than the discovery of probabilities for which the writer escapes complete responsibility by always putting his arguments into the mouth of somebody else.

Such a method you might well expect to lead nowhere. Beyond question, however, no European philosopher has had more enduring influence than Plato. This has fluctuated. At times it has blazed; at other times it has only feebly glowed; but it has never been more than eclipsed, and unless men change beyond recognition it never will be. To enter into the details of any philosophic system is clearly beyond our present scope. Very broadly, however, we may do well to remind ourselves of the character or tendency of Plato's. So long as this world lasts, life will stay baffling, confusing, and often to all appearances desperate; nothing can ever quite clear from it the clouds of error, of ugliness, of sin, vice, and wickedness. Yet these are so far from comprising the universe, that in thoughtful moments, as you gaze on them until your eyes begin to see deeper, they grow to seem like the vapoury clouds of earth dimming the full reality of sunlight. Beyond falsehood, ugliness, and evil glow the radiant, quenchless facts of truth, of beauty, and of good. Seek these, and even though you never attain mastery of their infinitudes you shall forever find in their exhaustless depths more and more illuminating light. Reality, as we call it, is transitory, delusive, phantasmal. Beyond it, about it, above it stays the serene eternity of immutable ideals. Even a glimpse of ideals may help assuage the troubles, alleviate the miseries, correct the blunders of daily life, as we pass from cradle to grave. Nothing but recognition of ideals, and, if so may be, knowledge of what they may reveal to such understandings as ours, can ever help us towards the calm security of wisdom. He does best who throughout our passing years most tirelessly seeks.

There are men and there are generations to whom moods like this appeal beyond all others. Whether they know it or not, such men and such generations are the secular disciples of Plato. Even still, when we carelessly try to name ideals beyond reality—such as love grown to exceed the transitory delusions of the flesh—we are apt, with no thought of Fourth Century Athens a few years before Philip's victory at Chæronea, to call them Platonic.

Had this been all that the Fourth Century contributed to the literary tradition of Europe, the period would accordingly be memorable for bringing into our enduring literature the fact of philosophy and the form of the dialogue. These, as we have seen, belong to the first half of the Century. The next quarter of it added two more primal names to the literature of Greece. These are Demosthenes and Aristotle.

IV

DEMOSTHENES

Demosthenes and Aristotle were of about the same age, and are said to have died within a few months of each other. In 375 both were boys; by 350 both were past thirty; and neither survived for more than a year the death of Alexander. Chronology therefore gives no help towards deciding which to dwell on first. For at least two reasons, however, it seems best that we choose Demosthenes: he was a native citizen of Athens, so deeply concerned with civic and public matters that his career implies the history of his time; and his work established in lasting literature a distinct form of expression. The career of Aristotle, on the other hand, who was of Stagira on the seacoast near Macedonia, and first came to Athens as a student, is comparatively independent of history, and his work, although second to none in positive importance, is not so primal. Without him European literature would have possessed at least one phase of philosophy, in the works of Plato; while, until Demosthenes revealed himself as the supreme master of Grecian oratory, oratory had hardly taken its independent literary place. There is a third reason, too, for permitting him to interrupt our glances at Fourth Century philosophy; nothing else could more prudently remind us how, throughout such considerations as ours, we are compelled by the conditions of language to treat consecutively matters which were really contemporary. Had we touched on Aristotle

first, we might have been at more pains to remember that philosophy had not completed its
Fourth Century development before oratory, the
other characteristic form of great Fourth Century
expression, began.

Demosthenes, there is hardly need to say, no
more invented oratory than Plato invented philosophy, Herodotus history, or Homer poetry.
Like them he only carried a form of thought and
expression so far beyond the point where he found
it as not only to make its origin comparatively
negligible, but also permanently to influence its
future course. Masterpieces, though apt to survive alone, seldom if ever come into being so; the
very existence of a masterpiece implies the previous
existence of an often traceable tradition, or school,
thereby so crowned that posterity tends to forget
the foundations on which great works must always
rest. Without a cloud of dramatists encompassing
him round, for example, we could never have had
Shakspere; yet, though some hundreds of their
plays exist, the growth of Baconian heresy already proves how nearly the dust of no more than
three English centuries has buried them. When
such oblivion may overtake literature made in our
own language, and itself its own excuse for being,
we need wonder little that the Greek origins of
oratory seem important only to students of Greek
history.

This form of expression is distinctly different
from all we have previously considered. Broadly
speaking, the office of poetry is at once to stir and
to please, occasionally conveying information;
that of history is to inform, meanwhile exciting
attention and incidentally giving pleasure; that

of philosophy is to explain perplexities and pleasantly to stimulate thought. Whatever else, all the
literature we have as yet glanced at, from Homer
to Plato, may be regarded as having fulfilled its
purpose when those who read or hear it are duly
informed, stirred, and pleased. At least to this
extent, a finished work is the chief end contem-
plated by poets, historians, or philosophers; so
far as any of these desire to influence those whom
they address, their prime purpose is to influence
only opinion or mood, or at most to induce sympathy. The object of oratory, on the other hand,
is by no means accomplished when an oration is
written or delivered, nor yet when hearers or readers completely and sympathetically understand.
Generally speaking, unless an oration makes men
behave otherwise than they might have behaved
if let alone, it is only a display of rhetorical fire-
works. It is not an end in itself, it is rather a
secondary matter—an instrument or weapon useful for attaining such ends as are sought by
practising lawyers and practical politicians.

The course of Athenian history, at least from
the period of the Persian Wars, had tended to
give increasing importance to eloquent speeches.
Decisions of grave consequence, both political and
legal, were apt to be made by a majority vote;
the court which condemned Socrates, for example,
consisted of some five hundred citizens, a large
minority of whom voted in his favour. Such conditions, in days when nothing like what we should
now call public prints existed, made oratory almost
uniquely efficient. A man who, for better or
worse, could persuade an assembly to act as he
happened to desire was a man to be counted

with. When his momentary purpose was accomplished, however, his means of accomplishing
it became an outworn tool—at best a matter
of record, on which later tools could be modelled when required. By the time of Demosthenes, two requisites of such tools were clearly
understood: an excellent speech must apparently
appeal to reason, the more soundly the better;
it must also, and more subtly, appeal to emotion
or prejudice. The difficulties here involved are
obvious: your orator must be master of his craft
to the point of craftiness, yet he must often if
not generally appear artless, spontaneous, sincere, and fervid. At his worst he is an adroit
trickster; at his best, he has to control genuine
impulse with histrionic skill. Throughout he is
compelled to devote himself with all his art and
with all his heart to questions which begin to be
matters of the past as soon as his work is done.

In view of all this, the wonder is not that Greek
oratory has chiefly historical or legal interest, but
rather that any Greek orator should ever have
emerged, as Demosthenes unquestionably has
emerged, into the full eminence of world-literature.
The historical circumstances of his time, the known
facts of his life, and the substance of his extant
works are admirably summarised in the short
monograph about him by S. H. Butcher. He was
the orphan son of a well-to-do Athenian man of
business. Despite physical disadvantages which
have given rise to anecdotic tradition,—such as
the tale of how he cured thickness of utterance by
practising speech with his mouth full of pebbles,
—he was compelled at twenty or so to bring suit
against a dishonest guardian, and to plead his

cause in person. For the legal career thus accidentally begun he proved to have unusual gifts. From time to time he wrote a good many speeches for other litigants whom Athenian practice required to speak for themselves. He early took interest in public matters, particularly when they concerned foreign policy. He was passionately patriotic, enthusiastically cherishing ancestral Athenian tradition. He was an assiduous student of Thucydides. He was among the first to perceive the danger of Macedonian aggression. So long as there was any hope, he opposed Philip with such intensity that the word Philippic, originally the name given three or four of his orations, has ever since been a general term for political denunciation. After Chæronea he did his best to preserve what was left of Athens. He lived through the reign of Alexander. In the confusion which followed Alexander's death, he was forced to seek sanctuary in a temple not very far away. Pursued thither, already under sentence of death, he took his life, heroically disdaining unmerited indignity. And before long his name and his statue were held venerable in the city he had tried to save.

Of the surviving speeches attributed to him, twenty-five remained unquestioned when Butcher's monograph was published. Eleven of these are political, like modern speeches in Parliament or in Congress; the rest are forensic—seven concerned with public or political affairs, and seven with private law-suits. To appreciate or even quite to understand work so partisan and occasional needs more knowledge of history and of detail than most of us can ever possess. Trans-

lation, too, must generally throttle the life of
oratory almost as fatally as it disenchants the
magic of lyric poetry; the soul of both lurks quiver-
ing in the meshes of their original sound and
rhythm; cut or even disturb a single strand, and
something escapes. Yet through more than two
thousand years Demosthenes, at least in tradition,
has held his own. Even when he was alive, he
was generally recognised as the greatest master
of the art he professed and practised; whether he
succeeded or failed at any given moment, he did
what he tried to do better than it had been done
before, and on the whole as well as it could imaginably be done.

Although his policy failed, accordingly, for he
fought against the stars, he has none the less
been admired by posterity, recurrently studying
and imitating him as the primal model of what
oratory ought to be. He stands to all Europe,
Butcher clearly points out, in some such relation
as that of Edmund Burke to the parliamentary
eloquence of England. Both were consummate
masters of language; both counted with human
nature; both were faithful students of history;
both sincerely believed in the constitutional traditions of their national inheritance; both raised
occasional eloquence to the height of enduring
political thought excellently expressed; both have
thus won secure place not only in history but in
literature. Yet each, to do his work, was per-
force a man of his own time; and the time even of
Burke is dead and gone. How much of either
must be counted as humanly temporal, how much
may be accepted as humanly eternal, nobody can
quite tell. The one sure thing is that the methods

of Burke long survived the parliamentary conditions where they originated, and that the methods of Demosthenes, originating in the democratic
conditions of Fourth Century Athens, have more
or less directly affected European oratory ever
since. To go no further, Cicero was aware of
them, and Burke was aware of them and of Cicero
as well, and Daniel Webster, aware of both Cicero
and Demosthenes, was aware of Burke into the bar-
gain. Orators do things still—assert principle, for
example, appeal to prejudice, denounce opponents
—not only because these things must be done anyhow but also, and perhaps considerably, because
these were the methods fixed in tradition by the
master who finally brought oratory into literature,
while Philip and Alexander were conquering the
liberties of Greece.

V

ARISTOTLE

It was just before Demosthenes made his first
public appearance, pleading for himself against his
dishonest guardian, that Aristotle first came to
Athens.[1]   Born of a respectable family at Stagira,
a sea-coast town close to the borders of Macedon,
he is said, as traditionally descended from Æscula-
pius, the god of medicine, to have been compelled
in boyhood to supplement his regular education
by such anatomical studies as were then practicable.   His father appears to have had friendly
personal relations with the Macedonian court,

[1] The facts here are mostly taken from the popular monograph on Aristotle by Sir Alexander Grant (1877).

before the time of Philip. At about the age when men now begin university work, Aristotle was sent to complete his education at Athens. There he became a pupil of Plato; and there he remained for some twenty years. In the course of this sojourn he was recognised as the ablest man who had ever sat at Plato's feet; so, although he had gradually diverged from Plato's doctrine, being given to strongly independent thought, he probably aspired to the mastership of Plato's school when Plato died—much as a distinguished university man might now aspire to succeed an elderly college president whom he personally respected but whose teachings he believed old-fashioned. When a more orthodox successor to Plato was chosen, Aristotle left Athens, and is said presently to have been selected by Philip as the private tutor of Alexander. In Alexander's time he returned to Athens, with a comfortable endowment from the Macedonian crown. The name of the school he thereupon established—Lyceum—has become almost as familiar in tradition as that of Plato's Academy. He lectured, with unsurpassed effect, until the death of Alexander. The subsequent confusions at Athens drove him, as they drove Demosthenes, from the city. Just how he died is not known; very likely he succumbed to the organic disorders often brought on by a habit of life mentally active and physically indolent.

He had written copiously. So far as is known, his earlier work, some of which survives, often took the Platonic form of dialogue, but was apt to be controversially opposed to various phases of Platonic doctrine; it is thought to have been published,—that is, frequently copied and thus placed at the disposal of whoever wished to buy it. His later work, on the other hand, which comprised the whole body of his mature teaching, is often thought to have been kept only in private copies, used as notes for his incessant lectures, sometimes complete enough to be read unchanged, sometimes more like memoranda to guide impromptu discourse. These came near getting lost; at last, however, some two hundred years after his death, they were brought to Rome, duly edited, and finally published there. Meanwhile his reputation had not only survived but strengthened; it has never faded out of sight.

His works, as we now possess them, are probably a considerable part of those published at Rome during the First Century before Christ. In two ways they sharply differ from anything we have hitherto dwelt on: they imply a temper so intent on thought, rather than on expression, as to prefer verbal precision to literary grace; and, more profoundly, they attempt to reduce the chaos of experience to semblance of order not by speculative inquiry or occasional aphorism, but by dogmatic system based on critically scrutinised fact. They are not precisely what we should now call scientific; in the Fourth Century before the Christian Era, true science, for want of data, was possible only in its most highly generalised and purest form of mathematics, and even then was elementary. On the other hand, they bring into world-literature and permanently establish there the kind of thought, recurrent through the centuries and now for a while dominant, from which science—that is, knowledge finally to be verified

by observation or experiment—must sooner or
later result. Dante wrote better than he knew
when he called Aristotle "Maestro di color chi
sanno." [1]

The contrast between his method and that of
Plato may be seen at a glance. Both, for example, wrote about government, Plato in his Republic and his Laws, Aristotle in his Politics;
both touched on oligarchy and democracy. Here
is a bit from Plato's Republic, where Socrates is
talking with one Adeimantus.[2]

Socrates speaks first:

Can we any longer doubt, then, that the miser and money-
maker answers to the oligarchical state?

There can be no doubt.

Next comes democracy; and how does the change from
oligarchy into democracy arise? Is it not in this wise?
The good at which such a state aims is to become as rich
as possible, a desire which is insatiable.

What then?

The rulers being aware that their power rests upon their
wealth, refuse to curtail by law the extravagance of the
spendthrift youth because they gain by their ruin.

To be sure.

There can be no doubt that the love of wealth and the
spirit of moderation cannot exist together in citizens of the
same state to any considerable extent; one or the other will
be disregarded.

That is tolerably clear:

and, so on, for many pages.

Compare with this the manner in which Aristotle sets forth a similar opinion;[3] he may be
imagined a lecturer stating his own views:

[1] "Master of them that know," Inferno, IV, 131.
[2] VIII, 555: Jowett III, p. 261.   [3] Politics, tr. Jowett, III, 7.

The true forms of government are those in which the one, the few, or the many govern with a view to the common interest; but governments which rule with a view to the private interest, whether of the one, or of the few, or of the many, are perversions. . . . Of forms of government which regard the common interests[1] we call that in which one rules kingship or royalty; that in which more than one, but not many, rule aristocracy (the rule of the best). But when the citizens at large administer the state for the common interest, the government is called by the generic name—a constitution. . . .

Of the above-mentioned forms, the perversions are as follows: of royalty, tyranny; of aristocracy, oligarchy; of constitutional government, democracy. For tyranny is a kind of monarchy which has in view the interest of the monarch only; oligarchy has in view the interest of the wealthy; democracy, of the needy; none of them the common good of all.

Even so slight an example shows Plato suavely conjectural and Aristotle dogmatically authoritative. If you wish to dispute Plato, he may take refuge behind the shadow of Socrates; when you face Aristotle, you must tackle the Master himself.

The Master you must tackle, too, cherished no less a purpose than to reduce all knowledge, physical and metaphysical, to final system. In so doing he came into sharp contradiction of the master at whose feet he had begun his philosophic study.[2] Plato held that ideas are more real than facts. Somewhere, for instance, there is an immutable Idea of Man, of which the countless individuals whom we perceive as men are only various, transitory, incomplete, and delusive manifestations.

[1] I permit myself, to make this passage clearer, a slight rearrangement of Jowett's words.

[2] See Sir Alexander Grant, Aristotle, 8-10.

Aristotle, on the other hand, held—with what would seem a good deal more like common sense —that an abstract idea of Man can be derived only from generalisation based on observation of individual men, and that apart from them it can have no real existence whatever. We are straying already into thickets of philosophy where realists and nominalists have quarrelled, and may again quarrel long, quite aside from our own path. Our proper concern is nowise with philosophy, but only with the moods of the two philosophers who successively yet together brought philosophy into the tradition of European literature; and just here we must not wander far from Aristotle.

He did not achieve his purpose, of course; nobody can possibly know everything, and, even if anybody could, human life is not long enough to allow the lucky creature completely to state universal truth. Aristotle's copious work was nowhere near finished; a considerable part of it, furthermore, has very likely disappeared, ages ago. Two pieces of it, however, which happen to survive, at once concern such pursuits as ours, and historically indicate both how his mind worked and how it has influenced posterity. He wrote treatises on Rhetoric and on Poetry; in each case he examined the practice of the Greeks and based thereon a statement of generalised principles as to what had actually been done; in each case, his manner, and to all appearances his temper, was vigorously authoritative; in each case his generalisations have again and again been accepted as finally indicating not what Greeks had done by his time, but rather what everybody ought everywhere and always to do. His rational conclusions from observation have thus often been held omniscient and irresponsible commands.

The posthumous history of his works has had much to do with this distortion. As we shall remind ourselves later, there were six or eight centuries between the fall of the Roman Empire and the development of what we have complacently thought modern civilisation when little knowledge of Greek survived in Western Europe. During much of this period, Aristotle was only a name; when at last he became once more a teacher, such versions of him as first appeared among our forefathers were probably Latin translations from the Arabic translations of his writings which were studied, largely under the influence of Averroes, in the universities of Moorish Spain. At that time the general temper of European learning tended to accept authoritative teaching as final. The doctrine of the Church, for example, was generally assumed to be true; and the business of doctors was accordingly, once for all, to enlighten ignorance. This temper accepted Aristotle as the highest of merely human authorities; as the man who without divine inspiration came nearest to understanding what nothing short of divine inspiration could ultimately explain. Thus the father of our scientific spirit was for generations held infallibly above investigation; orthodoxy always distrusts experiment. In such guise he appeared to Dante, who set forth in final poetry the doctrine of Thomas Aquinas.

As for us, hastily summarising, we must be content to record that, somewhat as Euripides brought tragic poetry nearer earth than Sophocles, and as Thucydides brought history down from the half-

epic heights where Herodotus lingered, so Aristotle brought philosophy out of the poetically
speculative condition where Plato had made it part
of literature, and into its first enduring semblance
of systematic order. By themselves, Euripides,
Thucydides, and Aristotle are magnificently Greek,
classical, primal; compared with their great predecessors, they mark long steps from the past that
had been towards the future that, for better or
worse, was to be; they no longer quite aspire;
their task is rather to master and to subjugate.
At least, and perhaps most profoundly, their mood
is less youthful than the moods they inherited;
and of the three, Aristotle, who lived not in the
Fifth Century but in the Fourth, is most mature.

VI

THEOPHRASTUS; MENANDER

So far as important surviving literature goes,
no other names of the Fourth Century are comparable with the four at which we have glanced. For
historical reasons, however, we can hardly neglect
two more, those of Theophrastus and of Menander.
Both men flourished at Athens during the second
half of the Century; both lived into the next; both
left rather popular writings; and both had considerable influence on the literature of subsequent
times.

Of the two, Theophrastus was about a generation the older. Without entering into any details
of his life, we may remind ourselves that he studied
under Aristotle, that he is said to have succeeded
the Master as head of the Lyceum—or Peripatetic

—School, and that he wrote philosophical and scientific works meritorious in themselves, but of no lasting importance as literature. What makes him of literary consequence is that tradition attributes to him a short collection of character-sketches, now numbering thirty. They are colloquial, rather epigrammatic, and to all appearances based on life; taken together they give one some such notion of every-day Athens as you may get of George II's London from the engravings of Hogarth. A casual example of what the Characters, as they are called, brought into literary being may be found in the first sentence describing "The Stupid Man":

The stupid man is one who, after doing a sum and setting down the total, will ask the person sitting next him "What does it come to?"

And so on, for about a page of print. Incidentally, the Greek work here translated by Sir Richard Jebb as *stupidity* is *anæsthesia*, whose modern meaning is an excellent instance of how the centuries affect language; the fact that you know what a word means now is no reason why you should suppose yourself to understand what it used to mean. Again we stray. Taken by themselves, the Characters of Theophrastus would hardly deserve attention in a consideration so cursory as ours. They chanced, however, in far later times, to stimulate imitations among the English and the French. Without them, to go no further, we should hardly have had the *Caractères* of La Bruyère or the numerous "Character-Writings" of Seventeenth Century England. Without these we should hardly have had, in their present form, the sketches of character in the essays of Addison and of Steele. Without these sketches—Sir Roger de Coverley, for example—we should hardly have had the novels of Richardson and of Fielding; and without them the whole popular literature of the Nineteenth Century might have taken another turn. So Theophrastus has his place in the ancestry of prose fiction.

There is a tradition that Menander, some thirty years younger than Theophrastus, was more or less associated with him, perhaps as a pupil. The work of Menander, however, was nowise philosophic. At the end of the Fourth Century, he was among the most popular writers of comedy; and his light plays, surviving those of his contemporaries, became the standard examples of what Greek comedy had grown to be a century after Aristophanes. None of them now exists. Almost to the end of the Nineteenth Century, indeed, Menander was directly known only in occasional fragments quoted by later writers: of these the most familiar to English-speaking tradition is "Evil communications corrupt good manners," [1] imbedded in the Fifteenth Chapter of the First Epistle to the Corinthians. He was also known to be the original model from which certain Latin comedies of Plautus and of Terence had been translated, adapted, or imitated. From these extant works, even if no other evidence had existed, it would have been clear that Menander's comic method was completely different from that of Aristophanes, and distinctly subsequent. Instead of broadly satirising, with extreme license, the men and the incidents of the moment, Menander, with

[1] I Cor., 15, 33.

deft fluency, conventionally sketched, in plots now long since grown trite, typical phases of private life. His characters meanwhile appeared to have had some such generalised quality as marks the avowedly generalised Characters of Theophrastus. So much was to be gathered from his Latin imitators and from a good deal of critical and allusive mention. The relation of Latin comedy to that of Seventeenth Century France is a matter of common knowledge. Without Plautus and Terence, Molière could never have been just what he was and is. Molière, furthermore, improved on his models, being a decidedly more gifted poet than either of them. A probable conclusion appeared to follow, and was long accepted. The loss of Menander was supposed irreparably to deprive us of early comedy as much better than Molière's as his is better than the Latin.

Since 1895, we have had consolation for this grief. Somewhere in Egypt fragments of Menander have been discovered, by no means complete but consecutive enough to give a notion of his dramatic method, and of how he presented character. These are generally agreed to be disappointing. Apart from a certain swift and gay ease, they are on the whole inferior to any equal amount taken from his comparatively laborious Latin imitators. It seems at least possible that Plautus and Terence are about as much better than he was as Molière is better than they. If so, his true value proves, like that of Theophrastus, rather historical than positive. He made something which, whatever his reputation, we moderns might serenely have neglected if it had not later developed into a form more important than it ever attained in his hands. Traditionally, none the less, he stays among the great.

Neither he nor Theophrastus, however, looks very large beside even the polite merit of Xenophon, far less beside the greatness of Plato and Aristotle and Demosthenes. We have touched on the two later men only to complete our glance at what the Fourth Century contributed to the literary tradition of Europe. That Century had inherited not only the traditions of epic and of lyric poetry inherited by the Fifth, but also the dramatic poetry and the history brought by the Fifth Century—the century of Pericles—into final existence. To this inheritance the Fourth Century—the century of Philip and of Alexander—added two other forms of primal prose—philosophy and oratory; to this it also added two lesser phases of literature destined to ripen into the fiction and the comedy of modern Europe. So the Century ended. In the year 300, enduring European literature still stayed altogether and only Greek.

CHAPTER IV

FROM 300 B. C. TO THE ROMAN CONQUEST OF GREECE (146 B. C.)

I

HISTORICAL TRADITIONS

The Third Century before Christ was the last when Greece can be considered anywise independent; about the middle of the Second Century, in the year 146, the power of Rome, which had already mastered the Greek colonies in southern Italy and in Sicily, finally took possession of Greece itself. Thenceforth, until the collapse of the Western Empire, more than six hundred years later, Greece remained politically a part of the united Roman dominions. And from the beginning of the Third Century, indeed, the historical traditions familiar to subsequent literature belong not so much to Greece, the primal fact of European antiquity, as to Rome, the secondary.

This interposition of Rome, to which we must soon come, was more instantly evident in the middle of the Nineteenth Century than we may find it now, in the first quarter of the Twentieth. Until 1875, at least in America, we still called many Greek things by Latin names; one thought of Zeus, for example, as the Greek equivalent of Jupiter. And though the Olympic Hermes of Praxiteles was dug up a little too late for anybody

to describe him as Mercury, we might still be
perplexed by an offhand mention of the Venus
of Milo under the name of Aphrodite. That wondrous Grecian statue, by the way, is now thought
to have been made as late as the Third Century,
if not later; certain details, particularly of the
drapery, deny it a place in the Fifth Century or
even in the Fourth. There can be no question,
however, that it reminds one rather of the great
periods which were past when it was modelled
than of what generally marked that to which it
is now assigned.[1] Greek sculpture stayed Greek,
but not Athenian. Phidias and Praxiteles too
were dead and gone. The art they had grandly
practised was tending towards such literal precision as that of the Dying Gladiator, such writh-
ing restlessness as that of the Laocoön group,
or such graceful sentimentality as that of the
Belvedere Apollo or of the Hunting Diana—whom
nobody calls Artemis—in the Louvre.

Of late years, the period of Greek history between the time of Alexander and the Roman Conquest has usually been described by the word
Hellenistic. What was going to be Europe was
no longer only or quite Greek; yet Greek influence, though not of the first political or military
importance, was bringing regions formerly barbarian within the range of Hellenic civilisation.
It extended westward, and saturated the traditions of Rome, over which we must soon linger
long. It extended eastward, to various places
beyond the scope of observation so cursory as
ours. More memorably for us at this moment,
it extended southward, where until the days of

[1] See Ernest Arthur Gardner: A Handbook of Greek Sculpture: 1911.

Augustus Cæsar it dominated the diuturnal humanity of Egypt as Persians and Shepherd kings had dominated it centuries before, as Romans and Mahometans were to dominate it centuries later, as the British Empire has now benevolently dominated it for thirty or forty years. How large this Hellenistic Egypt looms in tradition we can see by comparing the names of two generals, both eminent under Alexander, and both founders of independent dynasties; one is Seleucus, the other Ptolemy. Just who either was and what he did only students of historical detail remember. Hardly anybody, for some two thousand years, besides, could have felt sure without reference to authorities whether Seleucus and his successors began their independent career in Mesopotamia. Even to this day, meanwhile, almost everybody could have told you that the Ptolemies flourished in Egypt, and fixed their capital at Alexandria. Historically, indeed, this Egyptian Hellenistic tradition is the most familiar of all. Just as we may summarise the Fifth Century as that of Pericles, and the Fourth as that of Philip and of Alexander, so we may summarise the Third as the first century of the Ptolemies.

At this time, too, Greek literature, so far as it persisted, tended to become less important in Greece than in Egypt. Athens, no doubt, remained, as indeed it remained throughout antiquity, a traditional centre of culture. In the year 300, Theophrastus had not yet finished his career there as a lecturer and a writer, nor Menander his as an enduring master of comedy; and the Academic school founded by Plato still flourished. Apart from these maintainers of already somewhat waning traditions, however, only two Athenian names of the Third Century or of the Second seem certainly within the range of our cursory consideration. Two facts about both are significant: both belong to the first half of the Third Century, and the importance of both has nothing to do with history but concerns only philosophy. One name is that of a philosopher—Epicurus; the other is that of a school of philosophy—the Stoics. Its founder was Zeno of Citium; conceivably to avoid confusion with an earlier philosopher, Zeno of Elea, his teaching has generally been remembered as proceeding not from him but from the place—the Stoa—where he taught. What he taught is another question. Like the doctrines of Epicurus, that of the Stoics would lead us into philosophic mazes. Two or three facts about their existence are all we can touch on now. In the first place, these two new and divergent systems of philosophic teaching tended, like many new-fangled notions throughout history, to supplant the orthodoxies—here the older schools of philosophy, Platonic and Aristotelian, Academy and Lyceum—whose founders were dead. In the second place, they were at odds with each other; very generally speaking, the opinions of Epicurus tended toward extreme emphasis on the material aspect of the universe, and those of the Stoics toward extreme emphasis on the spiritual. Naturally enough, each school was disposed to misrepresent the other, the Stoics declaring the Epicureans prone to wallow in sensual delight, and the Epicureans retorting that the Stoics were foolish dreamers. How far from conclusive either charge was we may perceive when we touch on the

Epicurean poem of Lucretius written when the
Roman Republic was at its last gasp, and on the
Meditations of the Stoic emperor, Marcus Aurelius,
written when the Roman Empire began to totter
down its fatal decline.   In the third place, nevertheless, a distorted echo of those antique disputes
lingers to this day.   Without remembering why,
we think of epicures as men content with fleshly
joys, and of stoics as men austerely ready without
the consolations of revealed religion to bear either
those ills we have or fly to others that we know
not of.   The words *epicure* and *stoic* will stay
part of our language as long as the language lasts,
transmuting yet preserving the chief if not the
only persistent tradition established for posterity
by Third Century Athens.

Though no tradition quite so familiar survives
from Ptomelaic Alexandria, the general influence
of Alexandria from the beginning of the Third Century to the time when European tradition became
rather Roman than Greek, was for our purposes
paramount.   In the year 300 Alexandria was both
a new city, founded within the memory of men
not beyond middle age, and the seat of a new
dynasty eager to secure itself on a throne commanding the most considerable commerce in the
contemporary world.   One means of doing so was
to make the new capital brilliant.   Brilliancy is a
matter both of fashion and of intellect; if either
shine anywhere, people flock to it from elsewhere.
What happened at Alexandria under the Ptolemies
was not unlike what happened at Paris under
Napoleon, and at Berlin between 1870 and 1914.
A powerful new sovereignty tried to make the seat
of its government at once gay and learned.   Only

the learned phase of Third Century Egypt, and indeed of Egypt through several centuries then to come, has traditionally survived; and only one feature of that has stayed traditionally familiar. Even to the present day, however, people generally though vaguely remember that among the treasures of Alexandria there was once an unprecedented library.

This library was originally, and long remained, a conspicuous feature of what was generally known as the Museum, or abode of the Muses. Though the word *Museum* had probably been used earlier, its wide familiarity and its general diffusion throughout modern Europe is probably due to the fame attained by the Museum of Ptolemaic Alexandria. This was not the kind of institution which its name would now usually imply; it was rather such as we should now call a university. By the time when it was established, Greek literature had passed through the stages at which we have glanced, from antique Homer to contemporary Menander. It had not yet, however, been systematically studied; for one thing, texts were in a state of confusion inevitable when they could be reproduced only by repeated process of often careless manuscript copying; incidentally, too, a good deal of spurious work had got mixed up with the genuine. One prime task of Alexandrian scholars was to separate the genuine texts of Greek literature from the spurious, and having done so to restore them, as nearly as possible, to their original form.

The methods and the limitations developed by these prototypes of the learning at present prevalent about us are excellently summarised in F.

W. Hall's Companion to Classical Texts.[1] For our
purposes, it is enough to note that the Greek
Classics, as we now possess them, remain substantially as they were fixed by the studious criticism of Alexandria; the Books into which they
were divided, for example, are generally of Alexandrian origin, and the accents and breathings
which have bothered schoolboys for two thousand
years are said to be Alexandrian inventions.
Compare this kind of thing with Athenian traditions of the same period—Epicureans and Stoics,
let us say, with whoever settled the standard text
of Herodotus or of Pindar—and you will feel the
most important difference between Hellenic and
Hellenistic temper: Greece remained on the whole
intelligent, while barbarous regions appropriating
Greek inheritance could not make themselves
much better, or worse if you prefer, than erudite.
The most enduringly familiar name from this
period of scholarly industry is typical; among
other things, an eminent Alexandrian professor,
named Euclid, produced in the Third Century before Christ an elementary treatise on geometry
which was not altogether supplanted as a text-
book when English and American boys went to
school in the Nineteenth Century of the Christian
Era. A good cursory impression of his surroundings and of their tendency and history may be
derived from a glance at the Encyclopædia Britannica article on the "Alexandrian School."

This encyclopædic summary gives hardly due
emphasis to a name deservedly conspicuous
throughout Roman times, but eclipsed later partly
because the works of its bearer have perished, and

[1] Pp. 32–39 (Oxford: 1913).

partly because admirable Latin imitations of them
have survived. Callimachus, the first remembered
librarian of Alexandria, was not only a man of
great energy and learning, but so industrious a
writer that he is said to have produced some eight
hundred books. Among these were specially admired elegies and epigrams, without which we
could hardly have had, in their actual form, the
elegiac poetry of Rome, or the poems of Catullus,
or the epigrams of Martial. The services of
Callimachus to the course of both learning and
literature were accordingly great. As we have
seen, however, only a few broken fragments of his
writings have been rescued from the wreck of
antiquity.

Another work finally accomplished at Alexandria
has been more fortunate. Among the people who
flocked to Ptolemaic Egypt were many Jews who
had mostly forgotten their ancestral language and
habitually thought in Greek. Chiefly for their
benefit, a translation of Hebrew Scripture into
Greek was undertaken in the Second Century.
The name this traditionally bears—the Septuagint
—is derived from a legend that it was accomplished by seventy-two learned men in seventy-
two days. Really, as it now survives, it seems
to have been the work of several hundred years.
Substantially, whatever its history, it still exists,
and throws much light on the state of Old Testament texts when the Ptolemies ruled the dominions
of the Pharaohs.

Ptolemaic, accordingly, we may on the whole
call the Greek traditions so far as they here concern us, both of the Third Century and of the half-
century which ensued before Greece was finally

conquered. How completely we are warranted
in doing so will be evident when we compare the
familiarity of this name with the oblivion which
has overtaken two others. The last stand of
Greece, in the year 146, was made at Corinth,
which the Romans presently captured, sacked, and
destroyed. The Greek general who tried to defend it proves to have been called Diæus, the
Roman general who defeated him was called
Mummius; to ascertain what either was called,
however, you must turn not to world tradition
but to your most conveniently accessible book of
reference.[1]

II

THEOCRITUS

What Alexandrian life was like when Alexandrian learning was founded happens to be compactly recorded for us in a little sketch which has
been called the most graphic of all Greek antiquity—the Fifteenth Idyl of Theocritus. Mat-
thew Arnold's translation of this, in his essay on
Pagan and Mediæval Religious Sentiment,[2] is
at once the best English version and the easiest to
find. It tells how two prettily frivolous Alexandrian women met and gossiped on their way to
a festival of Adonis, and thus puts in admirable
setting the graceful hymn they there heard sung;

[1] In my case here this happened to be Shuckburgh's Greece to A. D. 14.
Seignobos does not mention the needless names.

[2] Essays in Criticism, I, VI. The whole essay is worth reading, for
such purpose as ours; it contains also a translation of St. Francis of Assisi's
Canticle of the Sun.

the whole thing is compressed into 159 hexameter
lines, more than half of which are trippingly colloquial. Though feathery in lightness it implies
the atmosphere where for their little while these
butterflies hovered in Ptolemaic sunshine; the
hymn meanwhile, pretty as themselves and not
much more significant, tells us what sort of attrac-
tion lured them out of doors. You think of Tan-
agra figurines, perhaps, or of the curled portraits
painted, with demure eyes, on the wooden slabs
which replaced amid their new-fashioned mummy-
wrappings the archaic and conventional masks of
immemorial Egypt. There is a glittering court
above such beings, and a surging mass of many-
coloured bazaar-like creatures about and beneath
them; and dashing Greek soldiers keep things in
semblance of order. It is all bright, gay, fleeting,
transitory, ominous. To have known such life,
you feel, would surely have been a momentary
pleasure, just as it would have been to enjoy, when
he was the last new maker of poetic novelty, the
dainty art of Theocritus.

He was by no means the only poet of his time,
nor perhaps the most apparently important. We
have already glanced at the poetic excursions of
the librarian Callimachus. There were plenty of
others who knew by heart the poetry of ancestral
Greece, from Homer down, and who exquisitely
imitated both its lyric beauties and sometimes its
epic animation. What is more, they were not
altogether ephemeral. Much as modern Europe
came to understand the primal glory of Grecian
fine art only when men began to perceive how far
this outshines the secondary expression of Rome,
so the Romans themselves delighted in Alexan-

drian poetry before they fully recognised the transcendent beauty of those elder Greeks whom the Alexandrians venerated as the Masters. In the Æneid, for example, as every one can see, Virgil beautifully imitated a parodied Homer; but those who have read the Argonautica of the Alexandrian Apollonius Rhodius assure us that without this now obscured poet's account of how Jason dealt with Medea we should never have had quite as it lives for all time the tenderly pathetic story of Æneas and Dido. Before Virgil imitated Homer in the Æneid and Hesiod in the Georgics, too, he had already imitated Theocritus in the Bucolics, or Eclogues. This accident has doubtless had a good deal to do with the persistence of Theocritus as an influence on the poetry of later Europe; most probably. however, he might to some degree have survived without it. For he happened to introduce into lasting literature a form of poetry—the Pastoral—which, despite its evident artificiality, has proved to appeal recurrently and genuinely, at least to the whims of taste and in all likelihood to some less unstable phase of human emotion.

Not much is known about Theocritus. It seems probable, however, that he was early familiar with the countryside of Sicily, where even to this day you may sometimes hear among the hills the sweet, shrill notes of wooden pipes played by shepherds as they watch their feeding flocks. The sound is haunting, at once human and almost as straight from the heart of nature as the song of a bird; at a distance, the shepherd looks like a creature not of humdrum life but of poetic fancy. Get near enough, inspect him carefully enough,

and you will no doubt find him dirty, rude, cun-
ning, and foolish; but a glimpse of him is like a
peep into a world more primally innocent than
this coarse, naughty world of ours. So far as
Theocritus has lastingly influenced literature, he
did so by translating this pretty aspect of Sicilian
hillsides into graceful, trifling, mostly hexametric
poems, where the shepherds and shepherdesses,
though suggested by nature, are no longer what
rustics must really be everywhere, but are presented as rustics appear to sentimental passing
strangers. The name given his sketches befits
them. An Idyl has been thought of these two
thousand years as a fantastically artificial variety
of poetry; but the literal meaning of the Greek
word is almost exactly what a *Glimpse* means in
English. You catch sight of something that sets
your fancy playing; you look at it no more, but
let your fancy play; which was very pleasant to
Ptolemaic courtiers and fashionable folks of Alexandria. This was the public to which, amid the
decadent Hellenism of the Third Century, Theocritus appealed as the best new maker of verses.

Somehow, his appeal has never quite died.
The names of his idyllic personages linger always
familiar—Daphnis, for example, Thyrsis, Tityrus,
Amaryllis, Corydon, and Lycidas. Virgil, as we
have already observed, acceptably imitated him for
the revived fashion of Augustan Rome; and Virgil
was imitated far and wide twelve or fifteen centuries later. And Spenser's first work was the
Shepherd's Calendar, which tried to bring pastoral conventions a little nearer the nature from
which they had been wandering ever since Theocritus first led them astray. When we remember,

though, that Spenser's own lament for the death
of Sir Philip Sidney disguises Sir Philip as a shepherd called Astrophel, we shall remind ourselves
at once how deep and how vagrant the influence
of the pastoral has proved.   It has given English
literature our two noblest mortuary poems, the
Lycidas of Milton and the Adonais of Shelley.   It
has shown itself, on the other hand, in such graceful trifles as the Pastor Fido of Guarini, the Aminta
of Tasso, and the Sad Shepherd of Ben Jonson.
Without it, we might hardly have had in their
actual form the ballets of Italian opera, nor the
Dresden china figures which made gay with flowery
colour the light boudoir of the Eighteenth Century.   Without it, Marie Antoinette might hardly
have played the milkmaid in her toy village at
Trianon, nor English-speaking children have told
you all about Little Bo-Peep.

And this recurrently fascinating prettiness was
the last thing established among the literary traditions of Europe by the antique, unique originality
of primal Greece.

CHAPTER V

THE GREEK TRADITION

There could be no greater mistake than to suppose that we have glanced at all the literature of Greece. Any systematic account of the matter, even though extending no further than the point where we have now arrived, would call instant attention to many names and tendencies of the full classical period, from the time of Homer to that of Theocritus, on which we have not touched. Furthermore, there is one fact about Greek literature which, though commonly forgotten, gives it unique interest quite apart from its merits. So far as the relations of literature with living language are concerned, this first of European literatures has never quite stopped. From the remote antiquity when Greek epics were reduced to writing until the present day every century has produced something normally expressed in Greek, by men who thought and spoke the Greek of their times. The Greek language, of course, has altered a good deal in the course of its three thousand years; you would hardly expect a modern Athenian instantly to grasp a sentence written, or still more spoken, after the manner of Periclean Athens. For all this, classical Greek, throughout recorded history, has stayed more or less intelligible to the Greeks, somewhat as Chaucer is to Twentieth Century Englishmen or Americans; and any of us who fails after a few minutes to make out what on the whole a page of Chaucer has to say ought to consult not the dictionary but the doctor.

At the same time, there is good reason, in such a scheme as ours, for considering as distinct the period over which we have now lingered as long as we can. So far as there was any European literature from the time of Homer to that of Theocritus, this literature was wholly and only Greek. Its allusions, for example—religious, historical, or literary—were either directly or implicitly Greek; if they touched on foreign things,— Egyptian, for example, Colchian, Macedonian,— they regarded them as more or less barbarous. Anybody was assumed to know who Theseus was, or Zeus, or Solon; nobody would have had the slightest idea of who Romulus was, or Jupiter, or Numa Pompilius; and the names of Moses or Jehovah or David would have meant no more to Socrates or Epicurus than those of Aztec or Peruvian heroes or gods or statesmen would have meant to big-spectacled students of Confucius and Mencius before the Chinese Empire crumbled into a make-believe republic. The sovereigns of Memphis, no doubt, and the deities, the Nile and the Euphrates, too, and Scythia and the misty shores of encircling Ocean, were not altogether unknown; but they, and names like them, were familiar only as things other than Greek, foreign, barbarian, different, remote, alien as the colossal torpor of the defaced Pyramids is to the quenchless life of the ruined Parthenon. Until the time of Theocritus nothing but Greece exhaled the spirit destined to animate immemorial Europe.

After that time came a change. A few names of those who have later written in Greek and of the things they have written about may serve to remind us of its nature and its course. In the

Second Century before Christ, the Greek Polybius wrote about the already portentous history of Rome until the end of the Punic Wars; in the First Century before Christ, it is thought, appeared the first of the collections of Greek lyrics—at the time both old and new—on which centuries later the Anthology—the Greek word for nosegay—was based; in the First Century of the Christian Era, Josephus wrote in Greek about the Jews; at the same time the Greek writings now collected in the New Testament were at least coming into existence; when the Second Century of our Era began, Plutarch was probably at his best, whose perennially popular Lives—as we shall soon remind ourselves again—concern Roman traditions quite as much as those of the Greek language in which he thought and wrote; it was during this Second Century that Marcus Aurelius made in Greek the Stoic memoranda which often seem the noblest spiritual record of Roman paganism; it was in Greek that the Byzantine Fathers, Chrysostom and more, set down their Christian doctrine; and throughout the history of the Eastern Church Greek has liturgically lived on, much as Latin lives in the Western. Until the fall of Constantinople, less than fifty years before the discovery of America, Greek remained the literary language of that region, where its course had stayed uninterrupted since literature began there. Even under the Turkish domination of the Sixteenth and the Seventeenth Centuries there are traces of Greek ballads and the like; and by the Eighteenth Century that modern phase of Greek was already growing up which is now said to bring forth more newspapers in proportion to the calculable number of their readers than any other contemporary tongue. Glance back at this record, and you will see that of all the things we have touched on only the Anthology is purely Greek. Everything else treats in later than classical Greek terms of matters which the elder Greeks would have held barbarian.

We need hardly remind ourselves, the while, that among living tongues few are much less known to foreigners than modern Greek. To men who habitually think in English, or French, or German, or Italian, or Spanish, for example, it presents itself much as a negligible dialect of barbarians might have presented itself to Periclean Athenians. This obvious fact implies the actual history of classical Greek. From the Second Century before Christ to the Third Century of the Christian Era the Greek literature on which we have touched was as familiar among educated Romans as Latin literature is to Catholic churchmen, or as French has been to cosmopolitan Europeans from the time of Louis the Fourteenth. Even then, however, your every-day Roman was apt to find the Greek language beyond his range, as bluff and unlettered Casca does in the second scene of Shakspere's Julius Cæsar.[1] Cassius, plying him with questions as to what has just happened when Cæsar refused the crown, asks:

> Did Cicero say anything?
>
> *Casca :* Aye, he spoke Greek.
>
> *Cassius :* To what effect?
>
> *Casca :* Nay, an I tell you that, I'll ne'er look you i' the face again; but those that understood him smiled at one another and shook their heads; but for mine own part, it was Greek to me.

[1] I, II, 277-283 (Cambridge edition).

From the time of Marcus Aurelius, it began to become Greek to everybody this side the Eastern
Empire. By the Sixth Century it was almost
unknown throughout Western Europe; so it remained for hundreds of years; in the Fourteenth
Century, a scholar so alert as Petrarch is said
never to have come across anybody who could
teach him to read the original text of Homer.
Though Greek traditions and even Greek works
grandly survived, they long survived only as they
had been transmitted or translated by men who
thought and wrote in Latin. It was thus that
Dante knew them; and thus we must henceforth
try to think of them at least until we come to the
period, a century or more after Dante's, when the
dead grammarians of the Renaissance finally restored to our ancestral possessions the literal records of Greek antiquity.

From then till now—that is, for more than five
hundred years—they have been so constantly and
so admirably studied that very likely they can
now be better understood and appreciated than
ever before. To-day we can hardly consider them
for any reason without turning to them, as we have
turned here, directly, forgetting while we do so
that in this aspect they are not so much the traditions of the centuries which were to ensue on
them as the facts on which those traditions were
based. Thus viewed, they reveal a few general
characteristics which we may do well to summarise.

In the first place, ancient Greeks, who first displayed the type of mind which was destined to
become European, and who happened to possess
a language of unsurpassed beauty and flexibility,

were little if at all hampered when they attempted the miracle of expression by the notion or the certainty that any previous and foreign people had already done what they were trying to do. Their problem, at least when we compare them with subsequent Europeans, was therefore simply to grasp the ideas they wished to set forth and to discover the words and the artistic forms most nearly suitable for their purpose. In the second place, their unsurpassed and in some respects disproportionate intelligence was artistically controlled by an instinctive distaste for unrestrained emotional excess. Though not remarkable for practical common sense, they had an artistic sense of the highest order. In the third place, this quality combined with the unique simplicity of their artistic problems to make their productions at once enduringly fresh and evidently excellent. Thus, though they had little if any conscious purpose of hampering the future, their accomplished works could not help seeming to be models of how such things ought to be done, and therefore affecting not only the subsequent expression of Greece but also that of all the Europe to which Greek influence has ever extended. So, finally, they brought into enduring existence the primal types of epic poetry, of lyric poetry, of dramatic poetry, of historical prose, of philosophical prose, of oratory, and of pastoral poetry which were destined to modify the thought and the utterance of all subsequent Europe.

For ages, however, subsequent Europe was generally to know these things not as they originally were, but only as they seemed when peered at through the veil of the interposed traditions of Rome.

BOOK II

THE TRADITIONS OF ROME

CHAPTER I

TO 100 BEFORE CHRIST

I

HISTORICAL TRADITIONS

A little while ago we touched on the fact that in the year 100 of the Christian Era Plutarch was probably at his best. His name is very familiar; ever since his Lives were translated into French and a little later into English, between three and four hundred years ago, they have been the most popular and therefore the most nearly original source from which our notions of antique worthies have been derived. So, although mention of him at this point violates our general purpose of considering the traditions of literature century by century, it is none the less just here that he is most worth our attention. For no one else so clearly marks the manner in which later times have generally fused the Greek traditions at which we have glanced with the Roman to which we now turn.

What little we know about him[1] is mostly derived from his own works. He was born at Chæronea, in Bœotia, during the reign of the Emperor Claudius, some four hundred years after the victory of Philip there had ended the liberty of Greece. He was educated at Athens, then still unruined and the traditional seat of philosophic culture. He

[1] Compactly summarised in Bernadotte Perrin's Introduction to the Lives: Loeb Classical Library, 1914.

represented Chæronea as deputy to the Roman governor of Greece. He travelled widely. He must have passed many years at Rome, where both political duties and his personal accomplishments made him intimate with the best society of his time. He lectured, mostly on moral philosophy. He ultimately went home to Chæronea and there passed his later years, widely recognised as a philosopher and a man of letters. He probably lived into the reign of Hadrian, when the prospect of the Roman Empire looked bright. He was a loyal Roman citizen, or if you prefer a loyal subject of the Cæsars. Yet, although he could read Latin, he never confidently mastered any other language than his native Greek. Quotations from the Greek classics abound in his works; he makes hardly any from the Roman. There are none, it is said, from Virgil; there is a little dispute as to whether one may be from Horace or not. Even so late as the Second Century of the Christian Era, it appears, a lettered Greek might still hold barbarous any literature except his own.

When we come to other than literary traditions, however, this had long ceased to be the case. If Greece remained the principal source of intelligence, learning, philosophy, and culture, Rome had already been for some three centuries the centre of law, of government, of authority. By Plutarch's time the whole antique world was almost equally familiar with the historical traditions of both; and whoever pondered on how life should be conducted could not neglect either. This problem was what most occupied him. His philosophic works, usually called Morals, and about

as long as the Lives, generally concern questions
of how people ought to think and to behave.   His
fondness for this kind of speculation permeates the
Lives themselves.   Fifty of them survive, all but
four in pairs—one Greek and one Roman; and
most of the pairs are followed by formal moral
comparisons.   The series conventionally begins, for
example, by parallel lives of Theseus and Romulus,
with a comparison of these legendary founders of
originally diverse national traditions; and, to go
no further, there are parallel lives of Demosthenes and Cicero duly compared, and of Alexander
and Cæsar where the comparison has been lost.
Throughout, antique worthies are treated rather
biographically than historically; they are characterised, with abundance of anecdote; and for all
the narrative power which has kept the work
popular, they are chiefly regarded as instances of
conduct which has at once exemplified and influenced national ideals, finally merging in the common human ideal of what we now call European
antiquity.   How much they have to do with our
own traditions, a single and typical fact must
serve to remind us: they are the basis, in our own
literature, of the Coriolanus, the Julius Cæsar, and
the Antony and Cleopatra of Shakspere.   What
is more to our purpose at this moment, the making
of them, somewhere about the year 100 of the
Christian Era, proves how by that time even a
Greek man of letters who had never found need
thoroughly to learn the Latin language recognised
that the heroic and historic traditions of what was
growing to be Europe already included not only
the primal traditions of Greece but also and
equally the secondary traditions of imperial Rome.

His Roman Empire was really, as it supposed itself, the third phase of consecutive Roman history and government. There had been a time, already remotely antique, when the government of Rome, then only local, was royal. A revolution, probably in the Sixth Century before Christ, had expelled royalty—of which the name was thenceforth detestable to Rome, much as it now happens to be among the citizens of the United States. The ensuing Republic—this word is the literal Latin for Commonwealth—had shown two divergent tendencies: amid the social disputes which for centuries had kept Rome recurrently turbulent, aristocratic privileges had gradually diminished; and through these same centuries, the military and administrative force of Rome had gradually extended until, in the First Century before Christ, a paradox was clear—an unstable central government was virtually bound to keep in stable order the whole civilised world. During that Century a new series of revolutions turned the central power into a military autocracy, to persist for about five hundred years. What we are apt to forget is that the title of its sovereigns, now held superior to any borne by kings, was originally unpretentious; the Latin word *Imperator* —or *Emperor*, as we call it in English—meant nothing more nor less than *General*, and *Cæsar* was a family name. Thus the imperial title— *Empereur*—of the Napoleons, like the imperial title —*Kaiser*—of German monarchs implicitly embalmed during our Nineteenth Century the secular abomination of royalty traditional to republican Rome.

What the actual history of this long development had been, no one knew when Plutarch wrote; it is more or less disputed even among our most learned contemporaries. Two facts about it, however, were already certain by the year 100 before Christ. A considerably legendary account of things which had occurred earlier than what our present chronology calls the Third Century before Christ was generally known, and conventionally accepted, by the Romans; and what had ensued during the Third Century and the Second was considerably a matter of historical record. These traditions, utterly strange to the classic traditions of Greece, were as familiar to Plutarch as those of his own Greek ancestry. More than any one else, except Livy, he has kept them so for us.

They begin with the legend of the wolf-suckled twins Romulus and Remus, shadowily demi-divine and said to descend through Æneas from the royal race of Troy. The founding of Rome was traditionally placed about the middle of the Eighth Century. The Seventh Century and most of the Sixth comprised the period of the seven Roman kings, from Romulus to Tarquinius Superbus. Their sovereignty came to an end through an aristocratic revolution excited by the reckless conduct of Sextus, the son of Tarquin. He violated the Roman chastity of the beautiful matron Lucretia. She sent for her husband Collatinus and their kinsman Brutus; she told her poignant story, and took her life in their presence. They roused the people, expelled the king, and established the republican sovereignty of annually elected consuls—at first patrician or noble. When Porsenna, of Clusium, tried to restore the Tarquins, the bravery of Horatius, who held the bridge unsupported, saved Rome, as every schoolboy knows who has read, or has had to read, the Lays of Macaulay.

So we come to the Fifth Century—in Greece the Century of the Persian defeats, of Pericles and of the Peloponnesian War. Compared with historic facts like these, the traditions of their contemporary Rome are surprisingly nebulous; yet among them you begin to discern enduring solidities. This was the Century of the legendary Appius Claudius and his hapless victim Virginia, again revived by the Lays of Macaulay; of the first Tribunes of the People, and crescent encroachment of plebeians on the hereditary privileges of patricians; of the no too historic worthies Coriolanus and Cincinnatus; of the codified Law of the Twelve Tables; of the first Dictator and of the first Censor.

The contrast between the Greek traditions of the following Century—the Fourth, the Century of Philip and Alexander—and those then gathering about Rome is different but hardly less marked. This was the period when Gaulish raiders besieged Rome itself, when the bearded Senate was slaughtered as it sat silently defiant, and when only cackling geese saved the Capitol; and it was the Century when Samnite enemies subjugated a Roman army, compelling them to pass under the yoke at the Caudine Forks; but it was the Century, as well, when Roman power began its final advance in Italy. By the year 300 Rome was no longer only a local sovereignty; the Republic was fatally tending towards Empire.

The Third Century—in Greek, or Hellenistic, tradition the Century when the Ptolemies began their royal course—brought Rome at last into the full light of history and left her, after perilously fluctuating fortunes, already virtually imperial. It began with Italian conquests, over Samnites, and Gauls, and Etruscans, and the Greek civilisation of Southern Italy. Then soon came the first of the Punic Wars which were ultimately to settle the naval mastery of the Mediterranean, and thus of the whole antique world. When this war began, Carthage, originally a Phœnician colony established in the region now called Tunis, was the most important of maritime powers. It already had firm foothold in Greek regions of Sicily. Here it found itself face to face with Rome. The First Punic War lasted between twenty and twenty-five years. In the course of them, Regulus, who had defeated the Carthaginian fleet, landed in Africa and besieged Carthage itself; the tale of how, defeated in turn, made prisoner and despatched to Rome with terms of peace, he advised that no peace be made and, impelled by honour, went back alone to his Carthaginian doom, by and by took its place in Roman legend.[1] Before 240 Roman victories had brought the Carthaginian general Hamilcar to terms, and all Sicily was yielded to the Republic. Then followed some twenty years of nominal peace, during which the Romans seized the Carthaginian island of Sardinia and the Carthaginians established themselves in not yet Roman Spain; the name of Cartagena records them there to this day. The Second Punic War, which virtually occupied the last twenty years of

---

[1] *Cf.* Horace, Od. III, V; and Kipling's tale—Regulus—which tells how bravely this has been expounded in English schools. Collected Works, XXVI, 279.

the Century, began with what to anything else than Rome would have seemed annihilating defeat. Starting from Spain, the Carthaginian general Hannibal crossed the Pyrenees, dashed across Southern France, passed over the Alps amid frost and snow, descended into Northern Italy, swept the Romans from his way there, destroyed the flower of their army in Central Italy at the Trasimene Lake, followed this victory—despite the tactical delays of the dictator Fabius—by one more overwhelming still at Cannæ just below the spur on the boot of Southern Italy, and betook himself to comfortable winter quarters at Capua; and all this in two years. But Capua, as the saying goes, corrupted Hannibal. Thereafter the Romans began to retrieve themselves. Four years later Marcellus took Syracuse, for all the legendary engineering skill of Archimedes; the next year, the Romans recaptured Capua. In five years more they had driven the Carthaginians from Spain, where Scipio—later to be Africanus—won his first fame. He soon proceeded to attack Africa. Hannibal, recalled home to defend Carthage, he crushingly defeated. And the year before the Century ended, Carthage was compelled to accept peace on Roman terms.

The Second Century thus found Rome victorious. During the first half of it, the principal Roman advances were to the eastward in regions which two hundred years before had been among those earliest brought under the Macedonian power of Philip and of Alexander. Just about the middle of the Century, the Third Punic War began, which lasted only three years. Carthage, though subdued, still existed, and as long as it

existed stayed at least a possible menace. The
tradition of Cato, again and again urging upon the
Senate that Carthage must be blotted out,[1] implies the story. This time, the city was almost
literally razed, under the orders of the younger
Scipio Africanus,[2] son of the Æmilius Paulus who
conquered Macedon and grandson of the Æmilius
Paulus who fell at Cannæ, but by adoption grandson of Scipio Africanus the elder. In the same
year when Carthage thus vanished, the victory of
Mummius at Corinth finally reduced Greece to
the dominion of Rome. Fifteen years later,
Scipio had virtually achieved the Roman conquest of Spain, thereafter, until centuries later
Barbarian invasions destroyed the Empire, a Roman province. What was meanwhile happening
at Rome is implied in the story of the Gracchi,
grandsons of the first Scipio Africanus, and the
"jewels" of their mother Cornelia. Radically disposed, as has often been the case throughout history with generous youth of quality, each in turn
attempted economic and social reforms, unwelcome
to the class they sprung from; and each was consequently murdered. For all this turbulence in
Rome, Roman conquests continued. They reduced
to Roman sway the region beyond the Alps which
still bears the popular name of Provence. And as
the Century ended there surged forward the dominant figure of Caius Marius. Born a man of the

---

[1] He is said to have closed speech after speech with the words "Censeo
Carthaginem esse delendam"; the common English version of this is "Car-
thago delenda est." Provokingly enough, I have not lighted on the original authority for either.

[2] For an account of how Carthage fell, see Appian, VIII, 113–136. This
passage, thought to have been condensed from Polybius, may be found in
the Loeb edition of Appian, I, 601 seq.

people and always illiterate, he displayed extraordinary political and military ability. He subdued the African king Jugurtha, whose heroic struggle against Rome led only to the deadly chill of the Mamertine prison. Beyond the Alps Marius met and separately annihilated the Northern hordes of the Teutons and of the Cimbri; and when the Century ended, he was for the sixth time Consul. In that year, 100 before Christ, Julius Cæsar was born; and Cicero was six years old.

II

LITERARY TRADITIONS

PLAUTUS; TERENCE

The names of Cicero and of Cæsar loom so large in the perspective of European tradition, and each is in its kind so ultimate, that we are apt to forget a noteworthy fact about them. Except for Plautus and Terence, on whom we shall presently touch, they were earlier than any other Latin writers now extant except in fragments. By their time, nevertheless, the colossal and growing strength of Rome had been deeply affected by the finer civilisation of primal Greece. This is so far the case, indeed, that we possess hardly any monuments of earlier and purely Roman days. There are a few old walls, and cellars like the so-called Mamertine Prison, mostly uncovered by recent excavations; there are a few arched structures, such as the Cloaca Maxima, the great sewer which still drains the Forum; there are some cores of concrete, the usual method of Roman building from beginning to end. That is about all—sturdy, durable, unlovely. The triumphal arches, the aqueducts, the amphitheatres which ruinously fill one's fancy when one hears the name of Rome, belong not to the Republic but to the Empire. Everybody knows, to be sure, the austere stone coffins of the ancestral Scipios. A few portrait busts, too, survive from times little if at all later than those we have touched on. They are magnificently, uncompromisingly literal and living, incomparably stronger than the softened and Hellenised sculpture which put them out of fashion; but for all their calm dignity they lack the charm of grace. They are not rude, though; and neither was the society to which Cicero and Cæsar were bred.

So far as this society possessed a national literature it was only about a hundred years old. The most eminent of its poets was Ennius, who appears to have combined a considerable strain of Greek blood from Southern Italy with intensely Roman patriotic feeling. He fought in the Second Punic War, came to Rome about the beginning of the Second Century, and was held in high personal esteem by Scipio Africanus. He wrote copiously and variously—among other things, comedies, tragedies, satires, and a very long epic poem, called Annals, celebrating the traditions of Rome. Until the Æneid replaced it, this was held the Roman national epic. It had much to do with fixing the originally Greek hexameter as the poetic idiom of heroic Latin verse as well.[1] Only fragments of it survive, however,—some six hundred lines in all and few consecutive. Worse ruin still has overtaken

---

[1] Somewhat as Marlowe's "mighty line" established blank verse in England.

the other works of Ennius. For our purposes, he is little more than a name. One thing about him nevertheless seems clear; this chief classic of the First Century Romans owed much of his eminence to the fact that he had variously adapted the originally barbarous Latin language to what everybody acknowledged to be the finer poetic forms of the Greek. Whoever knows English poetry from the time of Henry VIII through the reign of Elizabeth will recall numberless instances of a similar process in our own literature. Throughout the life of Ennius this tendency to soften the asperities of native Roman culture was vigorously opposed by Cato, who seems to have been more impressed by the political instability, the enervating luxury, and the flexible morality of the Greeks than by their consummate intelligence or their exquisite æsthetic sense. Though the name of Cato stays traditionally great, however, little of his work remains, except in fragments. Historian, orator, and Roman, he has left us hardly more than the notions we associate with the word *censorious* when we think of his official title Censor. As a satirist, Ennius was already superseded, during the Second Century, by the more characteristically Latin Lucilius, himself now extant only in fragmentary lines, mostly quoted for linguistic purposes by later grammarians. Though the still remembered name of the tragic actor Roscius, who flourished about 100 before Christ, reminds us that Roman tragedy was once important, not a single example of the tragedy of Ennius exists, nor indeed of any Roman tragic poetry until we come to Seneca, at his best under the Emperor Nero. Of the comedies of Ennius, too, we have nothing but the names; they were never held his happiest efforts. His contemporary Plautus, however, survives; and so does the younger comic poet Terence who was born not long before Plautus died. Of all the Latin literature produced earlier than Cicero's time, the only works at once important and complete are now twenty comedies by the one and six by the other.

As we have already reminded ourselves,[1] these Latin comedies were adapted or translated from those of Menander and other writers, now lost, whose light touch animated the last form taken by dramatic poetry among the Greeks. The survival of Plautus and Terence at once testifies to their popularity, preserves—except for Aristophanes—all that we certainly know of antique comedy, and has greatly influenced the standard comedies of Italy and France. What is more, there can be no doubt that throughout the centuries, even to this day, men who have studied or familiarly read them have agreed in finding them amusing. For at least two reasons, however, they are no longer so to those who casually glance at modern translations of them: so far as they anywhere pretend to describe human experience, they deal with a state of society both foreign and past even when they were alive at Rome; and they have been so widely and so long imitated during the last five hundred years that nothing could now prevent their fun from seeming rather conventionally stale. That this is by no means the whole story, however, any reader of Shakspere can remind himself by turning to the Comedy of Errors. This is a free adaptation of a comedy by Plautus,

[1] Cf. p. 137.

called Menæchmi—Menæchmus is his name for the brothers whom Shakspere names Antipholus. Shakspere's other twins, the two Dromios, do not occur in the Latin play; and furthermore he considerably modifies the laxity of personal morality which Plautus assumes as normal. In more than one aspect, however, the Comedy of Errors may give us a better notion of what Plautus did than we might obtain by puzzling or nodding over direct translations from his Latin. Without him this gay, nonsensical confusion could no more have existed than his own plays could have existed without the Greek models on which he based them; and if we may trust the scholars who know him best, he not only allowed himself to modify his Greek plots as he chose but also set forth under Greek names various phases of contemporary Roman character and conduct. Just such free treatment marks the work of Shakspere, and for that matter of all the English dramatists in Shakspere's time; wherever their scenes are set, or at whatever period, the language and the behaviour of their characters, typical or individual, resembles what was current in the England which knew or remembered Queen Elizabeth.

Plautus appears to have been, like Shakspere eighteen hundred years later, a man of obscure origin who had considerable experience of life and of the theatre before he produced his craftsmanlike and fluent plays. He wrote, it is thought, for between thirty and forty years, of which twenty or so were in the Third Century. Conceivably, therefore, he might have known old men who could remember Menander, still alive and at work less than a hundred years before him. Terence be-

longed to a younger generation, and can hardly
have known Italy till after Plautus was dead.
He is said to have been born in Africa, and originally to have been a slave. His talent and at-
tractive qualities early improved his condition; he
was precocious and died at thirty or so—born well
after the Second Punic War, dead well before the
Third. The six comedies he has left us, less ex-
uberant than those of Plautus and more highly
polished, are supposed to be more like the Greek
works on which the art of both was modelled;
substantially, indeed, they may be rather translations than adaptations. Even so, they flow as
freely and as gracefully as if they were original.
The most familiar line from them is at once a case
in point and a typical example of how the meaning of familiar quotations is apt to change. At
the beginning of the Heautontimoroumenos, or
Self-Tormentor,—the retaining of the untrans-
lated Greek title goes far to show that the play
was probably presented as a mere translation,—an
elderly man, pestered while at work by questions
from a meddlesome neighbour, testily asks whether
the tormentor has so much time to spare that he
can attend to matters which are none of his business. The ensuing pun is hard to translate; it
may roughly be indicated as "I am a man; so
any man's business is mine." At all events, it is
a mere play on words; but the words in question
happen to be capable of serious meaning. "Homo
sum," they run, "humani nil a me alienum puto"; [1]

---

[1] The original pun is double, on *homo* and *alienus*, even treble if we in-
clude *nil* :

Men.   Chremes, tantumne ab re tuast oti tibi
          Aliena ut cures ea quæ *nil* ad te attinent?
Chrem.   *Homo* sum: *humani nil* a me *alienum* puto.—
                              Heautontimoroumenos I, 75-77.   (Loeb.)

taken by themselves they may be rendered "I am a man; no human lot can seem quite strange to me." And so, through centuries on centuries, this verbal pleasantry has been regarded by posterity as a noble philanthropic maxim, straight from the heart of still uncorrupted republican Rome.

If our concern were with dramatic history, we might dwell on these prototypes of later comedy long, defining them, and clearly distinguishing between them. Here it is enough to remember what is true of both. The highly conventional plots of both are taken directly from the later comedies of the Greeks. The scenes of both are generally laid in Greece—even Plautus is said to use the word *barbarous* when mentioning Rome. The names of the characters in both are apt to be Greek. All this may well remind us of the relation to Italy similarly evident in so many of Shakspere's plays. Shakspere, however, early began to individualise his characters. Nothing like such individualisation occurs in either Plautus or Terence; their characters, even when compared with those of Aristophanes, and still more with those of the tragic poets of the Fifth Century, turn out to be nothing but broadly indicated types, such as Elizabethans would have called humorous. Perhaps the nearest things to them in English may be found by turning to the earlier, and no longer very animated, comedies of Ben Jonson. In theatrical matters there must always be an element of make-believe; in surviving European drama, this element is hardly anywhere more obvious than you will find it when you ponder on

Plautus and Terence not only separately but together.

Thus taken together, they are doubtless robust, fluent, and—like Shakspere and his contemporaries —nationally idiomatic. Thus taken together, the while, they clearly mark another phase of European literature than the primal Greek, with which we have hitherto been concerned. The Greek, from Homer to Theocritus, betrays no evidence that the men who made it were ever hampered by consciousness of foreign models, superior to anything their own country had made. These earliest survivors of Latin literature, neither of whom was born until well after Theocritus—the latest Greek on whom we have touched—was dead, imply from beginning to end an ingenuous belief that if literature is to be made in their still hardly tamed language, it must be made according to standards already fixed by that elder civilisation which first brought into being the intellectual idiom of subsequent Europe. In this sense, even if they were so in no other, they were characteristically Roman. Just as the literature of Greece is fundamentally primal, so that of Rome, for all its classic dignity and all its sententious gravity and all its large urbanity, is fundamentally secondary. What is more, Plautus and Terence, earliest of enduring Latin writers, imitate not the greatest works of the literature they hold supreme but only one of its later and least profoundly memorable phases. Something similar we shall find recurring throughout European literature. Again and again, the decadence of an extinct art has lured men back to understanding of its masterpieces.

These two first survivors of the literature of Rome, in short, may best be regarded as variously typical rather than as positively excellent. Their work, and nothing else, remains to remind us of what Roman literature was like in the year 100 before Christ.

CHAPTER II

THE FIRST CENTURY BEFORE CHRIST

I

HISTORICAL TRADITIONS

At least historically, the First Century before Christ comprises more names and facts unforgotten by posterity than any other throughout European tradition. It was the Century of Marius and Sylla, of Mithridates, of Spartacus, of Catiline, of Pompey and of Julius Cæsar, of the conquest of Gaul, of the crossing of the Rubicon and of the battle of Pharsalia, of Brutus and Cassius, of the battle of Philippi, of Antony and Cleopatra, of the battle of Actium, and of the final concentration of Roman power under the imperial sway of Cæsar Augustus. These very names almost tell their tale; after two thousand years they are as familiar as ever.

The general outline of the story which hovers about them, too, is not only traditionally but historically true. This was at once the Century when expansion of Roman dominion showed itself most indomitable, and that when the ancient forms of republican government proved hopelessly inadequate longer to control the colossal power of Rome. Both tendencies appear wherever we happen to glance at the first half of the Century. At home as well as abroad, there were incessant wars and rumours of wars. Though these have been so recorded, and of late years so studied that historians can discuss them in detail, the tradition of them, which is our immediate concern, stays confused in the distance. As we think of the confusion, however, certain facts grow more or less clear. There was a Social War, in which the peoples of Italy demanded Roman citizenship; they were ultimately defeated, and thereupon the citizenship was paradoxically given them. Thus, throughout later Roman history, citizenship came to imply not residence at Rome but political rights in the Roman Empire: it was enjoyed, the pious will remember, by the Apostle Paul, who had never been near Rome till he came there with his appeal to Cæsar. On the Social War there presently followed, at about the same time, the first war against the threatening Asiatic power of Mithridates and the first Civil War, at Rome itself, between Marius and Sylla; very broadly speaking this internal conflict was between the new and comparatively democratic tendencies embodied in Marius, and the old traditions of the aristocratic Republic embodied in Sylla. At home and abroad, the fortunes of war fluctuated. There was a time when Marius found himself a fugitive, almost literally alone, and saved himself only by asking a Cimbric soldier sent to despatch him if the fellow dared kill Caius Marius; there was another, a little later, when, forbidden to land in Africa, he bade the officer sent to prevent him go tell the governor that Marius was to be seen sitting on the ruins of Carthage. Yet, not much later, while Sylla was fighting Mithridates, Marius came back to Rome, and died there dominant. In two or three years, Sylla, victorious in Asia, was at Rome once more, and wreaked his vengeance as he pleased, with slaughter and pillage in the very Roman streets. He soon died, in his turn. This, very generally, was the story of Rome during the first quarter of the Century, when Cicero and Cæsar were boys, and grew to be young men.

The next quarter of the Century brought them both into the full light of history, and Pompey, too, who was just about of an age with Cicero. War with Mithridates broke out again; and at the same time the revolt headed by the gladiator Spartacus threatened parts of Italy itself. In both cases, the power of Rome, for all the political and social disease at its heart, proved indomitable. Pompey came forward, upset the policies established for a while by Sylla, cleared the Italian seas of pirates, and at last finally subdued Mithridates. In the same year, Cicero, then Consul, exposed and suppressed the conspiracy of Catiline, and fancied for a little while that he had saved the Republic. But Cæsar, suspected of having to do with the conspiracy, was coming towards what the traditions of the future were long to declare his own. With Pompey and Crassus he formed the first Triumvirate; preserving semblance of the ancestral forms of the Republic, they virtually seized the sovereignty, in the year 60. The following ten years comprise the whole story of Cæsar's conquests in Gaul; while these were in progress, Crassus was defeated and killed in Asia. By the year 50, Pompey was master of Rome, but Cæsar of all the North and of his Gallic war veterans; the rivals were face to face, and Cicero, with no other choice than that between them, seems—like conservative men so placed throughout history—to have been

concerned mostly with speculations as to which
of them the devil would presently take as hind-
most.

Traditionally, the third quarter of the Century
is clearest of all.   In the year 49, Cæsar crossed the
Rubicon, a little stream which divided the region
of Northern Italy legally under his command from
the territory legally under the command of Pompey.   The die was cast, he is reputed to have said.
A year later, he proved himself the winner.   At
Pharsalia, in Thessaly, Pompey was overwhelm-
ingly defeated; and seeking asylum in Egypt, with
Cæsar close at his heels, he was treacherously
murdered in his boat.   The following months
Cæsar passed in Alexandria, the first imperial
Roman lover of Cleopatra.[1]   He gradually made
her sole queen, last of the Ptolemies; then swiftly
followed his victorious campaigns in Pontus,—
whence he wrote "Veni, vidi, vici," [2]—in Africa,
and later in Spain.   By that time he was absolute
sovereign of Rome, where Cleopatra had followed
him, his acknowledged mistress, with their child
Cæsarion; but, preserving the forms of the Republic, he bore only such titles as *imperator*, or
general, as *pontifex maximus*, or chief priest, as
consul, and as *dictator*—an office finally conferred
on him for life.   The style of royalty stayed immemorially detestable to Roman tradition.

At this point the story becomes more familiar
still to all who know English literature; for the
Julius Cæsar and the Antony and Cleopatra of

[1] See the impish but not therefore negligible Cæsar and Cleopatra of
Mr. Bernard Shaw.

[2] Originally, it is said, written to the Senate, these words were finally
inscribed on a banner borne in the triumphal procession which celebrated
his Pontic victory.   They mean, "I came, I saw, I conquered."

THE FIRST CENTURY B. C. 183

Shakspere have translated the prose of Plutarch
into changeless English poetry. Accurate or not,
they are surprisingly faithful to their authority,
which records what happened between the year
44, when Cæsar was assassinated, and the year
30, when Cleopatra took her life. The throbbing
distinctness of individual character which makes
them so memorable is of course due to Shakspere;
but the course of the story where these characters
live and move is straight from Plutarch. Cæsar,
dominant at Rome and throughout the Roman
dominions, was imposing peace on the world, by
that time turbulent throughout living memory.
In modern terms we may roughly generalise his
policy as the declaration of practicable law enforced by an army whose chief function was to
regulate all civilisation and thus make the world
safe. This policy involved at least a modification, if not the complete abolition, of many liberties enjoyed by citizens, and particularly by men
of rank, under the time-honoured constitution of
the Republic. The wars and rumours of wars
which had convulsed the Republic ever since anybody could remember had made conspiracy and
rebellion matters of habit. A consequent conspiracy, led by conservative Roman gentlemen,
lured Cæsar to the Senate house, and there stabbed
him to death, at the foot of Pompey's statue.
Thereupon anarchy for a while broke loose again;
and among others Cicero was murdered. Very
soon, two distinct parties defined themselves: that
under Brutus and Cassius, which endeavoured to
sustain some semblance of the old republican
principles; and that under the new Triumvirate
—Cæsar's nephew Octavian, his brilliant adherent

Mark Antony, and a rather shadowy person named
Lepidus—which was determined finally to assert
the dominant policy of Cæsar. About two years
after Cæsar fell, these forces met at Philippi
in southeastern Macedonia. Brutus and Cassius
were utterly defeated. The words with which the
Brutus of Shakspere salutes the self-slain bodies
of Cassius and of their faithful officer Titinius
imply the story of Europe for centuries to come:

> O, Julius Cæsar, thou art mighty yet!
> Thy spirit walks abroad, and turns our swords
> In our own proper entrails.[1]

Julius Cæsar is perhaps the clearest of Shakspere's plays; certainly it is among the easiest to
read. Antony and Cleopatra, at first confusing,
demands but abundantly rewards closer attention. With astonishing fidelity to Plutarch, it
tells how the unity of the triumvirate failed to
master its trinal diversities; and how Antony,
betaking himself to Egypt, was there ensnared by
the wiles of Cleopatra. Whatever she may have
been in life, Shakspere has made her an incarnation
of damning harlotry:

> Age cannot wither her, nor custom stale
> Her infinite variety.[2]

After fluctuating efforts to break her spells, Antony finds himself face to face with Octavian, already called Cæsar, in a final struggle for world-
empire. Lepidus has meanwhile faded out of
sight; though he flits across the stage once or
twice more, he is virtually disposed of in the mar-

[1] Julius Cæsar V, iii, 94–96.   [2] Antony and Cleopatra, II, ii, 240–241.

vellous scene[1] where all three triumvirs get perilously drunk on Sextus Pompey's galley, and he is
presently bundled helpless over the side into
safety. There is a naval battle off Actium, on
the southerly part of the coast of Epirus; in the
midst of it, Cleopatra, who has insisted on seeing
the fray, gets frightened, and bids her ship take
flight. Antony infatuated instantly follows her,
and thus

> For lazy glances flung away the world.

Back in Alexandria, and there besieged by victorious Cæsar, he falls on his sword and dies in
the arms of Cleopatra,

> A Roman by a Roman
> Valiantly vanquished.[2]

Thereafter, rather than be displayed in the triumphal train of Cæsar, she applies the asp, a
deadly serpent, to her breast:

> Come, thou mortal wretch,
> With thy sharp teeth this knot intrinsicate
> Of life at once untie. Poor venomous fool,
> Be angry, and despatch. O, could'st thou speak,
> That I might hear thee call great Cæsar ass
> Unpolicied. . . .
>
> *(To her attendant)*
>
> Peace, peace;
> Dost thou not see my baby at my breast
> That sucks the nurse asleep?[3]

[1] Antony and Cleopatra, II, vii. This should be compared with the
original passage in Sir Thomas North's translation of Plutarch's Life of
Antony—the version used by Shakspere.

[2] Antony and Cleopatra, IV, xv, 57–58. *Cf.* Plutarch's account of his
death.

[3] Antony and Cleopatra, V, ii, 306–313.

And when Cæsar, coming too late, finds her dead, he speaks her epitaph for the centuries:

> She looks like sleep,
> As she would catch another Antony
> In her strong toil of grace.[1]

With her the kingdom of the Ptolemies ended. Egypt was fully Roman. The second Cæsar was lord of all.

At that time he was only about thirty-two years old. He lived to the age of seventy-seven, dying in the year 14 of the Christian Era. For more than forty years, which included the whole last quarter of the First Century before Christ, he was more absolutely sovereign than any European had been before, and his power has never since been surpassed. Whether he was great, or cool, or only fortunate is not now our concern. Like his uncle, Julius Cæsar, he preserved the forms of the immemorial Republic. His banners bore the legend S. P. Q. R.[2]—the Senate and the People of Rome. His title was only *Imperator*, which had always been borne by Roman generals. *Cæsar* was his family name. *Augustus*, the name by which he is traditionally remembered, was originally an innocent honorific, meaning something like our own word, *august* or *reverend*. And *Princeps*, or *prince*, need have conveyed to sensitive ears nothing much more troublous than Americans of 1799 might have detected in its English equivalent *first*, when Lee eulogised Washington as "First in war, first in peace, and first in the hearts of his

---

[1] Antony and Cleopatra, V, ii, 349-351.

[2] Wickedly parodied, years ago, by some precursor of American Trusts, who declared the initials to stand for "Small Profits. Quick Returns."

countrymen." He pretended to exercise his authority as the formal successor of republican magistrates—proconsuls, for example, tribunes and censors; in fact, however, he came thus to embody the state. Among other things he was *Pontifex Maximus*, or chief priest of the Roman religion. The history of this title is a curious instance of how time and circumstance modify not only the meaning of words, but all the associations which gather about them. Literally, *pontifex* signifies *bridge-builder;* the fact that in primitive antiquity the safety of Rome required special and constant attention to any bridge across the Tiber seems to have put such structures under the particular guardianship of the local gods and their priests. Long before the time of Cæsar, nobody remembered that the pontifical office had ever had anything to do with bridges; but the title survived as that of the chief ministers of the Roman gods. It has never quite lapsed. It is borne to this day by the Pope, still believed by millions on millions to be successor of St. Peter as Christian Bishop of Rome and apostolic head of the Catholic Church. In its religious phase, indeed, the antique Empire of the Cæsars structurally survives even now.

The theory of our ancestral Church implies that of finally imperial Rome. After generations of anarchic bloodshed, there came into existence a new ideal of empire. This is nowhere more excellently celebrated than by the great poem written to assert it when Augustus was all-powerful, the Æneid of Virgil:

> Behold, at last, that man, for this is he,
> So oft unto thy listening ears foretold,

Augustus Cæsar, kindred unto Jove.
He brings a golden age; he shall restore
Old Saturn's sceptre to our Latin land
And o'er remotest Garamant and Ind
His sway extend; the fair dominion
Outruns th' horizon planets, yea, beyond
The sun's bright path, where Atlas' shoulder bears
Yon dome of heaven set thick with burning stars.
Against his coming the far Caspian shores
Break forth in oracles; the Mæotian land
Trembles, and all the seven-fold mouths of Nile.[1]

Till that time, imperial power had meant only
armed conquests—Assyrian, Babylonian, Egyptian, Persian, Macedonic. Now at last there appears a sense of duty, animating the gross body of
power. The mission of Rome was to bring to
troubled mankind the solace of *Pax Romana*—of
world-wide Roman peace, strong in the majesty of
the law. Three lines of that superb prophecy of
Anchises summarise for all time the hope of this
newly golden Augustan age:

Tu regere imperio populos, Romane, memento;
Hae tibi erunt artes: pacisque imponere morem,
Parcere subjectis, et debellare superbos.[2]

(Remember, Roman, thine imperial charge;
These be thy arts: enforce the rule of peace,
Sparing the conquered, beating rebels down.)

By what means Augustus attempted to make
real this ideal purpose, we need not inquire. Traditionally the forty years of his reign are a period

---

[1] Æneid, VI, 791–800; translated by T. C. Williams (Boston, 1908).

[2] Æneid, VI, 851–853: Williams translates this passage thus:
But thou, O Roman, learn with sovereign sway
To rule the nations. Thy great art shall be
To keep the world in lasting peace, to spare
The humbled foe, and crush to earth the proud.

of emergence from the storms of anarchy into the calm sunlight of world-order. Two familiar likenesses of him embody the spirit of his age. The first is the youthful bust, softened from the literal austerity of elder Roman sculpture, but still strong in its gracious rendering of beauty and promise; its features were parodied again and again by imperial portraits of the great Napoleon, whose face probably had some manner of resemblance to them. The other likeness is the statue which shows Augustus imperial—idealised, no doubt, as the bare head and feet would imply, and the symbolic devices on his fretted cuirass, but mature, calm, majestic, just, and sovereign; first of those destined to reincarnate the mighty spirit of Julius Cæsar, he walks abroad, on his way to the posthumous honours of divinity.

When the First Century before Christ closed, this was his aspect, after some thirty years of imperial sovereignty. The first half of the Century had been a whirl of anarchy and bloodshed; the last quarter of it, uniting the world under the beneficent sway of Augustus Cæsar, had promised a diuturnal future to the peace of Rome. And by the beginning of our Christian era, Latin literature, hardly in lasting existence when the Century began, had produced its most memorable masters. To the first half of the Century Cicero belongs, and Cæsar, and Lucretius, and Catullus; to the full serenity of Augustan promise belong Virgil, and Horace, and Ovid, and Livy. To these eight, and to a few of their lesser contemporaries, we may now turn.

II

CICERO

Among the most interesting books about Rome is Monsieur Gaston Boissier's Ciceron et Ses Amis.[1] Based on the letters of Cicero, it at once gives a remarkably animated account of him and of his times, and shows why he is now the most fully recorded and clearly defined personage of all classical antiquity. This is not because of the circumstances which made him historically conspicuous, nor yet because of the copious orations and philosophic works which have always been recognised as the chief classical model of Latin prose. It is due to the fact that more than nine hundred letters actually written by him, or to him, still exist. For centuries between his time and ours, no doubt, they were virtually lost and forgotten. Now that they have been restored to us again, for something like five hundred years, they often seem the most precious part of his work. Their general characteristics are admirably summarised in Boissier's introductory chapter; no other such collection of any period so variously and so clearly preserves at once the personality of a great public man and the atmosphere as well as the detail of the circumstances about him.

At the time when the first of these extant letters was written Cicero was about thirty-eight years old.[2] Sprung from a respectable family of

---

[1] An English translation of this, by A. D. Jones, was published in 1897.

[2] The original texts, arranged chronologically and abundantly annotated, may be found in the volumes edited by Tyrrell and Purser (third edition, Dublin: 1904).

country gentry, he had received both at home and abroad the highest education of his time; he was equally familiar with the traditions of Greece and of Rome; he had gone to the bar; being blest with extraordinary diligence and wit he had there distinguished himself; and he had early taken active part in politics. His career had thus been of a kind happily usual throughout the modern history both of England and of America. By nature and by training he was attached to the state of things amid which he had been born and bred. Whoever has his way to make likes to be sure of his bearings; whoever must stake his future cherishes respect for the rules of the game. To such a man no environment could have been much more disconcerting than that where Cicero found himself. The anarchic disturbances of civil war had made everything uncertain. At Rome neither life nor property was safe; and the old Roman aristocrats, who looked with patronising contempt on "new men," such as he was, had often become at once luxuriously corrupt in private life and cynically unprincipled in political conduct. A wellborn demagogue is a very dangerous animal. The conspicuous talent of Cicero had nevertheless brought him forward, both as a lawyer and as a public man; he had already made a considerable fortune; and if his work had stopped then a number of his forensic speeches and his denunciation of Verres would already have established his reputation as the most accomplished orator who ever spoke Latin.

In this aspect he is traditionally best known now. It is a commonplace that his methods have at various times been studied and imitated by public

speakers of widely different subsequent periods—
never more admiringly than in England and
America from the middle of the Eighteenth Century to the middle of the Nineteenth. It is rather
less generally understood that these methods of
his had in common with those of his imitators the
profoundly characteristic feature of being deliberately based on excellent foreign models. He was,
and he remains, the greatest Roman master of the
subtle art most enduringly mastered among the
Greeks by Demosthenes; but just as surely as
Demosthenes considered only the general principles
of his art and its best models in his native language, so Cicero never wrote a line of oratorical
Latin without a consciousness, intensified by life-
long study and culture, of his effort to rival in
what had lately been a barbarous tongue the lof-
tiest achievements of primal Greece. An often
forgotten result followed, and has never quite lost
influence. Cicero, conventionally accepted as the
most admirable master of Latin prose, really wrote
not the current Latin which everybody used for
daily purposes of thought or speech, but rather a
consciously literary dialect which attempted to reproduce effects fully attainable only by the more
subtle refinements of the Greek language. Such
work, whatever its merit, cannot escape evident artificiality; yet, accepted as itself a faultless model,
it has been held up for hopeless imitation by European schoolboys almost to this day. This is as if
some mongrel race, two thousand years hence, were
assiduously to be taught English by courageous
attempts to parody heavily Latinised examples
of our style, like the blank verse of Paradise Lost or
the balanced periods of Doctor Johnson. The clas-

sic literature of Rome never had, like the primal
Greek, the full and free grace of instinctive idiom.
It had, however, a studied polish much higher than
any fabricated by its imitators; and for such polish
there never will be a better name than Ciceronian.

The most widely familiar examples of Cicero's
oratory are probably his speeches against Catiline,
immemorially studied at English and American
schools. In the body of his extant work, these
come rather early. Only eleven of his letters, all
addressed to Atticus, have been preserved from
years before his consulship; and his correspondence
does not begin again until his consulship was over.
The traditional story of his political triumph, indeed, is principally based on orations which he
made at the time. What is to be said for the other
side must be gathered largely from inference; for
one constant, and constantly imitated, feature of
his oratory was fierce denunciation of opponents.
Before accepting Cicero's views of Catiline, one
may prudently ponder on the methods of Ser-
geant Buzfuz, a pretty sound Ciceronian, in the
case of Bardell *v.* Pickwick. These views, however, have long been sanctioned by tradition;
and may very probably have been sincere on the
part of the great magistrate who set them forth.
Elected to the consulship, he found the structure
of the State threatened by a new conspiracy, led
by Roman gentlemen of better origin than he. His
adroitness and eloquence suppressed it without
bloodshed at the capital; to Romans who remembered the atrocities of Sylla, this may well have
seemed a return to the golden age of the legendary
Republic. And Cicero, one of whose foibles was
the self-conscious self-esteem of a self-made man,

and who had been officially proclaimed *Pater Patriæ*, or Father of his Country, could ingenuously write of himself—though laughed at for the writing—such an alliterative hexameter as

> Cedant arma togæ, concedat laurea laudi.[1]
> (Let arms yield to the gown, the laurel-crown[2]
> To public commendation.)

His time, however, was out of joint.   Five years later he was in exile, his house and effects at Rome confiscated and looted.   For the rest of his life there is no other contemporary authority comparable with his correspondence, which now becomes copious.   Read it as you will, there can be no doubt that the crashing course of history was beyond human control, and that his life-long hope to see preserved or restored the antique constitution of the Republic was futile.   His exile, to be sure, lasted less than two years.   Through the greater part of Cæsar's campaigns in Gaul, through the struggles between Cæsar and Pompey, as well as at the time when Cæsar was murdered, Cicero was mostly at Rome, with fluctuating fortunes and influence, and sometimes with what looked like fluctuating principles.   Meanwhile he produced the greater part of his collected works, orations both legal and political, and the political or philosophical treatises which consoled or occupied his generally enforced periods of comparative leisure. After the death of Cæsar, he did his utmost to resist the resistless power of Cæsar's imperial tendency: his orations against Antony, conventionally called Philippics by reason of their essential

[1] De Officiis, I, 22.
[2] A Roman military victor was crowned with laurel.

likeness to the fiery but futile speeches in which
three hundred years earlier Demosthenes had denounced Macedonian aggression on the liberties of
Greece, at once defined his position and sealed his
doom. He was among the first to be proscribed
by the second Triumvirate—Antony, Octavian,
and Lepidus. Starting to escape, if he could,
from a country estate where he had taken refuge,
he was put to death in his private conveyance by
pursuing soldiers of the Triumvirs. His head and
his hands were hacked off; they were brought to
Antony as proof that this opponent need no longer
be reckoned with; and it is said that before the
relics were exposed in the Forum, the wife of
Antony—just then the "shrill-tongued Fulvia"[1]
of Shakspere's Cleopatra—displayed her matronly
Roman charity by piercing the dried and silenced
tongue of Cicero with one of her hairpins.

True or not, that ferocious anecdote defines the
Rome where the first consummate literary expressions of what we now call culture were produced.
This quality of culture, evident throughout Cicero's letters, as well as in every line of his more
studied literary works, makes him generically different from any Greek; at least in this aspect,
indeed, he seems almost modern. His letters are
those of an accomplished gentleman, in the finer
sense of the word; they show his complete urbanity of social habit—among other things he was
reported the best diner-out of his times, and his
witticisms were repeated far and wide; they also
show his politely alert familiarity with intelligent
thought, with fine art and with literature, Greek
and Latin; they could have proceeded only from

[1] Antony and Cleopatra, I, i, 32.

a man who knew how to enjoy the cream of life. Here if ever in the whole course of literature you find yourself in thoroughly good company; and thoroughly good company implies highly trained minds and manners. His orations, whether legal or political, could have been produced by nothing less than assiduous and life-long study, under the most skilful teachers, of an extraordinarily adroit and subtle art. Whether, under any circumstances, oratory has quite so much practical value as we are apt to assume is beside the point; Cicero could do at will whatever can be done with it. Here again we find him in a position possible only when the refinements of a highly developed civilisation are for a while matters of course. And his numerous philosophic and political treatises more than imply the same kind of surroundings. Speaking generally, they seem to have been produced, with remarkable speed and ease, by an almost overactive mind which found relief and recreation in what to most of us would be hard intellectual work. He hardly pretends to be an original thinker, and indeed may nowadays be conventionally credited with less original thought than he really displays. He had read, however, almost everything that was worth reading; he knew what he thought about whatever he had read. And, often modelling his form on the tradition established by Plato's dialogues, he was apt to put into the heads of Romans—Cato, for example, Scipio, or Lælius, as well as contemporaries of his own— thoughts and speculations which had caught his fancy while reading or talking about the philosophy and the literature of the Greeks. Once more, such expression implies not only a very highly culti-

vated condition of society, but also that phase of
culture, recurrent throughout subsequent Europe,
which eagerly recognises the standards made lasting by a finer though foreign civilisation of the
past. All this sounds as if his times were like
ours; yet, in those very times, Fulvia—a great
lady of his own race—could be believed to have
dealt with his relics as the French mob dealt with
those of the Princess de Lamballe in the first out-
bursts of their Revolutionary madness. He was
pre-eminently such a man as we might find delightfully cultivated now; and he lived and died
when persons of quality might behave like German soldiers in Belgian villages or Bolsheviki in
Russia.

A little poem by Catullus,[1] of which the deliberately equivocal grace has thus far eluded all attempts to translate it, pleasantly implies the relation of Cicero to his contemporary men of letters.
Addressing him by name, and calling him most accomplished or most eloquent of the offspring of
Romulus, it thanks him as the best of patrons or
advocates for some present or civility, or service,
in the name of the worst or most unworthy of
poets. Generally rendered literally as if it concerned Cicero's professional skill, and sometimes
thought ironic, it may just as well be taken as an
ingeniously pretty play on words; if we may trust
the dictionaries, the Latin *patronus*, which doubtless means counsel as related to client, applies
equally to the relation of a generous patron to
any kind of artist, and Cicero was at once a lover
of letters and rich enough to express literary ap-
proval by substantial gifts. So, the word *diser-*

[1] XLIX: Disertissime Romuli nepotum, etc.

tissime may signify as you please either most skilful in the choice of words or most delicately appre-
ciative in the criticism of anything.

Cicero was really both. It was probably only
when the works had survived the man, and become the permanent masterpiece of Latin prose,
that the marvel of his literary achievement over-
shadowed, through the centuries, the other aspects of his astonishing career. He had found his
language still somewhat rude; he had made it,
whatever his conscious artificialities, exquisitely
polished; to its native robustness he had added
something as near as ever might be to the lovely
subtleties of Greek flexibility. Thus he had produced something different from anything previously
in existence, and something which could be admired,
reverenced, and imitated wherever men could read
and could try to write in Latin—as men did
throughout the Middle Ages, and as orthodox
Churchmen, to go no further, still do. So, thinking
of him as incomparable, we seldom remember that
he was bravely trying all his life to do in Latin
what had already been done in another language,
and that his models in this other language were
not the oldest. His oratory has been reiterantly
celebrated, through generation after generation, until we are apt to forget that the form of literature
which he thus established in Rome, as the earliest
of its great literary achievements, was late to develop in Greece. This by itself, and still more when
we think of it together with the comedy of Plautus
and Terence domesticating at Rome a late phase of
Greek poetry, would imply the nature of that Latin
literature which in European tradition followed on
the primal Greek. Cicero has uninterruptedly

persisted as an acknowledged literary master; it
has been only in comparatively recent times that
we have come to perceive how, despite his ultimate
skill, his historical place in world-literature cannot
help being secondary.

For ages meanwhile he was probably regarded
not chiefly as an orator, legal or political, but as a
philosopher. Dante[1] groups him, in the "philosophic family" clustered about Aristotle, with the
shadowy Greek sages Orpheus and Linus, and with
Seneca "the moralist." His philosophic works,
secondary not only in style but in substance, were
more congenial to the mediæval mind than his
comparatively mundane letters, which almost got
lost. Even if we had lost them, however, and his
orations too, his philosophic works would preserve
the wonder of his Latinity. They would reveal, as
well, the breadth of his culture, the activity of his
mind, the selective power of his intelligence, and
the fundamental earnestness of his character. The
revival of his letters, indeed, is reported somewhat
to have shocked his admirers, not quite prepared
to find him so human. To the letters we must
turn for the man, and the oftener we do so the
more willingly we shall do so again. Tradition, of
which the letters preserve the historic basis, has
made and kept him a great moral philosopher, a
great advocate, and the greatest classical model of
Latin prose.

[1] Inferno, IV, 141.

III

CÆSAR

The parallel Lives of Plutarch sometimes appear oddly or at best artificially mated. In grouping Cicero with Demosthenes, however, he was simply and clearly right. Both were orators unprecedented and unsurpassed in the languages which they moulded to suit themselves; both were alike professional advocates and public men; both were at times what we should now call prime ministers; both tried to defend the ancestral constitutions of their countries from irresistible change; both failed; both met with violent deaths amid the crash of the systems they had hoped to save; and the forces which destroyed both had lately been incarnate in imperial conquerors. With equally simple good sense, Plutarch grouped together the lives of these conquerors, Alexander and Cæsar. The one carried Greek, or Hellenistic empire to a point which for a little while seemed fated to dominate the civilised world; the other brought into final being that Roman Empire whose principles are not yet altogether extinct. We have needed centuries clearly to discern the contrast between the two. So far as we can now perceive, the fleeting empire of Alexander was animated by no deeper ideal than that of overwhelming military force; whatever the purposes of Cæsar himself, the diuturnity of his empire came ultimately to animate it with the ideals of divine sanction and earthly peace.

These ideals, variously persistent through the generations, have made the Cæsar of tradition and

of legend grandly unlike anybody who could ever
have existed in the flesh. The accident that his
empire was mostly Western and controlled Europe
has doubtless helped his legend. Amid English
ruins you will still find tower after tower traditionally bearing his name; to find the name of
Alexander likewise remembered, you must voyage
as far as Egypt or India. It was no such trifle
as this, however, which once made the German
Emperor, William II, reverently salute in the ex-
cavated Forum the spot where they declare the
body of Cæsar to have been burnt. It was honest,
even though men may now generally hold it piti-
fully mistaken, belief that the great Roman whose
visible presence vanished here in smoke and flame
was the first apostle of the true duty of sovereignty—to enforce by arms the rule of peace.
Pax Romana had long endured; *Pax Germanica*
should soon rise, the German sovereign planned,
newly to embody the spirit of it.

The well-known facts of Cæsar's life have been
repeatedly studied. We have no such record of
him, however, as reveals the real Cicero in the
copious correspondence on which we lately touched;
nor indeed much contemporary record beyond his
own military reports. He was of the highest social rank, traditionally descended from Iulus the
son of Æneas, and thus both from the royal race
of Troy and from the goddess Venus. He was also
a man of the highest fashion, with all the accomplishments and, if we may believe scandal, with all
the private vices which make fashion abhorrent
to the uncouth or the godly. He had the gift of
fascination, particularly for women; though most
of his portraits look rather grim, the profiles re-

veal traces of that aristocratic beauty so evident in the later members of his family from Augustus to Nero; and nobody anywhere ever more carelessly contracted and disregarded personal debts. As a politician he was adroitly unscrupulous; as a military man he was a genius of the highest order; and to find another such combination of military capacity with administrative, Europe had to wait for Napoleon. Above all, he had the faculty of perceiving at critical moments just what could be done, and of doing it with lightning decision and more than lightning exactitude. Here lies the problem concerning him which can never be decided. There is an excellent case for declaring him to have mastered the secrets of a confusion little less than chaotic for every other human being of his time, and thus deliberately to have reduced anarchy to order. The case on the other side is about as good; he may equally well have been no more than the shrewdest of opportunists, fortunate enough when only seizing occasion fully to avail himself of that tide in the affairs of men which taken at the flood leads on to fortune.

At this point, intentionally or not, such of his writings as have survived do him good service. Like Frederick the Great, he dabbled in letters, and was at his worst as a poet. His verses, however, and various other pieces of his work have long since vanished. His military reports are preserved: seven Books on the Gallic Wars and three on the Civil Wars which ensued. The merit of these is emphasised by the chance that supplementary matter by other hands is generally published with them; there is an eighth Book on the wars in Gaul, and there are separate Books about his wars at

Alexandria, in Africa, and in Spain. As literature these appendices are negligible; as literature the authentic work of Cæsar is masterly. With unparalleled simplicity and compactness, with hardly a trace of emotion or partisan feeling, he sets forth what happened, or if you prefer what he chose that people should believe to have happened. His effects are implicitly strengthened by the fact that like Xenophon he writes of himself not in the first person but in the third, as if somebody else were giving a thoroughly competent account of his campaigns. He seldom stirs you, so that his incidental story of how a daring soldier, leaping overboard with the standard, rallied hesitant troops to the invasion of Britain[1] comes with all the force of surprise. From beginning to end, though, he impresses you as a writer who knows exactly what he means to say about a commander who always knew exactly what he meant to do. To this extent, the whole range of literature contains nothing more saturated with the temper of mastery than the Commentaries of Cæsar.

More than probably this effect is deliberate. Though pretending to be only matters of succinct record, these reports were almost unquestionably intended at once to justify him in the opinion of his partisans and if so might be to convince doubters that his course had been right. To do this, he must evidently represent himself as calmly dominant over self, and men and affairs. He does so with such assurance and such confident dignity that you never hesitate to take him at his word. You can hardly help accepting his facts as true; you cannot resist the impression that the

[1] Bell. Gall., IV, 25.

man who states them has something like the colossal impersonality of greatness; you may well find
yourself wondering whether the tales of his
dissolute youth and his unscrupulous maturity are anything more than echoes of malicious
gossip, of partisan denunciation, or of ribald songs
chanted by his half-drunken soldiers. Whatever
their deliberate purpose, these writings appear un-
affectedly genuine. If they really are so, the man
who wrote them seems far more likely to have
moulded chaos to his will than only to have taken
shrewd advantage of whatever happened to occur.

Though no earlier document exactly resembling the Commentaries now exists, it is thought
that, like any other masterpiece, they were not
unprecedented. The generals of Alexander are
known to have written compact professional reports of their own campaigns. If we still had these,
the works of Cæsar might more than probably
prove to be as faithfully modelled on Greek originals as those of Cicero are, or the comedies of
Plautus and of Terence. Here again chance has
favoured him. As they stand, his Commentaries
appear to us almost as primal as the hexameters
of Homer seem. And certainly the temper of
them—firm, judicial, masterful, solidly dominant
—is magnificently Roman. Hardly any other
known works can be found more nearly to justify
a secular legend or tradition of which they calmly
record the origin.

How various this tradition has been, three aspects of it in European literature may serve to
remind us. So far as the person of Cæsar goes, to
be sure, Dante gives to him only a line: [1]

[1] Inf., IV, 123.

Cesare armato, con gli occhi grifagni,
(Cæsar in armor, with his falcon eyes,)

appears among those pre-Christian worthies who
are doomed eternally hopeless to live in longing.
One meaning of Cæsar none the less pervades the
Divine Comedy: first of human beings he embodied the supreme ideal of earthly empire, and
in the lowest depth of hell his assassins Brutus
and Cassius, traitors to God's anointed, suffer the
worst tortures of all but one; only Judas Iscariot,
traitor to God Incarnate, has sinned more deeply
than they. In Shakspere's Julius Cæsar, on the
other hand, they live heroic, mistaken if you will
and futile in their attempt to turn the course
of history, but nevertheless impelled to the deed
which involved their fate by hatred of the tyranny
already fatal to the wisdom and the dignity of the
tyrant. And when the Emperor Napoleon III
tried to set forth his ideals of government,—hon-
estly cherished, if we may believe those who knew
him best,—he presented Cæsar as the foremost
Saviour of Society in all history. Which Cæsar
was, or what, nobody can ever be sure. The
facts fit all three versions of him, and more. If our
concern were with facts, he would remain vastly
impenetrable. Yet he would remain, even as a
fact, perhaps the greatest of all European humanity. As a tradition he is incontestably so. No
man before him and none since rises quite so
dominant as he, humanly fallible as you will, but
in his sovereignty the supreme traditional incarnation of the ideal of divinely sanctioned Empire.

IV

LUCRETIUS

Cicero and Cæsar, in their several ways the first masterly makers of enduring Latin prose, were not primarily men of letters. The literary eminence of Cæsar, indeed, is almost accidental; and that of Cicero, except for his philosophic treatises, —now generally esteemed less memorable than his orations or his letters,—might perhaps be regarded as incidental to his finally hapless public career. Fairly to estimate even him, we can never neglect the catastrophic history of his times, often best known from the records he made in the whirling days when no one could be sure whither things were bound. By chance, there have happened to survive from these very times the first enduring Latin poets—Lucretius and Catullus. Tradition has often forgotten just when they lived. Classical literature has so long and so generally been studied as a matter of grammar, prosody, and the like, that, unless a classical author happened to figure in history as well as in letters, very competent students of the classics often neglect his historical position. In this instance the neglect is regrettable; for different as Lucretius and Catullus are they imply together the feelings of artistic, sensitive, passionate natures surrounded by historical catastrophes of which they must be poignantly aware, yet which they can nowise influence or control.

They died within a year or two of each other, while Cæsar's Gallic Wars were at their height, and well before his crossing of the Rubicon.

Though Lucretius was probably some ten years or more the elder, neither could remember an Italy unshaken by civil wars, and both were grown men when Cicero was Consul and Catiline conspired. Ten years later, both were dead. In both, as we shall soon remind ourselves, you feel the full influence of the culture which had come to Rome from the primal civilisation of Greece. Both were none the less Roman. As we have already seen,[1] Catullus addressed Cicero as "Disertissime Romuli nepotum," which may roughly be rendered: "Finest of all the sons of Romulus"; and the opening invocation of the poem of Lucretius begins with the words

Æneadum genetrix, hominum divumque voluptas,
Alma Venus, . . .
(Mother of all who from Æneas spring,
Of men and gods the joy, dear Venus, . . .)[2]

Fourth or Fifth Century Greeks, to be sure, would have known that Æneas was a Trojan prince, but not that Romans claimed descent from him; and to Greeks the names of Romulus and of Venus would have been as unmeaning as those of Adam and Eve would have been to Cicero, or as those of Jimmu and of Daigo are now to Europeans unskilled in Japanese mythology. To both Lucretius and Catullus, however, as their allusions indicate, the native traditions of Rome were no less familiar than the exotic traditions of Greece.

In both of these poets, furthermore, you feel a

---

[1] Cf. p. 197.
[2] C. F. Johnson (1872) translates these words:
   Mother of Romans! joy of men and gods,
   Benignant Venus . . .

note of personal passion unlike anything which we have hitherto met. Here at last is something comparatively modern. Like many men of our own days, they were at once self-conscious, part of a highly complicated and swiftly altering civilisation, so placed that although they could poignantly perceive and feel they were powerless to act, and not only stirred to the depths but bewildered. Both, as Romans of the First Century before Christ, were Roman in sentiment yet veneered with a surface of alien polish. Here their likeness ends. Like so many men of letters nowadays, each felt the same conditions in his own peculiar way. No two men in all literature are much more different from each other.

Little is positively known about either. Somewhere near the year 400 of the Christian Era, to be sure, St. Jerome noted a tradition about Lucretius which has faintly persisted—perhaps because it is agreeable to orthodox Christian opinions of pagan philosophy. According to this legend, renewed in literature by Tennyson's admirable monologue Lucretius, the poet's wife, displeased by his addiction to philosophic speculation, secretly gave him a love-potion which had the unhappy effect of unseating his reason and ended in suicide. Tennyson makes him revolt from slavery to the flesh:

What Roman would be dragged in triumph thus?
Not I; not he, who bears one name with her[1]
Whose death-blow struck the dateless doom of kings
When, brooking not the Tarquin in her veins,
She made her blood in sight of Collatine
And all his peers, flushing the guiltless air,

[1] Lucretia. *Cf.* p. 165.

Spring from the maiden fountain in her heart.
And from it sprang the Commonwealth,[1] which breaks
As I am breaking now.

Without some hovering consciousness of the breaking Republic, the mood of Lucretius may be hard to understand; but the moment you grow aware of the conditions of Rome throughout his lifetime it seems the only mood rationally imaginable. The conditions of our own times, at the beginning of the Twentieth Century, too, are very like those of his. "Even though no single line or passage of his," I have written elsewhere,[2] "may quite stir the torpor of our modern habit, his whole work may well make us tremblingly wonder whether, after all, his be not the final word. We need not vex ourselves with scholarly search for whence he derived the substance of his Epicurean philosophy; we cannot now linger over the relentless details of his philosophic system, nor yet dwell on the reasons why, at sundry times between his and ours, he has been neglected or forgotten. What no one who reads him can help recognising is the still vibrant passion of his mood, and that quality of it for which I can find no better name than despair. We men are conscious beings, in a world of consciousness where we vainly fancy that, at least for the fleeting while of our conscious lives, things may somehow come under our control. Hence comes our vain aspiration, our vain effort, our hopelessly foredoomed futility and disenchantment. There is but one course which can console the wise; it is humbly to recog-

---

[1] The Latin word *Respublica* (Republic) literally means Commonwealth.
[2] The Ideals of Empire : Harvard Graduates Magazine, June, 1917, p. 463.

nise that consciousness can truly be no more than
passive.   In a universe of conscienceless force, re-
sistlessly pursuing its course from none can tell
whence to none can tell whither, the acts of men
and of nations are only manifestations thereof, as
irresponsibly ungovernable as earthquakes or tem-
pests.   So, indeed, are the gods themselves, differ-
ing from us only in the deathless duration of a
consciousness which permits them, like us, to see
what only delusion can make either us or them
fancy for an instant capable of deflection.   Doubtless there are epochs when, for a while, things may
seem to be subsiding from chaos into order; there
are lifetimes, too, so far from troubled that lucky
folks may sometimes pass from cradle to grave
happy in the delusion of security.   Such days as
those when Lucretius lived, however, can afford
no such anodynes.   Blind force, his reason assured him, had made the gods and the world,
fathomless antiquity, the vanished empires of the
forgotten past, Homeric Greece and Troy, Persia
and the Grecian victories, Rome itself—then at
once dominantly imperial and mortally stricken.
Men can observe, marvel, even momentarily enjoy if they admit that all the power conceivably
theirs lies in the wondrous chance that they possess the power of contemplation.   They may not
even murmur such words as 'Thy will be done';
for will itself is a delusion.   The only fact is force,
material, irresistible, unchangeable, everlasting."

The mood here indicated pervades the poem De
Rerum Natura (On the Nature of Things), which
is both the only extant work of Lucretius, and
the only surviving example of the once copious
philosophical poetry of antiquity.   As we have

already reminded ourselves,[1] this form of literature
existed among the Greeks; but of its Greek phase
only traditions remain and perhaps a few scattered and fragmentary lines. Accepting, if we
may believe those who know your philosophy, the
atomic theories of the Greek Democritus and the
moral principles of the Greek Epicurus, the Roman
Lucretius, modelling his didactic hexameters on
those of the Sicilian Empedocles, endeavoured to
explain the universe in terms which should make
tolerable the world-crash of his unhappy and be-
wildering environment. Far too intricate for detail here, his system is not hard to grasp and in
general conception is curiously modern. All life,
he holds, all existence comes from mere clash of
atoms in void. There is no such thing as immortality. Religion, as men conceive and practise it,
is a debasing superstition; he tells, for example,
the story of how Agamemnon sacrificed Iphigenia
in Aulis, and ends the episode with the line

> Tantum religio potest suadere malorum.[2]
> (Such sins and crimes religion can evoke.)

There are gods, no doubt; but the gods, like the
men and the worlds, are powerlessly sentient and
contemplative creatures of force and fate, itself
blind, invisible, unconscious, inexorable. The tremendous grandeur of irresistible law has never-

---

[1] *Cf.* p. 115.

[2] I, 101.   C. F. Johnson translates this line:

> Such and so great are superstition's crimes.

Monroe's literal prose version is "So great the evils to which religion
could prompt."   Compare these two learned renderings with my untutored
one, and you cannot help understanding the original.   This is the best way
for the unlettered to approach classical texts—by harnessing a team of
ponies.

theless a consoling splendour. Submit; grant that
effort can avail nothing, that struggle is useless,
and presently you shall find in wondering sub-
mission to the wonders of eternity a vast surcease
of the pain inherent in contradiction and rebellion.
In understanding lies the secret of salvation.

Despairing if you will, the fervour with which
Lucretius writes—a fervour excellently imitated
in the poem about him by Tennyson—grows con-
tagious. He has one priceless poetic gift: he can
command sympathy. His power of observation,
too, is amazingly sensitive; and his power of intensely emotional statement is all his own. He
makes quiveringly alive what from any one else
might well have dried into a process of pitilessly
sincere reasoning. On general principles, a philosophic poem is at best respectably dull. ˙ The
poem of Lucretius, if you will read it without
pausing to scrutinise or to criticise, may now and
again prove absorbing. In itself, this is an artistic
miracle.

He left it unfinished. It ends abruptly, in the
midst of a long passage based on the terrible description of the Plague at Athens in the Second
Book of Thucydides.[1] Cicero, they say, had
something to do with preparing the swift, rough,
palpitating hexameters for publication. If so, he
had the tact to leave them individual and not to
polish them into a grace which, whatever its merit,
could never have been Lucretian. For something
other than grace, and greater, was needful to set
forth what the breaking of the Commonwealth
meant to a great spirit who greatly cherished the
great traditions of ancestral Rome.

[1] *Cf.* p. 83.

V

CATULLUS

In spite of its passion and its power, such philosophic poetry as that of Lucretius could never
have been popular. To enter into sympathy with
it demands harder thinking than every-day people
enjoy. With Catullus, the other great poet who
survives from the last days of the Roman Republic,
the case is different. His passion seems genuine,
his artistic sense is exquisite, and both are devoted,
at least in his best work, to the deliberate setting
forth of what appear to be his own personal emotions. This self-revelation, this implicit autobi-
ography, is at once permanently human in its appeal and consonant with the literary mood of
Europe during the past two or three centuries.
Compared with any one on whom we have as yet
touched, he therefore seems much more like the
men we have known and lived with.

Though those who care for his work thus come
to know him, as it were, with a feeling of intimacy,
they know little about him. He seems to have
belonged to a respectable family at Verona, or
somewhere near there; and so to have been a
Roman citizen of the kind whose political rights
were granted only after the Social War. As a
class these newly acknowledged citizens were
probably more proud of their dignity and more instinctively patriotic than the habitual inhabitants
of Rome; they were also probably disposed to
idealise, as the secular home of Roman traditions,
the mother city of the Republic. Catullus is
thought to have come to Rome, with good intro-

ductions, at the age of twenty or so, and to have
been at first dazzled and later disenchanted by the
brilliant and corrupt society he found there.   He
appears never to have studied in Greece or Egypt,
but at one time to have travelled rather extensively
in Greek regions, thus resembling a modern youth
of good condition who has replaced university
training by observing foreign civilisation for himself.   At thirty or so, he retired for a while to his
pleasant native regions, where he is said to have
died prematurely.

His extant work consists of one hundred and
sixteen lyric poems, widely different in length and
in character, and arranged in no evident order.
The first of them, however, dedicating the little
book to his fellow countryman Cornelius Nepos, a
man of letters whose social graces appear to have
exceeded his artistic gifts—at least so far as his
writings are preserved—indicates that this confusion may have been chosen by Catullus himself.
Throughout he imitates or adapts, with a fresh
felicity of his own, the lyric forms of the Greeks,
implying a knowledge not only of the primal Greek
lyric poetry but also of the fastidious and prettily
overwrought parodies of it which were fashionable in Ptolemaic Alexandria; some of his work is
known to have been modelled on what were then
held the masterpieces of Callimachus.   For two
reasons he thus became exceptionally important
in the tradition of European literature: with
strong individuality, he made excellently Latin a
number of literary forms hitherto excellent only
in the original Greek; and the accident that the
Greek language was long forgotten throughout
Western Europe, while knowledge of Latin has
always persisted there, has kept him throughout

the centuries not only a name but a fact. Secondary, like all Romans, in his relation to the Greeks, he has been in his relation to posterity almost primal; for no earlier Latin writer of lyric poetry came anywhere near him, and in some respects no later lyric poet in any European language has ever surpassed him.

His influence, for example, is evident at various times in the poems which now and again have survived from among those perennially made for weddings. His two or three elaborate works of this kind, probably if not certainly modelled on Greek originals, have a grace and a charm which has recurrently appealed to later writers with similar tasks before them; and beyond any of his admirers and imitators he has managed to suffuse them with what seems genuine as distinguished from conventional feeling. He can be approached but hardly surpassed. And something like this is true of much else among the various things that he wrote. One might thus study him long. In the end, however, approach him as you will, the poems most clearly characteristic of him, as well as most certain and most unfailing in their appeal, are those which record what seems to be the story of his personal affections.

Scattered through the present order or disorder of his collected works, these, which number something like a fifth of the whole though nowhere near a fifth of his lines, may be so arranged as to tell a fairly consecutive story. They concern a mistress whom he conventionally calls Lesbia. She is thought really to have been Clodia, a woman denounced in one of Cicero's orations as equally conspicuous for rank, for accomplishments, for unscrupulousness, and for profligacy; this lady was a sister of the Clodius whose escapades with certain celebrants of female mysteries led to the divorce of Cæsar, and to the traditional saying that Cæsar's wife must be above suspicion. So far as one can make out, Catullus, coming to Rome young, enthusiastic, and disposed to idealise everything Roman, was completely fascinated by this Clodia or Lesbia; and when she smiled on him, beyond his wildest hopes, fancied that their love was mutual. Nothing could long disguise from him the fact that he was only one of numberless admirers to whom now and again, when so disposed, she carelessly accorded her capricious and frequent favours. To follow and to reconstruct the story in detail is beyond our scope now. Some notion of it may be derived from the three poems concerning her which are now most nearly familiar. The first two—the second and third in his collected works—concern Lesbia's pet sparrow: one tells how prettily she plays with the bird, the other laments the grief brought her by the bird's untimely death; and if literature contains a daintier poem than either, it is yet to be discovered. The third poem is only a single elegiac couplet, made when he had come to understand what manner of woman Lesbia was; in his collected works it is the eighty-fifth:

Odi et amo. Quare id faciam fortasse requiris.
    Nescio, sed fieri sentio et excrucior.
(I hate and I love. Why I do such a thing perhaps you
        may wonder.
    I know not, but that I do I feel and in torture writhe.)[1]

[1] Theodore Martin (1861) translates this couplet thus:

I hate and love—wherefore I cannot tell,
But by my tortures know the fact too well.

No translation can begin to convey the searing
scorch of that burning Latin simplicity. *Excru-
cior* literally refers to the agonies of crucifixion,
not yet sanctified by the history of Christianity.
Conflicting and intermingling love and detesta-
tion, over which the victim has no manner of
power, are like the nails that fasten hands and
feet to the cross. And the lightness of the ten
words which come between the first three and the
last makes the climax the more tremendous.

He can be horribly obscene, no doubt; but to
remember this any healthy mind must recall the
ugly passages which sink from memory beside those
where he sets forth his tenderness, his sensitive-
ness, and his suffering. And in one of his most
unspeakable depths he bids us call to mind that
if a poet himself be chaste there is no need that his
lines be. Whatever you think of this morality, it
has been more or less practised throughout the
history of literature. Catullus very likely echoed
it from some Greek, perhaps known to the curious,
just as, when Herrick wrote at the end of his Hes-
perides, under King Charles I,

Jocund his muse was, but his life was chaste,

he almost translated Catullus. And anyhow the
conventions of classical antiquity permitted a
range of utterance by no means agreeable to the
still somewhat Victorian prejudice of those who
read English. Decency, after all, is a question of
manners or fashion; an innocent dancing-school
waltz would have shocked the most cynical Roman
who ever surfeited himself at an orgy. Emotion,
on the other hand, is coeval with humanity; that

of Catullus appears to be genuine. Whether it actually is or not may of course be disputed. Again and again, throughout literature, you will find poems which may be taken either as passionate statements of tremendous love-affairs or as ingenious pieces of half-dramatic imagination. You can never make quite sure which is which; only, some make you believe in them and others do not. From the time of Rousseau to the present day confession has been in much literary favour; a good deal of Byron's popularity depended on it, for example, and, to go no further, so does the appeal made by Mrs. Browning's Love Sonnets from the Portuguese. This is one reason why the reckless self-revelation of Catullus—the first enduring example of such a mood in European literature, for surviving Greek lyrics of the kind are either fragmentary or artificial,—seems now so strangely modern. Whatever he really was, he must always appear to be poignantly individual.

In a very different way, the passion of Lucretius is equally poignant. Not self-revealing, it is almost as self-conscious. These poets were contemporary, and contemporary with Cicero and Cæsar. If it is possible to generalise the mood excited in sensitive spirits by the crash of the Republic, and the spectre of world-chaos—terribly like what has happened about ourselves since 1914—we may perhaps call it an intensely personal sense of that eternal conflict between man and his environment which was so grandly and so objectively set forth in general terms by the tragic poets of Fifth Century Greece.[1]

[1] *Cf.* p. 56.

VI

SALLUST

Cicero and Cæsar, Lucretius and Catullus are the four great names of Roman literary tradition between the beginning of the First Century before Christ and the final establishment of the Roman Empire. There were other writers during the last half-century of the Republic; but in general we may consider them either as virtually negligible, like Cornelius Nepos, or as substantially lost, like Terentius Varro, whose Menippean Satires exist hardly more than in name. The only secondary Latin author of this period whom we cannot quite neglect here is Sallust. His two surviving monographs—one about Catiline, the other about Jugurtha—are at once the first examples we possess of serious historical writing in Latin, and implicitly indicate the persistence through those crashing years of characters neither so dominantly active as Cicero or Cæsar nor so passionately sensitive as their contemporary poets.

The personal history of Sallust, so far as it is known, is creditable only to his practical intelligence. A man of obscure origin and unprincipled ability, he managed, by taking the democratic side and denouncing the vices of the decadent aristocrats, to bring himself ultimately into a position where he could comfortably and safely emulate and surpass them. He had the tact, or the luck, to attach himself to the fortunes of Cæsar. Favoured by Cæsar, he so enriched himself with the spoils of African provinces that the splendour of his Roman villa—the Gardens of Sallust—has never been

quite forgotten by legend; and here, while Antony and Octavian, not yet Augustus, were plot-
ting and struggling for mastery of the world, he
passed his later years in magnificent and luxurious
literary leisure.

The most considerable fruits of this were five
Books of Histories, believed to have been concerned
with what happened throughout the Roman dominions during the years which ensued on the death
of Sylla. Of these only fragments remain. His
monographs on the conspiracy of Catiline, however,
and on the African wars with Jugurtha some fifty
years earlier, are preserved intact. In manner and
in temper they are curiously unlike what we know
of the self-seeking and self-made millionaire who
wrote them. It is generally agreed that he modelled his literary methods on those of Thucydides.
First among the Romans, accordingly, he wrote
history as if it were not so much a mere record of
fact as a sound basis for reflection and reasoning.
Himself a partisan, he more than probably gave
a partisan turn to his work, intending rather that
his readers should think with him than that they
should think rightly. Like Thucydides, however,
he had the art—or perhaps better he learned from
Thucydides the art—of seeming to write dispas-
sionately. In consequence, when you read his clear
though never quite great narrative, you find yourself quietly disposed to believe what he says, and
never either excited or repelled by the intensity
of his partisan feeling. He can deal with actu-
alities as if he stood grandly aloof from them—
which is perhaps the most subtle method of leading
the doubtful unwittingly to agree with you. So
his Catiline and his Jugurtha, who lived and plotted

and fought and died, have been throughout the centuries the Catiline and the Jugurtha of European tradition.

To complete our impression of the period of Cicero and of Cæsar, this glance at their more prudent and fortunate contemporary has appeared worth while. To linger over him, however, after he has duly reminded us that supple skins can be kept intact even amid world-chaos, would be unduly to emphasise a matter not of the first importance in such a scheme as ours. And matters of the first importance are close at hand. For, if the commonly accepted dates be true, Virgil had begun to write some years before Sallust comfortably died.

VII

VIRGIL

Though Virgil was only thirty years younger than Cæsar, he belongs not only to another generation but to another world. Born when the fate of Rome seemed still in the balance, he had the fortune to pass his mature years amid the full security of Augustan promise. Ardently sympathising with the new and more serene spirit of this time, he expressed it first and best. During life he was recognised not only as the most excellent exponent of its ideals but as the longed-for master who had finally achieved the miracle of making the poetry of Rome rival, if not surpass, that of Greece. From his own day to ours the tradition thus begun has never lapsed. Though it has greatly varied and fluctuated, it has always been familiar. Meanings he could never have dreamt of have been read into his lines; he has been enveloped in clouds of superstition; he has been dissected by generation after generation of often ignorant grammarians and schoolmasters; during the Eighteenth and Nineteenth Centuries his right to eminence has been disputed, particularly by the stupid erudition of German scholars; but there has never been a time when his works themselves have not been known to every human being who has seriously studied the literature of Europe. Thus, if only thus, he would be unique.

The history of this unique diuturnity has been admirably, if somewhat dryly, summarised in Comparetti's Virgil in the Middle Ages, which traces it not only as it persisted throughout what has pretended to be literature and scholarship, but also as it took the form of fantastic popular legend, transforming the most eminent of Augustan poets into the most potent of antique enchanters. Fairly trustworthy historic facts go far to account for both phases of tradition.

Virgil, son of a well-to-do farmer somewhere near Mantua, was born there in the year 70, a time when the still recently conferred rights of Roman citizenship must generally have inspired something like enthusiastic Roman patriotism. He grew up in this pleasant Italian country, itself a part of the provinces assigned by the first Triumvirate to Julius Cæsar; and as he approached maturity Cæsar was his virtual and beneficent sovereign. He was sent to school for a while at Milan, and later studied under the best teachers at Rome. Never robust, and said to have been shy and amiably awkward, he seems to have returned to

his native region, and there to have devoted
himself to literary work. What must have appeared a great misfortune, when he was approaching the age of thirty, proved to be the making of
him. During the subsident confusion which ensued on the battle of Philippi, the lands of his
family were seized, for distribution among the dis-
banded soldiers of the second Triumvirate. To secure restitution, if he could, he went back to Rome.
There his literary power was recognised. He became a friend of Octavian, soon to be Augustus
Cæsar; a friend, as well, of Mæcenas, the most
generous patron of Augustan letters; of Horace,
too, a little later, and of whoever else came to distinction in the culture of the finally growing Empire. There can be little question either that he
was personally lovable or that amid general social
license his character was remarkable for simplicity
and purity. The rest of his life passed prosper-
ously, partly at Rome and more amid the wondrous
landscapes about Naples. He lived through the
first ten years or so of Augustan empire. Dying in
the year 19, at the age of fifty-one, he escaped even
premonition of its decline. He knew and he
loved all Italy, from the Alps to the Sicilian sea.
He saw it growing to be the centre of earthly peace,
established and sustained by the newly conscious
imperial power of Rome. And his three great
works crescently and sincerely celebrate its limitless promise.

One aspect of all three works deserves our attention before we turn to them separately. Though
by Virgil's time the dominion of Rome vastly exceeded anything in the earlier history of Europe,
the culture of Rome remained, as indeed it always

remained, to a considerable degree exotic. In
literature the primal achievements of Greece, already matters of an auroral and early clouded
past, appeared—as they are—unsurpassed and un-
surpassable. So the conscious effort of the Romans
had been to produce, in their own language, something which might vie with them. Well before
this effort began, the Greek classics were no longer
living and contemporary things; but rather the
reverend subjects of industrious but pedantic
Alexandrian scholarship. Two phases of our own
ancestral literature are here similar. The effort
of Elizabethan Englishmen to rival the literatures
of continental Europe and that of Americans after
the Revolution to rival the literature of England
were impelled by motives very like that which
impelled Romans to rival the literature of Greece.
In all three cases, the patriotic fervour of the effort
led to expressions distinctly different—and in the
case of Elizabethan England magnificently and
independently different—from anything earlier;
but neither literature in America, nor the literature
of the Elizabethans, nor the literature of Rome
could ever have existed without earlier and alien
models and standards. In the Second Century before Christ, as we have already seen, Latin writers
had brought comedy to a point fairly to be held
excellent; but so far as extant works go they had
achieved no such success in other fields. During
the first sixty years of the First Century, however,
the work of Cicero had produced masterpieces of
oratorical, philosophic, and epistolary Latin prose;
that of Lucretius had produced a Latin masterpiece of philosophic poetry; that of Catullus had
produced beautiful Latin lyrics; and that of Cæsar

and of Sallust had brought historical Latin prose at least to the point of dignity. There remained, the more evidently, three conspicuous phases of Greek literature still unapproached in Latin. These were the latest, and at Alexandria probably the most widely acceptable at the time,—the Idyls of Theocritus,—and the two earliest—the didactic hexameters of Hesiod and the epic hexameters of Homer. It was Virgil's happy lot to establish something like all three in the lasting literature of Rome.

The first of his three great works, the Bucolics or Eclogues, consists of ten short poems in hexameter verse, comprising altogether less than 850 lines. They appear to have been begun at the time when he had returned from Rome to his native province, and to have been finished, revised, and published after what seemed misfortune had brought him to Rome again. If we may trust those who know their classics best, hardly anything could be more seemingly imitative than most of these pastoral verses. Though not sustained or literal translations they are such excellent parodies of Theocritus as could have been made only by one saturated both with the text and with the spirit of the fashionable poet most admired by Ptolemaic Alexandria. They generally profess to deal with shepherds or the like—simple country folk—who give utterance to exquisitely polished verse. Their first apparent difference from their models is that they seem even more deliberately artificial. Theocritus had really known the countryside of Sicily; and some vestiges of its human life here and there underlie the prettily fantastic graces with which he set it forth to please the courtiers of the Ptolemies. Though Virgil really knew the countryside of Italy, you would never imagine this from his beribboned shepherds, modelled only on the already make-believe creatures of Theocritan fancy. It is not always easy, indeed, quite to understand why such conspicuous make-believes should both have appealed to the taste of their own time and have had recurrent and often profound influence on European literatures at later periods.

That they have done so, however, there can be no question; and perhaps the most obvious phase of their influence was originally almost if not quite a novelty. The country-folk of Theocritus were elaborately and prettily conventionalised, no doubt, but that was about all. The country-folk of Virgil now and again symbolise or refer to real people and events of his time; and these come nearer the "old Algrind" of Spenser—an evident anagram for Archbishop Grindal—or his lament for Sir Philip Sidney under the guise of Astrophel, or his presentation of himself as Colin Clout and of Sir Walter Raleigh as the Shepherd of the Ocean, than they come to much of anything in the original Greek. Here Virgil showed something like originality; at least he turned pastoral poetry into a channel which it was to cut long and deep, among other ways through the Lycidas of Milton to the Adonais of Shelley.

Another difference which distinguishes them from their originals in Theocritus is consentingly recognised by almost all who have studied them carefully; though the Virgilian shepherds are utterly unlike any imaginable peasants, the places where they live and sing are not only real but really Italian.

The backgrounds of Theocritus have no such definite character as you will feel when from the
wide-branching beech-tree of Virgil's first line onward, you discover his fantastic personages to
merge in settings conceivable only by one who
had always known and loved the landscapes even
still perhaps the most gracious in Europe. And
in his day, these were Roman, and Rome was
on the verge of acknowledged empire. Thus
Rome was the more ready to recognise and to
welcome Virgil's merit. For more than two centuries before his time, there had been brave attempts to make Latin hexameters which should
rival those of Greece; and these had resulted in
countless noble lines and in many noble poems.
Until the gentle and exquisite grace of his verses
appeared, however, there was little which could
be held final. Here, at last, was a studied but
superbly mastered beauty of expression hitherto
unapproached in Latin and never surpassed. It
could not have the fresh vigour of the primal
Greek; but it could give a kind of delight not
quite to be found in any primality. Fifteen centuries later something like it was again to illuminate Italy, when the aspirations of primitive painting culminated in the conscious and serene mastery
of Raphael.

Among the Eclogues is one to which the course
of history gave accidental but great traditional
importance. The Fourth of the ten, containing
only sixty-three lines, and commonly called by
the name of Pollio, a friend and patron of Virgil
in Northern Italy and Consul in the year 40, is
not a pastoral dialogue but a celebration of the
hope for the whole future world to be expected

from a man-child not yet born. Whom it may actually have concerned can never be decided—some think this to be a child of Pollio, some a child of Octavian, some Octavian himself duly conventionalised as the coming incarnation of Empire. The coincidence of its date with the birth of Christ, however,—in the perspective of a few centuries forty years are not long,—combined with the obscure yet radiant glory of its prophetic promise, and with some of the terms by which this was set forth, to make centuries of early Christianity accept it as an unconsciously inspired Christian prophecy. The lines

> Jam redit et Virgo, redeunt Saturnia regna;
> Jam nova progenies cælo demittitur alto,[1]

for example, doubtless refer either to the return to earth of the inviolate goddess Justice, or conceivably to the Zodiacal sign under which the coming child was expected to make his appearance; but to many moods of historical Christianity they appeared almost literally to foretell the maiden motherhood of Mary. Thus the first published work of Virgil gave him not only classical eminence but a place, with the Sibyls, in the traditions of Christian Europe.

The Bucolics are commonly attributed to the years 41 to 39, during which Virgil passed the age of thirty. He is thought to have been just about forty years old when his next important work, the Georgics, was finished. As it contains, in its four books, less than 2,200 lines, his methods of poetic composition were evidently deliberate. The

---

[1] Lines 6–7: Once more the Virgin comes and Saturn's reign;
Behold a heaven-born offspring earthward hies.
(Tr. T. C. Williams: Boston: 1915.)

origin of this poem appears to have been to some
degree political or social. Roughly speaking, the
ten years or so when it was coming into existence
began with the battle of Philippi, which finally
defeated the murderers of Julius Cæsar, and ended
with the battle of Actium, which finally established
the power of Augustus. After something like a
century of civil wars, vexing all Italy with recurrent devastation and confusion, there was both
need and longing for peace and order; and no
single feature of such prospect was more desirable
than renewed interest in peaceful agriculture, the
necessary basis of all social prosperity anywhere
throughout history. With this in view, Mæcenas
is said to have suggested to Virgil the subject
which should at once direct attention to this public need and enrich Latin literature with a work
such as might rival or replace the Works and
Days of the Greek Hesiod. By a pleasant chance,
our most nearly life-like contemporary account of
Virgil, and of his daily surroundings, belongs to
just about this period. The Fifth Satire of the
First Book of Horace, thought to be closely modelled on a similar work of Lucilius about a century
older, describes with much detail, and pleasant
lightness of touch, a journey made by Mæcenas,
in company with Virgil, Horace, and other friends,
from Rome to Brundusium, now Brindisi, probably at a time when the disputes between Octavian
and Antony demanded the presence there of the
distinguished man who was not only the chief
patron of Roman letters, but also the most trusted
political adviser of Augustus. And somehow the
trivial line[1]

Lusum it Mæcenas, dormitum ego Virgiliusque,

[1] Horace, Sat. I, v, 48.

which says only that at the end of a tiresome stage of the journey Mæcenas refreshed himself by something like a game of tennis, while Virgil and Horace preferred a nap, tells more of them, and of their mutual relations, than volumes of comment.   Virgil is said to have introduced Horace to Mæcenas, who was evidently a good friend as well as a patron to both.   In circumstances like these the Georgics were slowly and conscientiously written.

They could not have been written without Hesiod as an antique and reverend model.   They could not have been written, either, without full knowledge both of the learning and of the conscious literary graces of Hellenistic Alexandria. More deeply still, however, they could not have been written except by one who had always and familiarly known the daily life of Italian country-folk—the skies above them, their hills and fields, their crops and their vines and their olives, their flocks and herds, their horses and their cattle, and the bees on which all antiquity depended for what it knew of sweetness.   For all the studied polish of the lines, too, these poems could not have been written without sincere belief both in the rustic enthusiasm which pervades them and in the beneficent promise of what was soon to be Augustan Empire.   The famous passage beginning "O fortunatos nimium"[1] rings true, as it celebrates the happy lot of husbandmen:

> Oh, more than blest, if their true bliss they know,
> Are tillers of the land! whose sustenance
> From civil faction far, the righteous earth
> Ungrudgingly bestows

[1] Georgics, II, 458 seq.

are the words with which Theodore Williams[1] renders the first three lines of it. They sound conventional, no doubt, but as you come to know
them, they prove genuine. So does the closing
passage of the whole work,[2] which Williams translates as follows:

> Thus have I made my songs of well-kept farms,
> Of flocks withal and trees, while Cæsar's power
> Was launching the vast thunder of his war
> Over the deep Euphrates, publishing
> By conquest his supreme and just decrees
> Unto the grateful nations, taking so
> His pathway to the gods.[3] The selfsame days
> I, Virgil, passed in sweet Parthenope[4]
> Busied and blest in unrenowned repose,
> I that erewhile, when youthful blood was bold
> Played with the shepherd's muse and made my song
> Of Tityrus beneath the beech-tree's shade.

The manner in which the last line of the Georgics,

> Tityre, te patulæ cecini sub tegmine fagi,[5]

echoes the first line of the Bucolics,

> Tityre, tu patulae recubans sub tegmine fagi,[6]

deliberately and rightly brings the two works together. Throughout the Bucolics, as we have
seen, the backgrounds are apt to be the real
landscapes of Italy; but the figures who flit before them are Theocritan and sometimes symbolic

[1] Boston, 1915, p. 64.   [2] Georgics, IV, 558–565: Williams, p. 121.
[3] A somewhat excessive allusion to the progress of Octavian, after the
battle of Actium, through Eastern provinces formerly subject to Antony.
[4] Naples.
[5] Literally, "Tityrus, thee I sang beneath the wide-spreading beech."
[6] Literally, "Tityrus, thou who liest beneath the wide-spreading beech."

conventions or fantasies. In the Georgics all this is strengthened into something like larger truth. The country-folk are real farmers or herdsmen, never individualised, but skilled in their daily and yearly tasks almost as they may be seen to this day. The growth in strength, however, is a true growth, and not a change of spirit. To both works, alike and together, might still be prefixed the three lines which Addison chose in 1701 as the text from which to preach his fulsome Letter from Italy:

> Salve magna parens frugum, Saturnia tellus,
> Magna virûm! tibi res antiquæ laudis et artis
> Aggredior, sanctos ausus recludere fontes.[1]

And when both works were complete, Italy as well as Augustan promise was finally safe in lasting literature. Addison's protest seems sincere that, if he had the power,

> Unnumbered beauties in my verse should shine,
> And Virgil's Italy should yield to mine![2]

Virgil's Italy, indeed, was as present to Addison as Byron's was to Nineteenth Century travellers. It is quite imaginable, too, that the Bucolics and the Georgics may have stirred Romans tired of civil wars, much as Childe Harold stirred Englishmen ready to waken from the pre-revolutionary torpidities of the Eighteenth Century. But times change and we human beings with them. In a

---

[1] Georgics II, 173-175. Williams (p. 53) renders the passage thus:

> Hail, O Saturn's land,
> Mother of all good fruits and harvests fair,
> Mother of men! I for thy noble sake
> Attempt these old and famous themes and dare
> Unseal an age-long venerated spring
> (And uplift Hesiod's song o'er Roman towers.)

[2] Letter from Italy, 53-54.

single century Childe Harold has quickly passed
from its original warmth of true popular appeal to
the chilly recesses of literary history; and in the
course of twenty centuries such artificial conventions as those of pastoral poetry and such primal
devices as would set forth didactic purpose in poetic
terms have mostly meant little to human beings, as
distinguished from scholars, fantastics, or pedants.
We can study them, we can admire them as much
as we choose; but without considerable effort of
historical imagination we cannot sympathetically
understand how anybody could ever have enthusiastically enjoyed them. So, if Virgil's work had
stopped here, he would have remained a beautifully sincere celebrant of Italy and of the imperial
policies of Julius and Augustus Cæsar; he would
have proved himself, too, the faultless master of
Latin style who could at last make the studied
grace of Latin hexameters rival by reason of its
very differences the vigour and splendour of the
primal Greek. Thus his place in European literature would have been secure; but it could never
have been thought comparable with that of Homer,
or of the tragic poets of Fifth Century Athens.
Eminence like theirs belongs only to the few who
can tell, epically or dramatically, what seems to
"that willing suspension of disbelief for the moment which constitutes poetic faith,"[1] a genuine
human story. How true this is anybody can remind himself by merely thinking of Virgil now.
Everybody knows, in a general way, that he wrote
the Bucolics and the Georgics; but everybody
remembers first that he wrote the Æneid.

If we may trust the accepted story, this last of
his works has survived against his expressed will.

[1] This definition occurs somewhere in Coleridge; I forget just where.

When he had finished the Georgics, he is said
soon to have begun the more ambitious poem
avowedly intended not only to supplant the older
Latin epics, of which the most important was the
now long-lost Annals of Ennius, but also to set
forth the spirit of Roman nationality, at last become Augustan Empire, in terms comparable with
the primal and unrivalled epics of Homer. To this
task he gave his last ten years or so. His rather
sudden death, at the age of fifty-one, left it incomplete; though he had both planned and written
it from beginning to end, he had not harmonised
all its details, and he was dissatisfied, as indeed
he might probably always have remained, with
what his fastidious taste held many crudities of
detail. He therefore left instructions that the
work should be destroyed. These were disregarded; in spite of them it was posthumously
published; and from the time of its appearance it
has stayed what it is and will permanently be—
the European masterpiece of deliberate as distinguished from spontaneous poetry.

Not only for its own sake but because through
nearly two thousand years it has been more or less
intimately known to every subsequent writer
whose work survives in the literature of Europe,
the Æneid should be read by all who care for
our literary traditions.[1] This is no formidable
task, for it contains in all less than 10,000 lines,
against the more than 15,000 of the Iliad, and
the more than 12,000 of the Odyssey. Thus
considerably shorter than either of its original
models, it obviously challenges comparison with

[1] To my mind, the blank-verse translation by T. C. Williams (Boston,
1908) more nearly approaches Virgilian effect than any other as yet made
in English.

both. The first six of its twelve Books relate the
adventures of Æneas on his wide-wandering voyage from sacked Troy to the shores of Italy, where
Roman Empire was destined to spring from his
descendants; these Books, sometimes in detail,
resemble the Odyssey—Æneas, to take a single
and obvious example, gives a long account of his
past adventures to Dido just as Odysseus gives
one to Alcinous. The last six Books of the
Æneid, which tell how, once arrived in Italy,
Æneas is compelled to establish his foothold there
by force of arms, similarly resemble the Iliad
with its surging battles and divine comminglings
in the fray. The moment you begin to compare
the Æneid with its originals, however, certain
clear differences will instantly appear.

For one thing, as we reminded ourselves when
we touched on Homer, the Iliad and the Odyssey, independent of each other, relate only episodes in the long story of the Trojan War; while
the Æneid, conceived and composed as a whole,
completely tells the traditional story of how fugi-
tives from conquered Troy came to where in the
fulness of time their descendants were to become
the final conquerors of Greece. For another, the
grand impersonality of Homer makes his noble,
swift, simple lines seem like a contemporary account of the matters they set forth; and the very
first words of the Æneid—

Arma virumque cano, Trojæ qui primus ab oris
Italiam, fato profugus, Lavinaque venit
Litora[1]—

[1] Arms and the man I sing, who first made way,
Predestined exile, from the Trojan shore
To Italy, the blest Lavinian strand.
—Tr. Williams.

distinctly assume, with their frank use of the first person singular, the point of view of Augustan Rome, where the poet is to tell of a legendary past, seen throughout from a remote, hard-won, and magnificent present. Homer writes heroically; Virgil writes of heroes and of heroic deeds, conscious of what had sprung from them throughout intervening ages. Again, the most salient feature of Homeric style is a grand simplicity, conscious —if conscious at all—only of how words should express meaning; and the style of Virgil is not only deliberately ingenious but full of such elaborate and imitative refinements as could have been devised only by a poet profoundly learned and admiringly familiar with the whole range of Greek expression from the original epics to the graces and affectations of Alexandrian fashion. Thus, though Virgil went far to fix poetic idiom from his time to ours, he can hardly have seemed to his contemporaries more nearly idiomatic in Latin than Milton seems to men who think in vernacular English. For all their obvious differences, indeed, the most nearly analogous poem to the Æneid in European literature is probably the Paradise Lost.

Both tell anew, and each in its way finally, stories which had long been immemorially familiar. Both imply in their writers the most extensive culture of their times. Both are intended to celebrate causes in which the writers passionately believed. In this aspect, the most obvious difference between them lies in the fact that when Milton dictated his lines the cause of the Puritans was politically lost, and that when Virgil made his lines the cause of Roman Empire stayed radiant with promise. The legendary founding of the eternal city was believed to have occurred more than seven hundred years before; some five centuries had already passed since the Republic had supplanted the still traditionally detested system of Roman royalty; fluctuating but never desperate in fortune, the power of republican Rome had gradually come to dominate the then civilised world, and in the same year, already a century past, had conquered what was left both of Greece and of Carthage; at last, the spirit of Cæsar and of Augustus had breathed a new soul into what had sometimes appeared the dying body of the Commonwealth. The closing of the Temple of Janus, after the settlement of the East, had symbolically proclaimed world-wide peace.[1] All this was in the patriotic mind of Virgil when he set himself the happy task of proclaiming for all time what through centuries was to remain the acknowledged ideal of Empire.

How he probably came to choose his precise subject, and how the legendary story of Æneas had taken form through the centuries, has been admirably summarised in Professor Nettleship's compact monograph on Virgil.[2] By Virgil's time Roman tradition had long held that the origin of Rome could be traced to the Trojan hero whose posterity had been destined to overcome the descendants of the victorious Greeks. And the course of history might be held to justify this final conquest. Nothing could ever deprive Greece of her primality, no doubt; nothing need ever ob-

[1] Cf. Æneid, I, 289; VIII, 714.
[2] Classical Writers, ed. J. R. Green, 1880. The preface is dated August, 1879. The chief fault to find with this little book is that it spells Virgil with an e—which is doubtless as correct classically as it is traditionally abominable.

scure her literature, her art, her philosophy, her
scholarship, the permanent sources and frequent
inspirations of the culture both of Rome and of
what, mostly through Rome, was to be all subsequent Europe. If the higher life of Rome thus
owed so much to Greece, however, this was by no
means all. For generation after generation Greece
had been declining from her Fifth Century culmina-
tion; her decline had bred in her luxury and cor-
ruption, physical and moral; these had influenced
Rome for the worse, as surely as the nobler phases
of Greece had influenced Rome for the better; to
counteract them there was need to revive the antique manliness peculiar to Rome herself. Roman
virtue had made and sustained the Republic; it
had ripened into the serene ideal of peaceful Empire; and it had sprung not from momentarily
dominant Greece but from the chief heroic enemy
of Greece—Troy, still living in the spirit. A later
story had already intermingled with the legend of
Æneas that of the Carthaginian Dido, thus giving
antique basis to the pitiless history of the Punic
Wars. Broadly speaking, Virgil no more invented
the substance of his Æneid than he created his
frequent borrowed lines or phrases, his antiquarian
and other learning, his Roman patriotism or the
metrical structure of his hexameter lines. His peculiar task was to fuse these and more in a work
which his pervasive spirit was to make his own—
much as, sixteen hundred years later, Shakspere
brought into world-literature story after story
ready for the purpose.

Like Shakspere, however, and all other masters,
Virgil was strongly individual. To define his individuality, not so sympathetic during the past

century as it has generally proved, is hopelessly beyond our power now. To feel it one need only read him, even in translation; and if one have not time or patience for all twelve Books of the Æneid one may perhaps feel it most instantly in the First and the Fourth of them, which mingle Homeric memories, the humanity of Euripides, the somewhat sentimental refinement of Alexandrian epics and profoundly Roman feeling in the tragic story of Dido. For more than one reason, however, the Sixth Book of the Æneid is more suitable to our present purpose. Compactly complete and moving toward a superb climax of Augustan ideal, it instantly suggests comparison with its obvious model, the Eleventh Book of the Odyssey; and, as we have already reminded ourselves, it stands in European literature midway between that first panoramic vision of the dead and the Divine Comedy of Dante.

At this point, indeed, it is well worth while in any event, to read the Eleventh Book of the Odyssey again; there are only 640 lines. Turning back to it now, you will probably feel more deeply than before its matchless freshness, the noble simplicity of its swift and unconscious conception and expression, the measureless antiquity of Greek tradition which it assumes, but above all its own comparative antiquity. Living though they seem by themselves, these west-bound voyagers on windy and trackless seas belong to another and an indefinitely earlier world than we have had in mind ever since we first touched on the literature, Greek or Latin, of historic times. When, beyond the stream of Ocean they come to the dim shores where the shadows of the dead can emerge, the

sacrifices they make resemble those of savages.
There is something almost swinish in the thirst
with which the phantoms crowd to drink the fresh
blood whence they may regain fleeting semblance
of the life they have lost, and in the terror which
forbids them draughts until they are unthreatened
by the sword. All this, no doubt, we may forget when we feel their renewed humanity, as when
unburied Elpenor tells his hapless story,[1] or as when
the mother of Odysseus appears and has to wait[2] until Tiresias has uttered his purely personal prophecy,[3] or as when she is suffered at last to reveal her
maternal tenderness[4] even though the filial arms
which try to clasp her meet through her visible but
unbodied form, or as when Agamemnon contrasts
his tragic fate—not yet avenged by Orestes—with
the happier conjugal fortune of Odysseus,[5] or as
when the spirit of Ajax stands angrily apart disdaining even in death to have speech with one by
whom in life he had been defeated.[6] We can
hardly help feeling the primitiveness of it all,
however, when we remember the confusion of the
shadowy dead,—classified only as women and men
in a semblance of being even less ordered than
theirs had been when they breathed in sunlight,—
and when we find Odysseus at last shrinking from
them, for fear that Persephone should send forth
the Gorgon whose gaze, turning him to stone,
might keep him too hers there forever.[7] And the
fair wind which wafts him back towards the living
comes like fresh air.[8]

Compared with this, the Sixth Book of the

[1] Od. XI, 51–83.   [2] Ibid., 84–89.   [3] Ibid., 90–151.
[4] Ibid., 152–224.   [5] Ibid., 385–467.   [6] Ibid., 541–564.
[7] Ibid., 630–635.   [8] Ibid., 640.

Æneid, a masterpiece of deliberate composition in some 900 lines, may seem according to your mood either vastly more mature or provokingly sophisticated. Its mysteries, unlike those of Homer, are not elementary and fearful but ritual and symbolic; they resemble the celebration of the Mass rather than the slaughter of victims. Like Odysseus, Æneas must make pilgrimage to reach his unearthly goal and hear the prophecy of his future; but his pilgrimage is not with companions to the edge of life, where he may summon the dead from the depths, it is with a single Sibyllic guide to the depths themselves, thrown open to him by the magic of the Golden Bough. These depths of Acheron have an order of their own, too, where the dead pass towards the Stygian ferry of Charon,

> As numberless the throng as leaves that fall
> When autumn's early frost is on the grove;
> Or like vast flocks of birds by winter's chill
> Sent flying o'er wide seas to lands of flowers;[1]

where beyond the burning flood of Phlegethon the wicked writhe in eternal torture; and where the good are happy in the Elysian Fields. So those with whom Æneas holds converse he finds each in something like his eternal place: Palinurus,[2] for example, whose tale is evidently told to rival that of Elpenor in the Odyssey; Deiphobus,[3] who similarly challenges comparison with the Odyssean Agamemnon; self-slain Dido,[4] passionately disdainful of her betrayer, as Ajax was of Odysseus; and old Anchises,[5] who combines the tenderness of Anticleia, mother of Odysseus, with the pro-

---

[1] Æn., VI, 309-312; tr. Williams. [2] Ibid., 338-383.
[3] Ibid., 494-546. [4] Ibid., 450-476. [5] Ibid., 679-901.

phetic foresight of Tiresias, but speaks prophecy
not so much of what shall happen to Æneas himself as of the Roman Empire and world order destined to spring from his seed. This prophecy is
rightly not in the midst of the narrative, where
Tiresias utters his prophecy to Odysseus, but is
made its magnificent climax. And the passage of
Æneas up from the Shades is not a terror-stricken
flight; it is rather a clear-eyed awakening from a
gravely exultant visionary dream.

In this Book, as everywhere in the Æneid,
those who can read the Latin, even though stum-
blingly, may find immortally beautiful passages.
On one we have touched already—the lines in the
prophecy of Anchises which foretell the imperial
ideal to be cherished by Rome.[1] Another may be
found in the passage where Dido turns forever to
the unfailing love of her dead husband Sichæus.[2]
Lovelier still are the words which at once predict
and lament the fate of young Marcellus, who had
he lived would have been the heir and the successor
of Augustus.[3] The tradition is probably true that
when these were read to the bereaved mother of
the princely boy, she swooned in ecstasy. No
translation, of course, can begin to convey the
final beauty of lines like these. None but scholars,
perhaps, can rightly pretend even truly to feel it.
But one thing is sure; they can dreamily haunt
through the discords of a prosaic lifetime a man
who first knew them as a stupid and reluctant
schoolboy.

[1] *Ibid.*, 851–853; *cf.* p. 188, *supra.*
[2] *Ibid.*, 472–474. It may not be quite fantastic to discern here implicit
commendation of the laws by which Augustus endeavoured to revive the
forgotten sanctity of marriage.
[3] *Ibid.*, 867–886.

Thus they and their maker have haunted through twenty unbroken centuries the poetic consciousness of Europe. We may well have seemed to linger over Virgil too long, and nowise to have revealed him. For our purpose, however, we have lingered rightly. No other poet so summarised what Europe had been until the days of promise when he lived. No other so confidently proclaimed the high hope which he was never to know unfulfilled by the future. No other has ever been so persistently studied, so blindly reverenced, so fantastically misunderstood, so incessantly unforgotten. No other has been transmuted by popular legend into the most potent of wonder-working enchanters. And no other could have given rise to the rhyming lines in which a Thirteenth Century poet, quoted by Comparetti,[1] tells how St. Paul, on his journey to Rome and lingering at Naples,

Ad Maronis mausoleum
Ductus fudit super eum
Piæ rorem lacrimæ:
"Quem te," inquit, "reddidissem!
Si te vivum invenissem,
Poetarum maxime!"[2]

VIII

HORACE

The trait of Virgil which most clearly accounts for his enduring eminence is that he not only expressed the ideals of his time but also summarised

[1] I have mislaid the precise reference.
[2] Anybody can read the sound of these words, which mean—Led to the tomb of Virgil, he shed over him a dew of loving tears: "What I could have made thee!" he said, "if I could have found thee alive, greatest of poets!"

its past beyond any other antique poet. For such encyclopædic range, indeed, his only rival or fellow in European literature is Dante, thirteen hundred years later. In the perspective of the centuries grandeur looks solitary; yet as a matter of human experience it has hardly ever come into existence except at times of great general activity. One of its essential features, too, involves something like a limitation; its very largeness prevents it from quite implying the moods of everyday life. These have never been expressed better than by the friend and contemporary of Virgil who stands second only to him in the tradition of Augustan letters.

The life of Horace resembled that of Virgil. The son of a wise but uneducated father, who had made a modest way in his country world, the boy, born in Apulia five years after Virgil was born in Northern Italy, was given the best education of his time. He studied at Rome, and later at Athens. At the battle of Philippi, he was an officer in the army of Brutus and Cassius; but no harm came of this. His very obscurity kept him safe; and it was not in his temper to be a passionate partisan. He came quietly to Rome, where he occupied himself with poetry. He became a friend of Virgil, who is said to have introduced him to Mæcenas. The friendship and patronage of Mæcenas made his unpretentious fortune. His later years were passed at Rome and at a farm which Mæcenas gave him in the Sabine hills, not far from Tivoli. In his own range of poetry, he was recognised and has remained unsurpassed; and the very nature of this work from beginning to end implies his excellent social quali-

ties. To go no further, the Fifth Satire of his
First Book, a work on which we have already
touched,[1] describes beyond compare his friendly
relations with Mæcenas and with Virgil, as they
were tested by a rather tedious journey from
Rome to Brundusium; and the Ninth Epistle of
his First Book, commending one Septimius to the
princely youth who was later to be the Emperor
Tiberius, has been held to comprise in its thirteen
hexameter lines the most nearly faultless letter of
introduction ever written. He was favoured with
the friendship and patronage of Augustus. After
Virgil's death, whom he survived for nine years,
he was distinctly the most eminent of living
Roman poets. And when he died, almost in the
middle of the forty years through which Augustus
was sovereign, he had incomparably expressed
the temper of that newly civilised life on which
the still high hope of Roman Empire and Roman
peace was based.

His fame at the time is no wonder. The survival of it, however, and its renewal whenever
subsequent history has allowed the growth of
social graces, may fairly be held astonishing.
Hardly anything is more volatile, more transitory,
more mutable than fashion. What it chases one
day it laughs at the next. Yet, though in widely
various guises it has over and over again smiled
with Horace, it has never laughed at him.
Whether in life or in letters a friendly sense of
his charm has proved itself through the centuries perhaps the most certain proof of polite
culture. Those who cannot respond to him are
not men of the world. The temper of this recur-

[1] *Cf.* p. 229.

rent phase of humanity he has generalised beyond any other poet. There is something significant in the genuineness of his appeal to the great gentlemen of England in the Eighteenth Century. Time was, and not so very long ago, when a speech in Parliament was hardly complete without some savour of his lines.

Among his characteristics none is more distinct than a self-consciousness which almost anybody else might have found dangerous if not fatal. He writes of himself and from himself again and again, yet he never loses urbane reticence: always confident, he is never confidential. As you grow to know him, accordingly, you come to feel the pleasure of an intimacy sure not to burden you with secrets. There is no detail of open life, at Rome or at his Sabine farm, too trivial for mention if it chance to fit his purpose; there is no pleasure or petty vexation, of memory or of passing circumstance, on which he hesitates to touch if it suits his mood. His mood, however, keeps him and thus keeps us all secure from the troubles of obtrusion. To go no further, Catullus before him and Rousseau in times almost modern will serve to remind us of what this means; so will the self-pitying laments of Ovid's exile. There is a shamelessness of the soul, prevalent nowadays, more subtly obscene for its very semblance of decency than any of the body. From this Horace was beautifully free.

His work may clearly be divided, both formally and substantially, into two groups. The first, with which it probably began and certainly ended, consists of his early Satires and his late Epistles, written throughout in hexameter lines. The sec-

ond, which broadly speaking was written after
the Satires and before the Epistles, consists of the
Epodes and the Odes, widely various in character
and in metre, which among other things made
permanent in Latin literature and thus in the
continuous literature of Europe the most enduring lyric measures of the Greeks. That their
charm has survived the use to which they have
been put as models for the Latin verse-making
of generation after generation of English schoolboys may fairly be counted among the miracles
of literary history. But there was something in
Horace, as no one knew better than he, which
nothing can quite kill.

Of this, particularly as it appears in the Odes,
tradition has now so long been aware that one is
almost startled to find him mentioned by Dante
only as a satirist. When Virgil and Dante are
met by the sovereign poet Homer[1] in the placid
shades where the great of antiquity live hopeless
yet longing, he is close followed by Ovid, Lucan,
and "Orazio satiro." [2] On reflection, however,
it is not strange that at various times the Satires
have seemed better than the Odes, just as the Odes
seem better to-day. The substance of satire is
easier to understand than that of any poem whose
merit lies greatly or even partly in lyric beauty;
the temper of satire, ridiculing foibles and denouncing abuses, subtly appeals to that com-
placent love of self-righteousness which lurks in
most of us; and the moral pretension of satire,
even though not always genuine, is apt at once
to make an unresisting reader forget for a while
that he is little better than one of the wicked,

[1] Inferno, IV, 79–102.　　　[2] Ibid., 89: "Horace the Satirist."

and to pacify the frequent discomfort of con-
sciences doubtful whether they may rightly enjoy entertainment without edification. The form
of Latin satire, too, presents to anybody who has
studied Virgil far less difficulty than any lyric
measure. It is regularly written in hexameter
lines, comprehensible when you have caught the
rhythm of the Æneid, and at the same time
fascinating by reason of the great difference of
their effect from that of epic poetry. Any one
who knows the classic poetry of France may observe a similar variety in the Alexandrine couplets,
or quatrains if you prefer, which equally suit the
passion of Racine and the irony of Molière. Any
one who will turn to Dryden or to Pope may observe the same kind of range in the English heroic
couplet. For satirical purpose, the hexameter
line was never used more skilfully and happily
than by Horace. Lucilius, his chief predecessor
in this form of literature, wrote hastily and carelessly; Juvenal, the chief Latin satirist of a later
time, wrote with truculent intensity; Horace wrote
with exquisitely polished urbane ease. This, indeed, is not wholly a matter of form. Lucilius
before him and Juvenal after him—like satirists
in other tongues than Latin from the days of
Juvenal to our own—were often abusive. Compared with almost any other writer of satire,
Horace is not; he is said, indeed, to have called
these poems not Satires but "Sermones," which
means *Talks* or, if you like a big word, *Colloquies*.
To understand why, you must perhaps read all
eighteen of them;[1] if you lack time or patience for

[1] The most fluent English translation is Sir Theodore Martin's. One
could wish, however, that he had managed to combine his urbane ease with
a regular use of the heroic couplet. His various metres produce a less firm
effect than that of Horace's invariable though flexible hexameters.

this, you will go far on the way, and be amused while doing so, by reading only three: the Fifth of the First Book, which recounts the journey to Brundusium; the Ninth of the First Book, which describes an encounter with a bore in the Forum; and the Fifth of the Second Book, which professes to continue the interview between Odysseus, or Ulysses, and the shade of the blind prophet Tiresias in the Eleventh Book of the Odyssey. Here Ulysses is troubled about financial matters, and is gravely advised to supply his needs by one or another of the less admirable means, such as inducing a rich old man to name you in a will, believed to have been habitually resorted to by agreeable but penniless Augustans.

Had Horace written no more than the Satires, he would accordingly have been memorable. Historically, indeed, they sometimes appear the most interesting part of his work; for they give many quietly amusing glimpses of Augustan life, much as the Tatler and the Spectator, so often prefaced with gracefully translated lines from Horace, keep alive the London of Queen Anne. Like the English essayists, too, he indulges in a good deal of urbanely conventional moralising—never fervid enough to disturb you. By themselves, however, the Satires could hardly have made him the Horace of tradition. At least nowadays, and for a good while past, he has been as conspicuously the author of the Odes as Virgil has always been of the Æneid. The name *Odes*, by the way, is not that by which they were called in Latin; their original title is *Carmina*, or *Songs*. This term, which instantly avoids any confusion of them with the Pindaric and choral odes of Greece, most conveniently describes or defines them.

Whether they were actually sung or not, to begin
with, their purpose, like that of the songs of
Burns or of the Irish melodies of Moore, is essentially lyric.

They are lyrics, at the same time, with at least
two other than purely lyric features: they were
studiously intended finally to domesticate in
Latin, as they did, the loveliest poetic measures
of the Greeks; and throughout them you will
find compactly sententious phrases, not Greek but
Latin in impulse, which express once for all—
beyond any power of translation—the things they
mean. To take three or four random, hackneyed
examples, nothing but the words themselves can
ever say just what is compressed into phrases like

> Integer vitæ scelerisque purus,[1]
> (Flawless of life and pure of guile),

or

> Eheu fugaces, . . .
> Labuntur anni,[2]
> (Alas, . . . the fleeting years flow past
> unmarked),

or

> Odi profanum volgus et arceo[3]
> (I hate and spurn the unholy crowd),

or

> Dulce est desipere in loco.[4]
> (It's pleasant to be careless when we may.)

---

[1] I, XXII, 1. I cannot resist the temptation to place beside these words,
and the quotations which follow, the prose into which the conscientious
editor of the Loeb Classics edition of the Odes (1914) has thought proper
to render them. Here he writes: "He who is upright in his way of life
and unstained by guilt."

[2] II, XIV, 1, 2: "Alas . . . the years glide swiftly by" (Loeb).

[3] III, I, 1: "I hate the uninitiate crowd and keep them far away" (Loeb).

[4] IV, XII. 28: "'Tis sweet at the fitting time to cast serious thoughts
aside" (Loeb).

It is probably this exquisite finality of expression,
rather than the almost faultless grace of his lyric
measures, which keeps the Odes of Horace perennial. The very first of those four phrases, however, will serve to remind us how little tradition
understands him. Taken by themselves, the words
"Integer vitæ scelerisque purus" appear to summarise with grand simplicity an almost holy ideal
of human character; thus they are quoted now,
and thus gravely chanted. In the Odes, they are
the pleasantly ironic opening of what has properly
been called a decorous comic song. Substantially,
this goes on to say with demure grandiloquence
that while this excellently sincere poet strolled in
the woods, composing a song about a pretty young
person named Lalage, a wolf who caught sight of
him turned tail and ran away; and the last two
lines of the Ode—

> Dulce ridentem Lalagen amabo,
> Dulce loquentem[1]—
> (Sweetly laughing, sweetly talking Lalage
> I'll love)—

are about as far as can be from anything serious.
Not that Horace was never in earnest; but you
have to watch carefully if you would make sure
whether he is or not.

To do so, you must know him well; and there is
hardly a poet in European literature more willing
and ready to be pleasantly known. Beyond almost any other he keeps familiar ease secure from
the imprudent dangers of undue familiarity. As
you grow to know him, too, you will feel that

[1] I, XXII, 23-24: "I will love my sweetly laughing, sweetly prattling
Lalage" (Loeb).

throughout his literary life he slowly and gently matured. His earlier Satires and the book of Epodes[1] which preceded the Odes appear, in the perspective of his complete work, comparatively coarse; at least you can detect there some vestige of his obscure origin, and feel what he meant when, years later, he wrote of himself as "ex humili potens"[2] (From humble state exalted). He was a man of his Augustan time, too. He lived from the years when since long before living memory Rome had been convulsed by civil wars into the tranquil dawn of Roman peace; and he welcomed both the authority and the reforms of the strengthening Empire, reviving the traditions of the Roman past, social and religious, encouraging the gracious influence of the Greeks peerless for their intelligence and their fine art, and stimulating the pursuit of truth by philosophy. To understand his Odes you must keep all this in mind. You may understand them best, indeed, when you look back at them after reading his latest and ripest works, the Epistles.

Of these there are two Books. The first contains twenty letters, widely various in length and topic; the second contains only two, both rather long, and both concerned with general principles of literature; with this second group they sometimes place the separate letter commonly called De Arte Poetica (On the Art of Poetry). All of these poems, like the considerably earlier Satires, are in hexameter verse; all use this verse with a studied yet colloquial ease of idiom, perhaps most nearly paralleled in English by the Imita-

[1] This word seems to mean something like *couplets* or *echoes*.
[2] Od. III, XXX, 12: "Risen high from low estate" (Loeb).

tions of Horace where Pope most clearly disclosed
his own lack of urbanity. If it were not for the
snarling animosity of our most eminent Queen
Anne poet, his composite Epistle to Dr. Arbuth-
not, otherwise called the Prologue to the Satires,
might now and again seem almost Horatian.
Nothing can seem anywhere near completely Horatian, however, at least when we come to the
mature Horace of the Epistles, unless the sensi-
tively urbane lines, at once colloquial, sententious,
and final, set forth what you instinctively feel to
be sincere philosophic purpose—an honest effort
to perceive and to say something as near truth as
human conditions will allow. The details of any
philosophical system, like those of any state of
religion, at which now and again we may have to
glance, are evidently beyond our present scope.
So to expound the views of Horace in other words
than his own, or to trace them to their clear or
conjectural sources, is happily no business of ours
now. Two facts, indeed, concerning the Epistles
as they complete his work are perhaps enough to
touch on here.

In the first place, when at last you think of his
writings from beginning to end, you can hardly help
believing that he really held such purpose as he
set forth in the Epistle to Mæcenas which stands
first in his First Book. Three Books of the Odes
had certainly been published, and with unsurpassed
success, when he wrote the lines[1]

[1] Ep. I, I, 7-12:

> Est mihi purgatam crebro qui personet aurem:
> "Solve senescentem mature sanus equum, ne
> Peccet ad extremum ridendus et ilia ducat."
> Nunc itaque et versus et cetera ludicra pono,
> Quid verum atque decens, curo et rogo et omnis in hoc sum;
> Condo et compono quæ mox depromere possim.

Go where I will, unceasingly I hear
A voice that whispers in my well-rinsed ear:
"Cast the old horse in time, before he fall
Dead lame, and halt, the gibe and jeer of all."
So verses now and all such toys I quit,
Work night and day to find the true and fit,
The lore of sages cull where'er I may,
And hive it up for use some future day.
                              (Sir Theodore Martin.)

Those who know him best assure us that from the first Satires and the Epodes through the Odes to the last of the Epistles they can feel, for all his urbanity, his tact and his occasional courtliness, something like a constant growth of polite earnestness both philosophic and, like that of all sincere philosophy, religious. Antique religion variously differed from what our ancestral generations of Christianity have made the word religion mean for centuries—and never more obviously than when the growth of Roman Empire had mingled the perhaps thin deities of early Rome with the vagrant gods of decadent Greece and with the more mysterious divinities of the East or of the unchanging ages of Egypt. But Rome could never have been Rome without the spirit which was destined to animate the Catholic Church. Horace was no prophet, as some have thought Virgil; he was no dissembled preacher of the gospel, as some have thought Seneca, two or three generations later; but like all good men he grew more serious with the years, and like all good fellows he grew so gently.

In the second place, when you want to know what he means, you must be on your guard against conventional distortions of his meaning. The first example of this danger which comes to mind will serve as well as a dozen to indicate it. The Sixth Epistle of the First Book—a poem discussing the general question of how to make life most nearly tolerable—begins with the lines:

> Nil admirari prope res est una, Numici,
> Solaque quæ possit facere et servare beatum.

(Not to be wonderstruck, Numicius, is almost the one and only thing which can make and keep a man happy.)

This translation of the first two words into four is clumsy enough, if you please. The first comment on them which comes to hand states them to signify "the *ataraxia* of the Epicureans," a rendering certainly more learned and probably more exact. But the hobbling English is enough to remind us that the words "nil admirari," literally meaning "to admire nothing," and commonly quoted as if *admire* meant *approve*, are by no means intended to recommend fault-finding. What they really signify Sir Theodore Martin takes four lines to suggest:

> The best, indeed the only means I know
> To make men happy and to keep them so
> Is this, Numicius: never to admire
> With too great fervour or too great desire.

The Latin word *admirari* implies rather surprise and wonder than approbation; at least in America, the English word *admire* has come to imply enthusiastic if uncritical delight in the object of admiration. So, believing themselves disciples of Horace, Americans too greatly desirous of turning up their noses are now and again apt to display the too great fervour expressly condemned by the two words they conventionally misunderstand.

We have lingered over Horace perhaps too long; but he is of the few with whom one can hardly help lingering. His own lines about himself, in the Ode which closes his Third Book,[1] prophetically summarise his history through the centuries.

> Exegi monumentum ære perennius,

they begin (I have made a record to outlast bronze);

> Non omnis moriar,

he writes five lines lower (Not all of me shall die). And the reason is that first of all, from humble state exalted, he has brought the songs of Greece into the verse of Italy.[2] He was right. For hundreds of years between his time and ours, Greek was little known in Western Europe. There has never been a time, though, when Grecian melody, in Horatian guise, has not gladdened all Europeans who would listen. Even still, most of us who come to know it at all know it first through him.

IX

ELEGIAC POETRY

TIBULLUS, PROPERTIUS

If our object were seriously to study Latin literature, we should now have to consider with care a kind of poetry, contemporary with the full powers of both Virgil and Horace, at which, con-

[1] III, XXX.   [2] Lines 9–14.

cerned only with the traditions of European literature, we need no more than glance. Among the
standard forms of Greek verse had immemorially
been the elegiac couplet, at once described and
exemplified in English by Coleridge's lines[1]:

In the hexameter rises the fountain's silvery column,
In the pentameter aye falling in melody back.

The grace and ease of this couplet, preserving the
grandeur of the hexameter yet recurrently soften-
ing its effect, had led to considerable development
of it, often for the expression of amatory senti-
ments, among the polished though not unduly
fervent poets of Alexandria, of whom Callimachus
is now perhaps the most nearly remembered. Catullus, to go no further, had already used it in
permanent Latin. Though such lines as his "Odi
et amo," [2] however, are tremendously intense,
their most ardent admirer can hardly hold them
mellifluous. To attain anything like the Augustan
polish of Virgilian hexameters, or of Horatian
Alcaics and Sapphics, the Latin Elegiac Couplet
needed development from the state where Augustan literature found it.

This development was duly given it by three
poets, one of whom died some years before Virgil,
one in the same year with Virgil, and the third
only three years later, when Horace had some eight
years more before him. Of the first, Gallus, only
fragments have survived. Of the two others,
Tibullus and Propertius, we have quite enough to
give us a clear impression not only of how they
wrote but of what they were like. Both, accord-

[1] See p. 37.   [2] See p. 216.

ingly, are worth reading and worth knowing.
However well you come to know them, nevertheless, you can hardly fail to find them comparatively
secondary, in genuine passion to Catullus, in
range and power to both Virgil and Horace, and
in traditional importance to the copious popularity of Ovid, whose work was presently to eclipse
theirs.

They are doubtless distinct. Tibullus, a few
years the elder, has a sweetness of expression, and
sometimes of sentiment, which has won affection
from those who know his verses well; these have
been sympathetically translated into English by
Theodore Williams,[1] on whose versions of Virgil
we touched a little while ago. Propertius, who
seems to have come to Rome from Assisi, thus
first and faintly brought into literary tradition,
has more power, but less amiable quality, and is
generally the object rather of admiration than of
spontaneous liking. For our purposes, however,
we may here think of them not separately but together. In the year 25, when Augustan empire
was at last apparently secure, both were writing,
and neither was thirty years old. Ten years later
both were dead. The work of both is wholly in
elegiac verse, which both use for various purposes,
Tibullus with more tenderness and more sensitive
understanding of nature and friendship, Propertius with more fervour, more feeling for Roman
grandeur, and more attention to mythology. Both,
meanwhile, are most instantly remembered, at
least traditionally, for the kind of sentiment which,
each individually, they set forth in common.
Both had, or as poets pretended to have, rather

stormy experiences in the matter of love. Neither was a miracle of constancy. Tibullus writes, at different times, of two mistresses, whom he calls Delia and Nemesis; Propertius, though he admits occasional vagrancy, reciprocated by his mistress, celebrates only the lady whom he calls Cynthia. In both cases, the love poems are not very systematically arranged, and the surviving texts, particularly of Propertius, are technically as well as otherwise corrupt; Roman love affairs at their best were not chivalrously romantic. Granting this, you may still extract from the poems of each what may very likely be, as is generally assumed, a true story of Augustan love, where the lovers and their mistresses are both human and individual. So, unless your mood be prying, you need not trouble yourself with the question of whether the stories are duly conventionalised records of amatory fact or only finished specimens of amatory poetical conventions. Should this question possess you, there can be little doubt that these elegiac lovers and mistresses appear comparatively unreal, or at best shallow, when you compare them with Catullus and Lesbia; but that they similarly appear haplessly human when you place beside them the pretty lyrics in which Horace touches on his pleasures with Lalage[1] or Neæra.[2]

Some such perplexity, you may presently remember, besets the love-poetry which came into literature twelve or fifteen hundred years later— the Sonnets of Italy and, to go no further, of Elizabethan England. Petrarch, Sidney, Spenser,

---

[1] *E. g.*, Odes I, XXII.

[2] *E. g.*, Odes III, XIV. The last stanza of this ode is particularly Horatian. The poem begins by celebrating the victorious return of Augustus from Spain. In honour of this event, the poet presently directs his

and Shakspere will occur to anybody; and perhaps also the fact that, though very likely make-believe, Laura, and Stella, and the nameless Dark Lady all seem genuine, while the seemingly cooler and more conventional sonnets of Spenser are almost demonstrably true. The one indisputable truth about all four is that Sonnet-sequences brought into literary tradition an exquisitely artificial kind of love-poetry which somehow seems at heart natural. Something very like this was brought into the lasting tradition of Latin literature by the elegiac contemporaries of Virgil and of Horace.

X

OVID

Tibullus and Propertius were probably old enough to remember the death of Julius Cæsar; Horace and Virgil were certainly old enough to remember the chaotic last days of the Republic. So the four Augustan poets on whom we have touched could personally feel the sense of relief and hope which the strengthening Empire brought

servant to go invite Neæra to sup, and incidentally to dress her hair prettily. But if she is "not at home," the invitation need not be pressed. Then comes the end:

> Lenit albescens animos capillus
> Litium et rixæ cupidos protervæ;
> Non ego hoc ferrem, calidus juventa,
>   Consule Planco.

(Grizzling hair cools tempers eager once for quarrels and strife; I would not have borne this, hot with youth, when Plancus was consul.)

Taken by themselves, the first two lines are as gravely final as the opening line of "Integer vitæ." Taken by themselves, with their slightly melancholy rhythm, the words "Consule Planco" delicately express the sense of bright, vanished times one can remember. Yet really it is all a pleasantry.

to the Roman world. With Ovid, their only important successor in surviving Augustan poetry, the case was different. Born after the murder of Cæsar, and in the year when Cicero met his end, he could know only by tradition what had preceded the sovereignty of Augustus. As he wrote of himself, when old and exiled,[1] he had seen Virgil, and he had heard Horace read, but Tibullus had died too early to be his friend, so of all his predecessors he had personal relations only with Propertius—who had succeeded Tibullus as Tibullus had succeeded Gallus in the elegiac poetry where Ovid claimed for himself the fourth place. This claim has proved just. Without him Latin Elegiacs might be a matter only of literary history. From the times when his lines were written they have never been quite neglected; and though his longest work, the Metamorphoses, is in fluent and easy hexameters, all the rest we possess are in elegiac form.

He was a country gentleman, of comfortable means though not of high rank. After what would amount to a university education, supplemented by travel, he established himself at Rome when between twenty and twenty-five years old, not long before Virgil died. He had an appetite and an aptitude not only for letters but for fashion. Through more than twenty-five years, he thoroughly enjoyed a state of society the more agreeable because active interference in public affairs had become so nearly dangerous that prudent men and women of the better sort felt unusually free to pursue pleasure. In this pursuit Ovid eagerly joined, contributing to it not only a wel-

[1] Tristia, IV, X, 45-54.

come presence but an inexhaustible stream of
poetry which at once gratified and expressed the
fashionable temper of the times. After Horace
died, he had no conspicuous rival as a poet. If he
had died himself at fifty, his career—though by no
means exemplary—would have been among the
most cloudlessly happy imaginable. His last years
might seem pathetically different, if he had not
so incessantly and monotonously insisted on his
troubles. With little warning, he was ordered,
probably because he knew too much about the
misconduct of Julia, the profligate granddaughter
of Augustus, into exile at Tomi, on the Black
Sea, not far from the mouth of the Danube.
There he lingered on, in climatic and social discomfort and barbarian surroundings, until the
fourth year of the Emperor Tiberius. And thence
he sent back to Rome, year after year, the com-
plaining elegiac letters, reiterantly begging for
pardon, which are collected in his Tristia—or
Sorrows—and in his Epistles from the Pontus.[1]

This dismal conclusion of his always copious work
is at once very different from the beginning of
it and yet a direct result of his first poems. There
is little question that these were substantially what
we now possess only in a second and revised version, under the title of Amores, or Loves. Formally following the elegiac tradition then lately
established by Tibullus and Propertius, they set
forth with unprecedented ease and fluency the
story of his relations with a married lady whom

---

[1] There was a region called Pontus on the Black Sea; but this, well eastward on the North coast of Asia Minor, was nowhere near Ovid's place of
exile. So the words *ex Ponto*, in the current title of his Epistles, mean not
from Pontus but *from the Sea*.

he calls Corinna. Who she was nobody knows, nor even whether she may not have been mostly or wholly a creature of erotic fancy. The sure thing is that even in Augustan Rome these poems were so shamelessly audacious and at the same time so admirably turned as to make a success not only of skill but of scandal. If you wish an impression of their polite indecencies, you may get it from the comparatively rude Elizabethan translation of them attributed to Christopher Marlowe.

Somewhere between the last original version of the Amores and the revised form in which they survive, he appears to have produced at least many of the imaginary letters known as the Heroides. These purport to be more or less reproachful communications, made for despatch by something equivalent to the Roman post-office, from deserted heroines of legendary antiquity to their variously vagrant lovers. The first is from Penelope to Ulysses, there is one from Briseis to Achilles, another from Phædra to Hippolytus, another from Ariadne to Theseus, another to Jason from Medea; and so on. Perhaps the most nearly interesting now is that from Dido to Æneas, evidently made to challenge comparison with the Fourth Book of the Æneid. Nothing could be more fantastically and sentimentally artificial than such pretty nonsense, and compared with the Amores it lacks the spice of effrontery. Beyond question, however, it was not only welcome when it was written but was written well enough to be enjoyed at far later and different times; without it, to go no further, Michael Drayton would never have swelled the flood of minor Elizabethan poetry with his England's

Heroical Epistles, and without these our own minor romantic traditions might very likely have lost the names of Surrey and Geraldine. On the whole, however, this rather milder sort of thing can hardly have gratified literary appetites whetted by the Amores for still sharper savours. So Ovid, always ready to please with tongue or pen, presently brought forth what has been called the most immoral, though not the most demoralising, poem ever written by a man of genius. This is his Art of Love, which begins

> Si quis in hoc artem populo non novit amandi,
> > Hoc legat et lecto carmine doctus amet.
>
> (If any one here in Rome has not learned the art of loving,
> > Let him read this and, taught by the song he has read, make love.)

His ensuing instructions, which fill three elegiac books averaging more than seven hundred lines apiece, abundantly justify his promise. This time even Augustan fashion was aghast; and one technical reason for Ovid's exile, many years later, was pretended to be the corrupting influence of his Art of Love on general behaviour and morals.

If he had died at forty he would have left us only these variously erotic elegiac poems. His reputation would have been fashionable, frivolous, very scandalous, and not much more conspicuous than that of Propertius or Tibullus. The work on which his great traditional importance is based was produced, or at least made public, not in the last years of the First Century before Christ but in the first years of the Christian Era. This fact is worth remembering: at the date conventionally assigned to the birth of Christ, Ovid was the only considerable poet in the full flush of his power. It seems probable that he found his reputation, when well on in middle age, inconveniently juvenile; and that one reason why he devoted himself to work more apparently serious and more dignified in form was a desire to throw into shadow the prolonged indiscretions of his literary youth. Whatever his motives, there can be no doubt that almost as clearly as Virgil is traditionally remembered as the author of the Æneid, and Horace as the author of the Odes, Ovid is traditionally remembered as the author of the Metamorphoses.

All the rest of his work, though not forgotten, is comparatively secondary to this pleasantly rambling collection, in fifteen inexhaustibly fluent hexameter Books averaging more than eight hundred lines apiece, of the mythological stories still perennially familiar. The title, which means *Transformations*, indicates its only pretence to unity. Beginning with the miraculous transformation of chaos to order, proceeding with carelessly easy transition to the miraculous transformation of stones thrown behind them by Deucalion and Pyrrha into men and women, and so to the miraculous transformation of Daphne into a laurel-tree no longer alluring to the desires of Apollo, it goes on through numberless tales of miraculous transformation, each told with spirit and grace, until at the close of the Fifteenth Book it relates how Julius Cæsar was miraculously transformed into a star, and complacently ends

> Quaque patet domitis Romana potentia terris,
> Ore legar populi perque omnia sæcula fama,
> Siquid habent veri vatum præsagia, vivam.

(Wherever Roman power rules the world,
If poets say true, read by the lips of men
Throughout all time I shall live on in fame.)

Beside the similar words of Horace, "Exegi
monumentum ære perennius" and "Non omnis
moriar,"[1] these lines look trivial. The contrast
implies the difference not only between the two
men, but also between the earlier phase of Augustan poetry and the later. In fact, however, the
two predictions have proved equally true. Long
ago,[2] we reminded ourselves how the pretty stories
of Hawthorne's Wonder Book and his Tanglewood Tales come mostly if not wholly straight
from Ovid. So do almost all the images of mythologic antiquity familiar to us through the masterpieces of Italian painting. So indeed do by far
the greater number of impressions, distinct or
misty, which still make people feel as if they knew,
or ought to know but cannot quite remember, who
the creatures of immemorial Greek and Latin
mythology were and what they did. Wherever
you open the Metamorphoses and fall to reading a story or two, you will probably have the
double pleasure of surprise to find the story told
with such graceful animation, and of subtly com-
placent satisfaction that you were so well informed
as to have a bowing acquaintance with it already.
If you are learned enough, meanwhile, to play
with the original lines, you may very likely find a
distinct difference between the impression they
make and the impression made by an equal amount
of Horace or of Virgil. In either of these greater
poets you will incessantly come across long-since

[1] *Cf.* p. 256.   [2] *Cf.* p. 12.

proverbial phrases, which have so passed into
tradition that you knew the words without
remembering where they were originally used.
"Facilis descensus Averno,"[1] for example—"the
downward path is easy" roughly expresses what
this means—will be recognised again and again
by men who might be at pains to tell you much
about the interview of Æneas with the Cumæan
Sibyl; and thousands have known the words
"Integer vitæ"[2] without the slightest notion that
when first used they were not meant seriously.
With Ovid, on the other hand, you will more probably feel that, while each of his tales is familiar
yet perennially fresh, the copious words in which
he tells them have nothing like so often lingered
in traditional memory. Admirably felicitous, at
least, they have proved less enduringly salient.
Only one phrase of his instantly comes to mind
completely apart from its context. When Apollo
hesitantly allows Phaethon to take his place as
driver of the Sun, he warns him against the
dangers of going too high and thus getting cre-
mated, and of going too low and thus getting
smashed; and utters the prudent counsel "Medio
tutissimus ibis."[3] ("You will go safest in the middle.") The wisdom of this advice has proved
separately enduring. So, no doubt, have other
bits of Ovid: "Conscia mens recti,"[4] for example, which means "a clear conscience," and is
usually misquoted "Mens conscia recti"; or
"Tacitisque senescimus annis,"[5] which means
"we grow old in the silent years," a pretty way of
saying "without knowing it." But in the poems

[1] Æn., VI, 126. [2] Cf. p. 25. [3] Met., II, 137.
[4] Fast., IV, 311. [5] Fast., VI, 771.

of Ovid such more or less familiar expressions are
far less obvious than the familiarity of the stories
where they occur.

As a light story-teller, indeed, Ovid is unsurpassed. Those who know their languages best
often liken his temper to that of Ariosto, which is
most nearly approached in English by the comparatively ponderous and acrid Don Juan[1] of
Byron. The Fasti, or Holidays, which came
later than the Metamorphoses, has been less
popular; written in elegiacs, it is a calendar of
Roman festivals, arranged month by month and
celebrating with occasional narratives these frequent incidents of the Roman year, which were
something like the Saints' Days of our ancestral Church. Without the Metamorphoses, the
Fasti, only half of which has been preserved,
might hardly have lasted very long; those who
have read it, however, do not grudge their time.
A cursory but adequate summary of both poems
may be found in Church's little monograph on
Ovid.[2] To get any fair impression of why these
innumerable retellings of Greek legend in the
prettily and fantastically modernised terms of
Augustan Rome have stayed alive through almost
two thousand years, you must read them, at least
here and there, as they were written. This was
the highest form of contemporary poetry when
our Christian Era began.

The later works of Ovid concern his exile from
Rome. In various ways his elegiac letters—the

---

[1] Incidentally, as Byron rhymes Don *Juan* with *true one* and *new one*,
those learned moderns clearly err who pronounce this title "Whän," after
the Spanish fashion.

[2] Ancient Classics for English Readers: 1876.

Tristia and the Letters from the Pontus—are memorable; they contain many passages which imply the history of his time, and many others which express his haplessly unheroic yet not unamiable self. The last lines of the last letter from the Pontus[1] go far to summarise his lamentations through eight despairing years:

> Omnia perdididimus[2]: tantummodo vita relicta est,
> Præbeat ut sensum materiamque mali.
> Quid juvat extinctos ferrum demittere in artus?
> Non habet in nobis jam nova plaga locum.
>
> (I have lost[2] everything: nothing but life is left me,
> So that mind and body still may feel their woe.
> Why plunge the sword again into veins that are dry
> with bleeding?
> There is no spot in me where a wound can now
> be new.)

By themselves, at the same time, these prolonged though by no means unreasonable laments could hardly have given Ovid more traditional importance than he would have if he had written only the naughty elegiacs of his gay and fashionable youth. The beginning of his work and the end may never be neglected by those who would study the last twenty years of the reign of Augustus. What makes him enduring, however, and almost if not quite great, is the exhaustless animation with which he retold for his own times and thus for all future time the pretty mythologic tales already immemorially antique when he told them.

[1] Ep. ex Ponto: IV, XVI, 49-52.
[2] Latin literary idiom allowed the plural for the singular in the first person, much as English now requires it in the second.

XI

LIVY

Virgil and Horace belong to the first half of the reign of Augustus, and so do Tibullus and Propertius. Ovid, who wrote mostly in the second half of the reign, has carried us beyond the end of it, and also beyond the limit of the Century when it began; as he was past forty years old, however, when our chronology shifts we may fairly call him a man of the First Century before Christ. This is even more the case with Livy, the only important writer of Augustan prose. Though he died within a year or so of Ovid, he was hardly ten years younger than Virgil, and he was busy with his colossal work from long before the Æneid was published until well after the Tristia drifted moaning back from the Pontus. No other considerable Augustan writer could remember both the death of Cæsar and the accession of Tiberius. To find another example of memorable work contemporary at once with the rise and with the decline of the period where it belongs we must wait for sixteen hundred years. In this respect, the relation of Livy to Augustan literature resembles that of Shakspere, contemporary alike with Marlowe and with John Webster, to the Elizabethan drama.

Livy, to be sure, was nowise Shaksperean in range, in imagination, or in creative power. In two ways, however, his huge history—of which during some forty years he produced no less than one hundred and forty-two consecutive Books—dis-

tantly resembles the historical plays of Shakspere: it put hitherto more or less dry records into
a form so acceptable that though by no means authoritative it became and has remained a permanent source of historical tradition; and the sentiment of it throughout is contagiously patriotic.
Ab Urbe Condita Libri (Books from the Founding of the City) is the title now given it. Beginning with a compact but fluent summary of
events and sovereigns from the time of Æneas to
that of Numitor, Amulius, and Rhea Sylvia, it
gets in the fourth section of the First Book to the
twins, Romulus and Remus, brought forth by this
legendary Vestal, and to the wolf who suckled
them. From this point it proceeds, or rather it
proceeded, with the story of Rome until the death
of Drusus, adopted son of Augustus, and brother
of the Emperor Tiberius, in the year 9 Before
Christ. Livy is thought to have had in view
eight more Books, bringing the whole number to a
complete hundred and fifty, and carrying the story
of Rome to the death of Augustus. If so, he died,
past seventy-five years old, a little prematurely.
Since this regrettable event, besides, more than
a hundred of the Books he actually produced have
been lost. What we now possess are only two
fragments of the whole, the first ten Books, and
a group of twenty-five others, beginning with the
Twenty-first and ending with the Forty-fifth.
Apart from these, we know him only from compact
summaries of the lost Books made while they were
still intact. The first ten Books carry the story
of Rome from the legendary period of Romulus
to the year 293, when Rome was beginning to
master all the neighbouring Italian regions. The

twenty-first Book begins with the year 218, when
Hannibal was sweeping on to Italy; the thirtieth
Book ends with 201, when the triumph of Scipio
concluded the Second Punic War; the remaining
fifteen Books cover about thirty-five years, to the
year 167, when Roman power had begun to extend in every direction—to Spain, to Gaul, to
Syria, and to Macedon, for example. By that
time, Plautus was dead and the work of Terence
was beginning.

The very mention of these names may remind
us of how much the loss of Livy's later Books, and
almost a full hundred of them, may mean. Livy
himself was a gentleman of Padua, born in the
year 59, who came to Rome like Virgil full of such
patriotic feeling as was more fervent among the
newly constituted citizens of the Northern provinces than it then remained at the heart of the Empire. He began to write his history almost at
the time when the sovereignty of Augustus was
finally established. He kept on throughout the
reign, of more than forty years. As his compact
but fluent Preface indicates, his notions of history were by no means like those now prevalent.
He regarded its function as chiefly moral. "This
is the great advantage," writes his leisurely English translator, "to be derived from the study of
history; indeed the only one which can make it
answer any profitable and salutary purpose: for,
being abundantly furnished with clear and distinct examples of every kind of conduct, we may
select for ourselves, and for the state to which we
belong, such as are worthy of imitation; and carefully noting such as being dishonourable in their
principles are equally so in their effects, learn to

avoid them."[1] With this edifying purpose, he was by no means careful in scrutinising the authorities on which he happened to light. So, his first ten Books, particularly the first of all, which deals with the Seven Kings, are of little historical as distinguished from traditional value. When he tells of the Second Punic War, to be sure, he relies mostly on Polybius, a careful and intelligent Greek writer who was born a few years before the war ended, and personally knew the surviving Roman heroes of it.[2] Here Livy is consequently more nearly trustworthy; but we must remember, at the same time, that even here he is writing about events which occurred more than a century before he came into the world. When, somewhere about his seventieth Book, he came to the Social War, and then to the conflicts between Marius and Sylla, he was on firmer ground; for he was old enough to have known old men who could remember the times he dealt with. And his last thirty or thirty-five Books concerned matters within his own memory. He was fifty years old at the point where his history stopped. Not a line survives to show us how he could set forth affairs concerning which he was himself an increasingly contemporary authority.

It has often been supposed, accordingly, that if his later Books should ever be recovered they would flood with light nooks and corners of the

[1] Tr. George Baker (Philadelphia, 1823): I, 3. The original is far less diffuse: Hoc illud est præcipue in cognitione rerum salubre ac frugiferum, omnis te exempli documenta in illustri posita monumenta intueri; inde tibi tuæque reipublicæ quod imitere capias, inde fœdum inceptu, fœdum exitu quod vites.

[2] There is an admirably spirited Eighteenth Century translation of Polybius by James Hampton. The most recent translation, Shuckburgh's, though more accurate, is nowhere near so readable.

First Century which without them remain obscure. Perhaps they would. More probably, however, they might disappoint us. His moral view of history was generally accepted by his contemporaries, who were apt to class history with oratory, as a kind of literature whose prime purpose was to influence conduct. And his general opinion of his own times is implied in the passage of his Preface immediately following that on which we have just touched:[1] "Now, either partiality to the subject of my intended work misleads me, or there was never any state either greater, or of purer morals, or richer in good examples, than this of Rome; nor was there ever any city into which avarice and luxury made their entrance so late, or where poverty and frugality were so highly and so long held in honour; men contracting their desires in proportion to the narrowness of their circumstances. Of late years, indeed, opulence has introduced a greediness for gain, and the boundless variety of dissolute pleasures has created, in many, a passion for ruining themselves, and all around them. But let us, in the first stage at least of this undertaking, avoid gloomy reflections, which, when perhaps unavoidable, will not, even then, be agreeable." He had a deep sense of the past grandeur of Rome, of the fundamental unity of Roman history, and of the

[1] Tr. Baker, I, 3–4. Here is the original: Ceterum aut me amor negotii suscepti fallit, aut nulla unquam respublica nec major nec sanctior nec bonis exemplis ditior fuit, nec in quam civitatem tam seræ avaritia luxuriaque immigraverint, nec ubi tantus ac tam diu paupertati ac parsimoniæ honos fuerit: adeo quanto rerum minus, tanto minus cupiditatis erat. Nuper divitiæ avaritiam et abundantes voluptates desiderium per luxum atque libidinem pereundi perdendique omnia invexere. Sed querellæ, ne tum quidem gratæ futuræ, cum forsitan necessariæ erunt, ab initio certæ tantæ ordiendæ rei absint.

superb ideal of Roman Empire. This did not blind him to decadent aspects of the period when he began as the prose rival of Virgil and Horace, and ended as that of Ovid. As a moralist, therefore, he might have been the original of a fragment of Horace's Art of Poetry often quoted without the context which would distort the portrait:

> Laudator temporis acti,
> Se puero, castigator censorque minorum.[1]
> (A praiser of old times when he was young,
> A scathing critic of his juniors now.)

Thus, although by no means disposed to proclaim all right with the world, he was doubly acceptable to Augustus, who at once desired to emphasise the colossal unity of the Roman State from the very beginning and in spite of personal aberrations appears sincerely to have wished that Roman character and conduct might be restored to something like the traditional austerity of the past. So Livy, in his own day, set forth what people generally assumed that history ought to be; and there was never a period when people were more profoundly disposed to think what ought to be preferable to hard and ugly fact. Except incidentally, therefore, his account of his own times may have been rather moralised than authoritative.

His traditional eminence is nevertheless deserved. He was not only the single writer of Augustan prose who could claim anything like such distinction as that of his contemporary poets, Virgil, Horace, and Ovid. He was a great master of narrative, too, a story-teller remarkable for the skill with which he told his stories. He was a mas-

[1] Horace: Ars Poetica: 173-174.

ter of literary oratory, as well; the speeches which occur throughout his work, though now variously old-fashioned, were originally among the passages most genuinely admired. More signally still, he was accepted by his own times, and indeed almost until ours, as the standard authority on Roman history; the tradition of the Roman Republic, through the centuries of European literature, has been based on what Livy wrote about it. And what Rome thought of him when he had hardly faded from living memory is best told in the words of Quintilian, the most eminent critic of literature under the Flavian emperors. Admitting Homer the first of poets, Quintilian asserts Virgil to be the second, and nearer the first than the third.[1] In elegiacs, he proceeds, Latin has rivalled Greek:[2] of this form he holds Tibullus the chief master, but he admits that some prefer Propertius; Ovid he finds too lewd, and Gallus too harsh. Satire[3] he says is wholly Roman; and the best satirist is not Lucilius but Horace.[4] "In history, too," he goes on a little later,[5] "I would hardly yield to the Greeks, nor fear to compare Sallust with Thucydides. And Herodotus will not object if we call Titus Livius his equal for matchless eloquence, not only in wonderfully pleasant and excellently hon-

[1] Quintilian: Inst. Orator. X, 1, 86: Secundus est Virgilius . . . propior tamen primo quam tertio.

[2] Ibid., 93: Elegia quoque Græcos provocamus.

[3] Ibid.: Satira quidem tota nostra est.

[4] Ibid., 94. Multo est tersior ac purus magis Horatius, et ad notandos hominum mores præcipuus.

[5] Ibid., 101. "At non historia cesserim Græcis, nec opponere Thucydidi Sallustium verear. Neque indignetur sibi Herodotus æquari Titum Livium, cum in narrando miræ jucunditatis clarissimique candoris tum in concionibus, supra quam enarrari potest eloquentem: ita quæ dicuntur omnia cum rebus tum personis accommodata sunt. Affectus quidem, præcipue eos qui sunt dulciores, ut parcissime dicam, nemo historicorum commendavit magis."

est narrative but also in speeches. Everything he says is thoroughly adapted both to his subjects and to his characters. No historian, in short, has ever more appealed to sympathies, particularly of the best kind."

Like Ovid, Livy outlived Augustus and the Century when Roman Empire was finally established. Even more distinctly than Ovid, too, he was a man of that epoch. At the time of the Christian Era Ovid was not yet forty-five years old, and Livy was almost sixty. They were the only important writers then surviving from the Century which had also added to the traditions of European literature the names of Cicero, of Cæsar, of Lucretius, of Catullus, of Virgil, and of Horace. When the Century began, enduring Latin literature hardly existed. When it ended, the greatest works of Latin literature had been produced. Tradition has been right in placing there the Golden Age of Rome.

CHAPTER III

THE FIRST CENTURY OF THE CHRISTIAN ERA

I

HISTORICAL TRADITIONS

At the date conventionally assigned to the birth of Christ, the name Cæsar was that of a family which had produced two dominantly great men: Julius, already forty-four years dead, who had virtually established imperial sovereignty on the ruins of the Republic; and his nephew Augustus, who for some thirty years had actually exercised increasingly acknowledged imperial sovereignty throughout the dominions of Rome. The change which had come over the name Cæsar a hundred years later is the chief historical tradition left us by the First Century of the Christian Era. From a family name it had developed into an imperial title; and though the first twelve men who bore it may not yet have been set apart, as they were later, in a distinct group, we may confidently describe the Century, for our purposes, as that of the Twelve Cæsars.

No other tradition of it, through time then to come, gathers quite so portentous as this. The names of the Cæsars have never been forgotten; even though we can hardly know what manner of human beings they really were, there have collected about each of their names more or less distinct char-

reign of Domitian to this day. The mould in which he cast wit remains unbroken. One perplexing result follows. Even Herrick, and still more Jonson, permits himself a degree of obscenity, of coarseness, and of vituperation which any one who knows Seventeenth Century England—the England of the Pilgrims and the Puritans, of the Authorised Version of the Bible and of Oliver Cromwell—must instantly perceive to give a distorted or at best a very incomplete notion of the world they wrote in. An obvious reason for this is that writing at a time with a great future before it they modelled their work on Martial's, produced when imperial antiquity was on the verge of its decadence. Classic now for eighteen hundred years, Martial has been traditionally held more certainly authoritative. But quite apart from his own countless passages which are free from evil, there is fair reason to doubt whether even Flavian Rome was quite so black as he often seems to paint it.

VI

THE YOUNGER PLINY

To correct or modify a too vile impression of Roman society under the Flavian emperors, one need only turn to the Letters of the younger Pliny.[1] Compared with their models, the far more numerous and less meticulously revised letters of Cicero, they doubtless have a secondary aspect of studious artificiality. Taken by them-

---

[1] Melmoth's admirably sympathetic translation, of 1746, is happily reprinted in the Loeb Classic edition of the Letters. No translation of Cicero's letters is anywhere near so good.

selves they give a remarkably wide survey of life
and character from the standpoint of a cultivated
and prosperous Flavian gentleman. In this aspect as well as in the fact that each letter is
politely confined to a single subject, they have a
certain analogy to the English essays of Steele
and of Addison. Like these, too, they present in
a new light the conditions about them. If we
knew England from 1675 to 1725 only through
what may broadly be called the Comedy of the
Restoration, we might hardly suspect that it
contained such men as Sir Roger de Coverley.
If we knew Flavian Rome only from the flash-
ing sketches of Martial and the lurid memories
of Juvenal, we might never dream that such men
as Corellius Rufus[1] and Spurinna,[2] or such women
as Arria[3] and the little daughter of Fundanus,[4]
were no less part of it than rascals like Regulus[5]
or the brutal slaves who played the devil with
Larcius Macedo.[6] The difference between the
Tatler or the Spectator and the Letters of Pliny
is that the former present life under the guise of
fiction and that the latter touch on it directly.
But so, to take another English example, does
Swift's Journal to Stella; and, to ramble on
through the later Eighteenth Century, the Letters
of Horace Walpole, the anecdotes in Boswell's Life
of Johnson, and the Journals of John Wesley are
contemporary.

The Letters of Pliny may here and there remind us of any or all of these, except that they are
revised in detail with something like Horatian
assiduity. You can hardly avoid the notion that

[1] Ep., I, 12.   [2] Ep., III, 1.   [3] Ep., III, 16.
[4] Ep., V, 16.   [5] Ep., I, 5; IV, 2, 7; VI, 2.   [6] Ep., III, 14.

when it came to style this excellent man attempted to out-Cicero Cicero, and therefore came nowhere near the comparatively free manner which often makes the letters of Cicero seem the best thing he left behind him. Apart from this polished hardness of surface, Pliny stays good reading still, particularly if you approach him, as you should always approach good reading, not too seriously. Turn his pages carelessly, as you might turn those of the Queen Anne essayists; read when the mood seizes you; and before long you will find, without knowing how, that he has given you a distinct notion not only of his amiable and accomplished character, but of the not yet desperate Roman world where he managed to keep out of serious trouble. His Greek philosopher, Euphrates,[1] for example, resembles Plutarch rather than the "Græculus esuriens"—which may be rendered in colloquial American terms "hungry little Dago"—of Juvenal.[2] His descriptions of country houses,[3] of natural curiosities,[4] of works of art,[5] and of literary pursuits[6] are very pleasant. His clear and interesting accounts of legal matters[7] deserve prayerful study by English and American lawyers who may prefer not to annoy their readers. And his Tenth Book, which consists wholly of his correspondence while a provincial governor with the Emperor Trajan, and appears not to have been

[1] Ep.. I, 10.
[2] Juvenal, III, 78. The well-known passage (58-80) where this occurs is worth comparing with Pliny's letter about Euphrates. Which seems more nearly true any one is at liberty to decide.
[3] E. g., Ep., I, 3; II, 17; V, 6; IX, 36, 40.
[4] E. g., Ep., IV, 30; VIII, 20, IX, 33.
[5] E. g., Ep.. III, 6; IX, 39.
[6] E. g., Ep., I, 8; VI, 21; VII, 4, 17.
[7] E. g., Ep., I, 20; II, 11, 14; IV, 9; VIII, 14.

elaborately revised for literary effect, has preserved an excellent model of what conscientious
administration ought to be.

Like the uncle who adopted him, he was born a
gentleman of Como, and passed most of his
life in high official and social condition at Rome.
Like many kindly men so circumstanced throughout history, he never forgot or neglected his native place, partly perhaps because there are few
more innocent joys than being recurrently welcomed home and heartily celebrated there as a successful favourite son. Apart from his letters about
the destruction of Herculaneum and Pompeii,
on which we have already touched,[1] his most
widely remembered are that concerning ghosts,[2]
and those which he exchanged with Trajan when
not quite sure how to deal with the uncompro-
mising behaviour of Christians in a world previously blest with religious toleration.[3] Even these,
we may fully admit, do not reveal him as exactly
a great man. If he had been, he could hardly
be accepted as beyond peradventure a typical
man of his time. The great must always be few
and solitary, rising constantly larger through the
perspective of the centuries. But only a time still
great could have bred so great a gentleman as we
come to know when we come to know the younger
Pliny.

VII

TACITUS

Whoever even begins to know the works of
Tacitus must instantly recognise him, too, as a

[1] *Cf.* p. 301.   [2] Ep., VII, 27.   [3] Ep., X, 96, 97.

great gentleman. At the same time he reveals himself, at least in literature, as a great man. The facts of his life are little known. We have glimpses of him in a dozen or more of Pliny's Letters,[1] one of which, addressed to him, begins "I predict, and I am apt to be right, that your histories will last."[2] They were evidently intimate friends, sympathetic too as officials and as men of letters. His wife was a daughter of Agricola, whose career, as he has recorded it, was among the most wholesomely distinguished of the First Century of the Cæsars. But where he was born, who were his ancestors, and when he died nobody now knows. His grandeur therefore, strongly individual though he be, has a touch of half-Homeric impersonality.

A few things about him are nevertheless clear. Probably born under Claudius, he was undoubtedly old enough to remember the worst years of Nero and the revolutionary horrors of the year 69. Under Vespasian, he was already in office. He was fully mature under Titus and Domitian; and if he outlived Trajan, under whose beneficent rule his principal works were written, it cannot have been for more than a little while. His later years were passed, to be sure, not in the dark days of the First Century, but in the brighter days of the Second. His personal memories, however, included the most ominous threatenings of the rising deluge which before very long was to submerge antique civilisation. And as he wrote only of times within the memory of men whom he

---

[1] Duly specified, for a wonder, in the scanty index of the Loeb Classic edition.

[2] Auguror, nec me fallit augurium, historias tuas immortales futuras. Pliny, Ep., VII, 33.

knew well, if not within his own, the final effect
of his work is like that of a grim epilogue to the
world-tragedy whose buoyant prologue was written a thousand years before in the Iliad and the
Odyssey.

His literary manner—style if you prefer the
word—has the conscious oddity of a time when
ingenious phrase-making had long been the fashion. He could master, however, a tendency which
masters most men. The power of his compact
words more than redeems their artifice; they defy
at once forgetfulness and alteration. To take a
few examples, of widely different kinds, try as
long as you like to put into English an aphorism
imbedded in the noble paragraph which closes
his life of Agricola:[1] "Is verus honos, ea conjunc-
tissimi cujusque pietas." What it means is clear
enough: "True honor is the loving respect of all
who are nearest"; but this gives hardly more
notion of what Tacitus has said than if the words
meant different things. Or take his statements of
a healthy virtue and of an insidious vice observa-
ble among the German Barbarians: "Sera juvenum
Venus," he writes,[2] "eoque inexhausta pubertas"
("Their animal passions come late, so they breed
with full vigour"); and again,[3] "Sine apparatu,
sine blandimentis expellunt famem; adversus sitim
non eadem temperantia." ("Without sauce or
ceremony they get rid of hunger; in combatting
thirst they are less moderate.") These English
words tell what he means but not how he put it;
you would be at pains to imprison in any other
terms than his the implicit sarcasm with which
he calls to mind the juvenile lasciviousness of

[1] Agricola, 46.   [2] Germania, 20.   [3] Germania, 23.

imperial Rome, and the profligate extravagances
of Roman feasting. Passages from his historical
work are still more characteristic. His narrative
is too trenchant for disguise even by translation.
Whoever has read of Galba's end,[1] and Otho's,[2]
and that of Vitellius,[3] can hardly forget how the
surging mob in the Forum overwhelmed the
stern old man for a little while imperial, or how
nothing in the life of the usurping Neronic deb-
auchee became him like the leaving it, or how the
Roman populace watched as they would watch a
show the last attempt to withstand the victorious troops of Vespasian on behalf of the fat sovereign whose end was too ugly to be pitied. "De-
formitas exitus misericordiam abstulerat"[4]—are
the four words which those last eight feebly try
to represent in English. It is just as useless to
attempt translation of the eight Latin words in
which Tacitus tells how when the terrified Vitellius
was beaten to death the crowd abused him as
vilely as they had fawned on him when he was
alive: "Vulgus eadem pravitate insectabatur inter-
fectum qua foverat viventem."[5] No other words
than his own can quite reproduce the power with
which Tacitus makes one feel the momentary thrill
of horror when frightened lookers-on suddenly perceived that Galba—the first fleeting incarnation
of Cæsar who could nowise claim kinship with the
mighty Julius,—was falling before their very eyes:
"Neque populi aut plebis ulla vox."[6] ("Neither
gentle nor simple uttered a single sound.") We
need his own very syllables fully to marvel at the
tremendous antithesis with which he contrasts the

---

[1] History, I, 39–41.   [2] Ib., II, 46–49.   [3] Ib., III, 82–86.
[4] Ib., III, 84.   [5] Ib., III, 85.   [6] Ib., I, 40.

opinions concerning Otho and Vitellius entertained
by Romans uncertain as to which must presently
be their sovereign: "Vitellius ventre et gula sibi
inhonestus, Otho luxu sævitia audacia reipublicæ
exitiosior ducebatur."[1] ("The belly and gullet
of Vitellius were held damaging to himself; the
lechery, cruelty, and recklessness of Otho more
threatening to the State.") And, memorable
though the passage be in any form, none but
those who have compared translations with the
original Latin can ever fully appreciate the firm
strokes of Tacitus when he records how the stanch
Helvidius Priscus behaved in the Senate on the
accession of Vespasian.[2]

Apart, however, from a style so individual that
if it fail to dominate it may repel, Tacitus has
qualities which no translation can obscure. He is
the last of the four great antique writers of history—the form of literature least damaged by
rendering into other languages.[3] He bears to
Livy, so far as Livy now survives, a relation analogous to that borne by Thucydides to Herodotus.
That Livy is less powerful than Herodotus is
pretty clear; that Tacitus can hold his own beside Thucydides is a tenable opinion. He lacks,
no doubt, the large primality of Greece; but no
subject comparable in range with the imperial
dominion of Rome could possibly have tested the
strength of a Fifth Century Athenian. And this
imperial dominion Tacitus exhibits to us in three
distinct aspects. His Life of Agricola presents
it as on the whole it must have appeared to those

[1] *Ib.*, II, 31.   [2] *Ib.*, IV, 4-8, and *cf.* 43.
[3] And the translations of his History and his Annals by Church and
Brodribb are admirably readable

beyond its range; here at last was an organised
system which could reduce the warring world to
wholesome and orderly peace, capable too of em-
bodiment in commanders as imposing for their
virtues as for their discipline of what otherwise
might have been only colossal brute force. His
book about Germany presents, as nothing else
comes near presenting, the barbarian vigour constantly and everywhere threatening the Roman
frontiers. The task of Roman Empire was not
only to bring order out of chaos within its bounds;
it must also resist incessant external pressure,
urged on by obscure forces—remote, shadowy,
exhaustless—which were ultimately to prove insuperable. If Tacitus had written only these two
monographs, he would have left us a uniquely
distinct record of how Rome was conditioned
throughout the first Century of the Cæsars.
Yet, even when considered together, the monographs appear of only secondary importance beside
his two greater works. His History originally re-
counted the story of Rome from the accession of
Galba until the death of Domitian; his Annals, a
vast preface written later, begins with the accession of Tiberius and originally extended to the
death of Nero. Though a great part of each has
been lost, enough remains tremendously to indicate the disease already fixed upon the Roman state.
To survive, Rome had need of health superb as her
strength; and she was stricken with a sickness beyond all medicine. Thus trebly presented, the
Empire resembles a clear-skinned giant overawing
enemies while cancer gnaws at his vitals.

Whether the story be altogether and positively
true is another question. That he meant it to

be we can hardly doubt; nor yet that his treatment of it went far to fix in tradition the view of it which has generally prevailed. A familiar passage from the Annals[1] will serve at once to illustrate this and to suggest his limitations as an authority. It tells of the great fire at Rome under Nero, and how the Emperor thought well to hold the Christians responsible for the disaster. It speaks of them as generally "hated for outrageous misconduct,"[2] and as an example of such moral filth as pours into a capital, "where from far and wide abominable and shameful things of all kinds gather together and are welcomed."[3] It implies that guilty or not they were on hateful terms with humanity.[4] His compact account of their martyrdom, to be sure, which immediately follows, would hardly displease John Foxe himself. Nobody, however, would dream these outcasts to be professors of the principles of the Gospel, and parishioners of Peter and of Paul; and nobody can deny that the historian who thus misconceived them is the same on whom we must chiefly depend for our belief in the abominations of Nero. Yet, right or wrong, that belief has been rooted in European posterity. The truth or the falsity of it need not concern us now. Our business is with the traditions of European literature. When we come to these we may well stay uncertain whether any writer of history has ever been greater than Tacitus, the last great historian of classical antiquity. A period which could produce, amid all its confusions, a figure such as his was not yet altogether decadent.

---

[1] Annals, XV, 38–44.   [2] Per flagitia invisos: XV, 44.

[3] Quo cuncta undique atrocia aut pudenda confluunt celebranturque: Ib.

[4] Haud perinde in crimine incendii quam odio humani generis convicti sunt: Ib.

VIII

JUVENAL

The last unquestionably great Latin writer lived at this time still great; thus chance, perhaps, has assured his greatness. Though little is definitely known about Juvenal, there can be no doubt that under Domitian he was a contemporary of Martial, of Pliny, and of Tacitus; that his relations with persons of condition were less cordial or less pliant than those of his friend Martial; or that he outlived the others. One tradition has it that, exiled in Egypt, he died there at eighty some two years after Antoninus had succeeded Hadrian as emperor. Though he chiefly wrote, however, in the freer days of the Second Century, his opinions of the world had become fixed in the First. The Fourth Satire, which burlesques Domitian by pretending that he summoned his Privy Council to decide how the largest turbot ever caught should be cooked, happens to be fixed in historic time; and substantially the lines which fix it apply to the other fifteen Satires as well. All are based on what existed

> When the last Flavian flayed the fainting world,
> And Rome still cowered before a bald-head Nero.[1]

During that period, to be sure, Juvenal appears prudently to have occupied himself not with satire but with the far safer pursuit of rhetoric, then used mostly as an elaborate exhibition of ingenuity. Our nearest approach to it nowadays

[1] Sat., IV, 37–38:

> Cum jam semianimum laceraret Flavius orbem
> Ultimus, et calvo serviret Roma Neroni.

is probably a conventional debate for a prize where, whatever the issue, the affirmative and negative sides are assigned by lot. Practice of such performances, though often leading to skill in popular appeal, is favourable neither to judicial opinions of life nor to sensitive personal sincerity. If you win your point, you have done your job; if you have done your job, you are noisily commended; and if you are thus commended for work well done, it is hard, at least for you, to avoid the conclusion that you are an unusually weighty moralist. This is particularly the case when you happen, in the turmoil of this world, to find yourself an under dog or even only to sympathise with such luckless animals. Juvenal was apparently beset by both of these insidious temptations. His Fifth Satire and his Seventh describe the plight of penniless literary Romans in terms generally thought to be personally reminiscent; and if any great European writer has ever assumed more incessantly than he that whatever prevails is therefore all wrong, the fact remains unremarked.

The form of satire, which he finally chose to set forth his views and of which he has proved the most influential exponent, is generally held the chief contribution of Latin to the tradition of world-literature. Every other form used by the lasting Roman writers—from Plautus to Tacitus— was more or less modelled on primal Greek masterpieces. No Latin imitation of Aristophanes, however, if indeed any ever amounted to much, has been preserved. The kind of discontent which animated Fifth Century Greek comedy developed in Latin a comparatively independent variety of expression. Even Lucilius, to be sure, who first

brought satire into literature during the Second
Century before Christ, so far yielded to Greek
allurements as ultimately to abandon all metres
but the originally Greek hexameter, thereafter accepted as the regular satirical vehicle of Rome;
but the Greeks seem never to have used it for precisely such purpose as, by Juvenal's time, was
already classical among the Romans. The principal satirists before Juvenal were the now lost
Lucilius and the still extant Horace and Persius.
Whether they would have sufficed to make satire
more than a minor form of European literature
may be disputed. When Juvenal had done his
work, he had not only obscured his predecessors
for all future time; he had made formal satire as
important as most forms of literature brought
into being by the Greeks.

Without troubling ourselves to define it, for
nothing is much more futile than to attempt precise definition of artistic matters and then worry
whether a given work comes within the limits,
we should probably agree that satire, as we know
it, is apt to be an appeal to dormant or dominant
prejudice. It assumes something, anything, or
things in general to be wrong or ridiculous. It
assumes itself, and anybody who will sympathetically listen, to be intellectually and often morally
superior. It exaggerates and denounces; it is
often clever and trenchant; it is sometimes fervid but seldom kindly. When it does not make you
resentful it grins or shames you into acquiescence.
It permits itself excursive liberties of structure;
whatever comes to mind at any moment may pop
out if to the point. Formal satire, to be sure,
is not at present the fashion; nowadays men find

any too firmly precedented artistic traditions life-lessly formal. But nothing can ever suppress the most powerful piece of satirical writing in our English language—the Gulliver of Swift. This exhibits individual man first as a giant among pygmies who can subdue him by their countless numbers; next as a pygmy among giants, the stupidest and pettiest of whom has enough brute strength and careless thoughtlessness to frustrate his best wits; then as sane in a world of madmen; and finally as foul amid the clean simplicities of beasts. "Sæva indignatio" (raging wrath) are the words chosen by Swift to describe in his epitaph how he writhed under the whips and scorns of time. With less lifelong meaning they might equally be applied to the political mood of James Russell Lowell when he threw off the Biglow Papers—the most nearly lasting expression of satiric temper as yet produced in the United States of America.

A frequent though not necessary phase of such temper is implied in the dialect made familiar by the stinging lines of Lowell. It purports to be the speech of plain folks as distinguished from those who have been trained in polite amenities, of the simple as distinguished from the gently nurtured, of your every-day hard-headed Yankee. A healthy fashion used to describe such men as the common people, thereby recognised as the source of common-sense. Nowadays we are apt to leave out the adjective, to use the word *people* not as Lincoln used it, including all sorts and conditions of men, but as if only the lowly could rightly claim rights. One consequent difficulty met us a little while ago;[1] when Tacitus described the thrill of

[1] *Cf.* p. 317.

JUVENAL 325

horror in the Forum as the crowd saw Galba top-
pling, he used the words "Neque populi aut plebis
ulla vox"; we now have no terms exactly to define
his distinction. We clumsily contented ourselves
with an inadequate translation: "Neither gentle
nor simple uttered a single sound." Both *populus*
and *plebs* we might carelessly have translated by
the same word, *people*. But *populus* implies responsibility, meaning people of the better sort;
and *plebs* implies irresponsibility such as we now
associate with people of the lower sort, sometimes
described by our comparatively new word *mob*.
The compilers of Sir James Murray's New English
Dictionary have discovered no earlier use of this
now established word than an evidently slangy one
in 1688, the last year of King James II; and they
note a comparatively familiar deprecation of it by
Addison in 1711.[1] It is really a contraction to a
single syllable—something like that of *bus* from
omnibus—of the Latin words *mobile vulgus*, which
mean the *unstable crowd*, such as Shakspere shows
us in Julius Cæsar and in Coriolanus. Its classical origin may be a line from the Tristia of Ovid,[2]
where after mentioning how shadows evident in
sunlight disappear when clouds gather he goes on

> *Mobile* sic sequitur fortunæ lumina *vulgus*.
> (So fickle crowds follow the rays of chance.)

That fickle crowds are not ill disposed, the scene
where Coriolanus presents himself as candidate
for the consulship[3] reminds us quite as clearly as
it exposes their fickleness; and that all the fault is
not theirs duly appears in the scene which follows.[4]

[1] Spectator, 135.
[3] Coriolanus, II, 3.
[2] Ovid: Tristia, I, 9, 11.
[4] Coriolanus, III, 1.

But they are not to be depended on for anything more than community of crude human emotion. This was memorably expounded some years ago by Monsieur Lebon, whose "Psychologie des Foules" has been at once summarised and anglicised by the playful translation of its title as the Psychology of Fools. The French word *foule* means very nearly what is meant by the Latin word *vulgus;* we have no exact English equivalent signifying numbers and implying a humanly fallible tendency to unreason and other imperfections of refinement. And by this time, our plunge into a mist of words and allusions may well have seemed to distract us from Juvenal. He has none the less been in mind all the time. Until we can feel with the mob, and welcome the dialect of Hosea Biglow, we can never understand either the pervasive subconsciousness of humanity or how uncompromisingly this underlies all trenchant satire. Classic though Juvenal's hexameters look, they are so saturated with springs of popular prejudice that their aroma has flavoured all the subsequent satire of Europe. And to describe the nature of this contagiously unamiable temper, our English language affords us no other word than what without our plunge, and perhaps despite it, would be the misleading term *vulgar.*

Unlike almost all the other lasting writers of classical antiquity, Greek or Roman, Juvenal was neither a person of quality nor disposed to gratify his betters. It is not from his temper but rather from his manner and his style—accidents of the period when he wrote—that we derive our impression of his grandeur. Compared with Tacitus and Pliny, he may sometimes remind us of Piers Plowman when compared with the Canterbury Tales. To know him you must doubtless turn all his pages more than once, and linger over phrase after phrase which has persisted through the ages: "Frontis nulla fides,"[1] for example (You can't trust looks); or

> Haud facile emergunt quorum virtutibus obstat
> Res angusta domi.[2]
> (It's hard for those to struggle up whose strength
> Is sapped in narrow homes);

or

> Sed quis custodiet ipsos
> Custodes?[3]
> (But who shall guard the guardians themselves?)

Standard English literature will nevertheless give you some impression of him. Truewit's comments on women in the Silent Woman of Ben Jonson[4] are an admirably free, and decently expurgated, translation into racy Jacobean English of passages from the Sixth Satire of Juvenal—itself the most unbridled denunciation of womanly misconduct in all the literature of Europe. And the two principal poems of Dr. Samuel Johnson—London and the Vanity of Human Wishes—are excellently lasting adaptations, by an Eighteenth Century English churchman, at the time a literary hack, of the Third Satire of Juvenal, which denounces Rome, and of his Tenth, which slashes rather than pricks the bubble of vanity.

As to the influence of Juvenal on our literature, you will find the Satires of Donne, although repellently crabbed and thus unlike him in style,

[1] Sat., II, 8.
[2] Sat., III, 164–165.
[3] Sat., VI, 347.
[4] Act II, Scene 1.

constantly inspired with his spirit and sometimes approaching his power. Without him Dryden could hardly have written Absalom and Achitophel, nor Pope when pretending to imitate Horace have been so bitterly un-Horatian. His temper underlies much of Byron's invective, such as occurs in English Bards and Scotch Reviewers. And the distorted perspective in which Juvenal sees the better classes of imperial Rome has been likened to that in which the far more sympathetic Dickens observes the better classes of Victorian England. He is rhetorical, he distorts and exaggerates; but he is fervid, and if not always and indisputably a sincere moralist he is at least sincere in his moral pretense; writing at a period still great, he writes in the grand style of classical antiquity; and while he thus appeals to the fastidious taste of culture, he veils under his grand manner a kind of feeling which those who would praise it will call popular, and those who would rather appraise it may more truly call vulgar. He speaks, perhaps, to the favoured few; but he speaks for the human, uncritical, suffering, and distorted many.

Another epilogue, if you like, you may find his work to the world-tragedy of which Homer made the prologue. He was contemporary with Tacitus. Both lived and wrote long after the year 100, but by the year 100 both were in full maturity of life and experience. We may best think of them, and of those who made literature about them, as then grouped together. As a group these men are secondary among the Latins only to the greater group which made the First Century before Christ the Golden Age of Latin Literature. Plutarch lectured and wrote in Greek for the same public which Martial, and the younger Pliny, and Tacitus, and Juvenal addressed in Latin. And the great literature of European antiquity ends with this Silver Age of Rome.

CHAPTER IV

THE SECOND CENTURY OF THE CHRISTIAN ERA

I

HISTORICAL TRADITIONS

As we have already seen, the memorable writers who came to maturity under the Flavians lived on and wrote long into the Second Century. Though they record or imply impressions and memories of terribly ominous and troublous times, they therefore survived to know something of what Gibbon summarised in his familiar sentence: "If a man were called to fix the period in the history of the world during which the condition of the human race was most happy and prosperous, he would, without hesitation, name that which elapsed from the death of Domitian to the accession of Commodus." [1]

Gibbon's Decline and Fall of the Roman Empire begins with an account of its condition during these halcyon days, and then tells its history from the death of Marcus Aurelius until the last trace of the Eastern Empire vanished when Constantinople fell before the Turks more than twelve hundred years later. The book is among the most remarkable ever written. The first volume appeared in 1776, the year of the American Declaration of Independence; the last in 1788, the year before the Constitution of the United States went

[1] Decline and Fall: chap. III (ed. Bury, I, 78).

into operation. Professor Bury's introduction to what is now the standard edition[1] clearly specifies various aspects in which the colossal work is no longer quite authoritative. The marvel is that it remains on the whole what it probably will always remain—so comprehensive and so firmly outlined a record of European history through a dozen centuries that for any who wish to see in perspective the period between antiquity and modernity it can hardly be superseded. Furthermore it is a work of admirably readable literature. Its prejudice against Christianity no doubt makes its treatment of the religion which has long dominated Europe misleadingly unsympathetic;[2] but, to go no further, its accounts of two facts immeasurably important both traditionally and historically —Mahometanism[3] and the Crusades[4]—are probably the best ever written, at least for such purposes as ours. We cannot too often remind ourselves that our concern is not primarily with history or even with literature, but rather with the traditions assumed as familiar throughout the growing literature of Europe. The fact that Gibbon's work is itself a great traditional fact in English literature would alone bring it within our scope. And, quite apart from this, it so records the general traditions of European history from the Second Century to the Fifteenth, that whoever wishes to remind himself of them should always have it at hand.

The first three chapters of Gibbon[5] summarise the condition of the Roman Empire during the

---

[1] Seven volumes: London, 1900.

[2] The famous chapters on this point are XV and XVI (Bury, II, 1-139).

[3] Chapter L (Bury, V, 311-396). Chapters LI and LII continue the story (Bury, V, 397-494; VI, 1-61).

[4] Chapters LVIII, LIX (Bury, VI, 259-365).   [5] Bury, I, 1-82.

Second Century, which he generally calls "the age of the Antonines." For us the chief tradition derived from this period may rather be called that of the Five Good Emperors who succeeded the first Twelve Cæsars. From the accession of Nerva, in 96, to the death of Marcus Aurelius in 180, the Empire enjoyed a succession of sovereigns who, whatever their personal failings, so conducted affairs of state that they seemed to realise the imperial dreams already classically recorded in the Æneid.[1] Though Nerva, to be sure, lived only two years, and died before the Second Century had quite begun, his beneficent policy was continued and developed by his adopted heir Trajan, the first Cæsar not of Italian birth. Born in Spain, somewhere near what is now Seville, Trajan was already in the second year of his sovereignty, and well past the age of forty-five, by the year 100. The details of his life and reign need not concern us now. He left behind him a tradition so excellent that, although he was pagan, Dante preserves the legend of how his soul, permitted the grace of momentary infantile reincarnation, was duly baptised and thus admitted to Paradise;[2] and the column which commemorated him in his own Forum still stands at Rome less mutilated than any other monument now so old there. He had no son, and probably adopted as heir the kinsman who succeeded him, Hadrian.

Under Hadrian the boundaries of Roman power were for a few years at their widest; and something like personal memories of him traditionally linger. That his presence left his name in such diverse parts of the Empire as Britain, where he built the

[1] Cf. pp. 188, 201; Æn., VI, 679–901.   [2] Paradiso, XX, 103–117.

first Roman wall, and Athens, where the ruins of his buildings are almost as apparent as those of his stupendous villa at Tivoli, and Egyptian Thebes, where an inscription on the singing Memnon is said still to record the fact of his visit, proves how widely he surveyed his dominions. The Castle of San Angelo at Rome was originally his domed tomb. The lovely images of Antinous combine with the tender legend of this favourite's fate to soften the mood in which we might judge his infirmities. And the lines which he is believed to have composed as a farewell to life are lastingly and sweetly human:[1]

> Animula vagula, blandula,
> Hospes comesque corporis,
> Quæ nunc abibis in loca,
> Pallida, rigida, nudula,
> Nec ut soles dabis jocos?

> (Gentle breathlet, ever fresh,
> Guest and comrade of the flesh,
> Whither goest thou now away,
> Pale and stiff, unclothed of clay,
> Laughing no more, no more at play?)

His adopted heir, Antoninus Pius, was emperor through more than twenty years. No reign ever more justified the saying that periods of happiness are without history; in tradition Antoninus hovers indistinct but benignant. His adopted heir and successor, Marcus Aurelius, was as good a man. Walter Pater's Marius the Epicurean introduces him in a story, itself almost if not quite literature, full of the spirit of his time. Though he con-

---

[1] See Spectator, No. 532 (10 Nov., 1712); and Elwyn and Courthope's edition of Pope (London, 1871), VI, 187, 393, 397.

scientiously opposed as revolutionary the conduct
of the Christians, his Meditations, which he jotted
down in Greek, prove him at heart to have been
something like a Stoic saint. The column raised
in his memory at Rome remains there the only
rival of the column of Trajan; and his equestrian
statue, now long placed on the Capitol hill, has
never been overthrown. With him ended the
period of imperial beneficence begun by Nerva;
it had lasted almost eighty-five years.

Justly or not, tradition represents the wives
of Antoninus and of Marcus Aurelius, both named
Faustina, as luxuriously corrupt. The elder Faustina left no son; the younger bore to Marcus
Aurelius the son who succeeded him, the Emperor
Commodus. His reign of thirteen years resembled those of Nero and of Domitian. Debauchery
and tyranny led to his murder. Then ensued
a brief parody of the appalling year 69, more
than a century before, when Galba, Otho, and
Vitellius had quivered momentarily imperial
between the last of the Julian dynasty and the
first of the Flavian. For some three months
Pertinax—traditionally only a cloudy name—
was emperor; he was killed by his own guards,
who are said thereupon to have sold the sovereignty to the highest bidder, Didius Julianus.
Three months later they had murdered him, too;
and the succession of the Cæsars had passed to
an able general of African birth, Septimius Severus.
In the year 200 he had been emperor for seven
years; he lived for more than ten years longer.
Among the shapeless ruins on the Palatine Hill,
those of his palace are perhaps the largest—they
say it was once seven stories high; and his

triumphal arch is the only monument of the Forum now imaginably recognisable by eyes that saw Rome in its splendour.

As we shall remind ourselves by and by, other Cæsars have lingered in tradition; but no subsequent line of imperial succession is anywhere near so distinct as the Twelve Cæsars of the First Century and the Five Good Emperors of the Second. Something of what impended may be felt by any who will call to mind again the works of art on which we have casually touched. The column of Trajan has something like Augustan dignity; the portraits of Antinous despite their beauty are sentimental; the column of Marcus Aurelius and still more his bronze statue appear in comparison almost rude; and the sculpture which frets the triumphal arch of Septimius Severus looks rather barbaric than classic. Gibbon was right in beginning with the accession of Commodus his tremendous narrative of the decline and fall of the Roman Empire; and we may believe ourselves equally right in summarising the Second Century of the Christian Era, the last full century of classical and purely European antiquity, as the Century which added to the historical traditions of Europe the stately line of the Five Good Emperors—Nerva, Trajan, Hadrian, Antoninus, and Aurelius.

II

LITERARY TRADITIONS

SUETONIUS, APULEIUS, PERVIGILIUM VENERIS;
LUCIAN, GALEN

Compared with the two First Centuries, before and after Christ, during which almost all the great extant writers of Latin literature came into existence, the Second Century is nowhere. In the year 100, to be sure, many of the writers grown to mature years under the Flavian emperors had not yet produced the works which make them enduring. But if we ask for names virtually unknown when the Second Century began, recognised when it ended, and still in some kind of existence, we shall find them surprisingly few and impressively unimportant. Suetonius and Apuleius are the most memorable Latin authors; whether the anonymous Pervigilium Veneris, which here and there may remind one of the lines attributed to Hadrian, was written under the Antonines or a century or two later may never be quite settled. Apart from these, our literary traditions from the Second Century are not Latin, but at least in language Greek. We have already touched on Plutarch, a full contemporary of the writers whom we have grouped as Flavian, and on the Greek Meditations of the last of the Good Emperors, Marcus Aurelius. When we were concerned with the First Century, we may remember, we mentioned nothing Greek at all; that period, indeed, was so rich in Latin that we did not even glance at Vitruvius, whose famous Latin treatise on architecture was written under Augustus, any more than when concerned with the great centuries

of Greece we had found place to touch on the
medical tradition of Hippocrates. In the Second
Century, Latin literature so subsided that we can
hardly help noticing, together with the Greek
dialogues of Lucian, the Greek medical works
of Galen.

None of the men of letters who came into
existence during the Century is comparable in
scale with their predecessors. Historically the
most considerable is probably Suetonius. He
was a younger friend of the younger Pliny; he
was more or less of an official, at one time a sort
of private secretary to the emperor Hadrian;
some indiscretion is thought to have caused his
retirement from public life; and almost throughout the reign of Antoninus Pius, he devoted his
later years to industrious literary leisure. Much
of the fruit of this is lost. The work by which he
is permanently known is his anecdotic biographies,
in eight Books, of the Twelve Cæsars. The six
emperors of the Julian line are given a Book apiece;
Galba, Otho, and Vitellius are put together in
the Seventh Book, and the three Flavians in the
Eighth. The new succession of Good Emperors,
under whom these accounts of their predecessors
were written are left untouched, much as Shakspere in his plays concerning English history
wrote nothing about the Tudors until, well after
the Stuarts had succeeded them, he had a hand
in Henry VIII. And it may be that the traditional group of the Twelve Cæsars originated
in the fact that these and only these were recorded
by Suetonius. For just his task he had more than
one qualification. He liked gossip; he was by
way of hearing court gossip concerning both
present and past under Trajan and Hadrian; and

at least in Hadrian's time he probably had access
to the long-since lost private archives of the
Cæsars. For many details about them, some not
scandalous, he has always been the principal
authority; he is a principal source, as well, of
the most abominable traditions about them indel-
ibly fixed in European memory. That he wrote
under what was virtually a new dynasty may rouse
our suspicion when we consider him as a serious
historical authority. Nothing can avert his importance in anecdotic tradition. And there can
be little question that he is the most important
historical writer of the Century succeeding that
which began when Livy was still at work and
ended when Tacitus, though not yet a great author,
was already mature.

Apuleius, the other Latin writer of the Second
Century who has indisputably survived, was an
African rhetorician and philosopher, little and
inconspicuously at Rome. Whoever desires light
on his life and character may find it pleasantly
shed in Mr. H. E. Butler's translation of his
Apologia,[1] and the adequate introduction prefixed to it. This Apologia, to be sure, an elaborate speech in his own defense, is interesting mostly
as an example of what had happened, by the
Second Century, to such forensic eloquence as we
find in Cicero and in Demosthenes. Their rhetorical devices look fresh as nature when compared with the vivacious but extremely conventionalised artifices of Apuleius. His importance
in literary tradition is wholly due to another
piece of his work—the fantastic tale which he called
Metamorphoses but which has long been nick-
named the Golden Ass. The story, modelled

[1] Oxford, 1909.

like that of Petronius on a now lost Greek phase of fiction developed at Miletus in Asia Minor, tells how a by no means austere young man is magically changed into an ass, and after many—often unmentionable—adventures as a beast of burden is at last restored to human form. Here and there it may still be found faintly amusing; it contains incidental descriptions of daily life interesting to students of history; and some of its excursions into philosophy and the like are said to be very useful to those who would know how the Second Century was disposed to speculate. So far as Apuleius distinctly survives, however, it is only by reason of the skill with which he retells, as a long episodic story, the world-old legend of Cupid and Psyche.[1] Walter Pater's version of this is perhaps the most surely delightful passage in Marius the Epicurean.[2] The tale is charmingly pretty; for all its sentimentality it has not only sweetness but significance; yet it is further even than Suetonius from what still suffused the writings of Tacitus and of Juvenal—the grandeur that was Rome.

So too, if indeed it belong to this period at all, is the anonymous Pervigilium Veneris, with what Marcus Dimsdale[3] calls "its haunting refrain":

Loveless, mayst thou love to-morrow; loving, still to-morrow love.

This translation has the unusual merit of preserving not only the meaning but the exact rhythm of the original Latin line:

Cras amet qui nunquam amavit; quique amavit cras amet.

---

[1] It runs from Book IV, 28 to Book VI, 24 (Loeb, 185–285).
[2] Part I, chap. 5. [3] Latin Literature (1915), p. 528.

The poem where it recurs is a kind of pagan hymn, probably composed for some festival of Venus. Though it may possibly be as late as the Fourth Century, it may have been written during the Age of the Antonines. Compared with anything on which we have as yet touched, except the five lines of Hadrian, it has for modern ears the quickening charm of a lyric movement half-way between those of our own times and the strangely different lyric measures of the Greeks. It has beauties, too, which make one always glad that it has not been lost. But it is neither primal, like the beautiful works of Greece, nor grand, like the enduring works of Rome.

And this is all that in the perspective of time now stays surely visible of what Latin literature brought to birth during the Second Century of the Christian Era.

The introduction to Fowler's translation of Lucian[1] clearly tells all that is known about the most ingenious and most nearly popular Greek writer of this period. He was a Syrian, probably born under Hadrian and dead after Commodus. During the first half or more of his life he seems to have travelled widely, as a rhetorician and a lawyer; and it is noteworthy that, although he tarried and probably practised for some time in Italy and even in Gaul, he is thought never to have found need of mastering the Latin language.[2] His copious work during his later years, when he had turned from rhetoric and law to philosophy, took the form of animated, witty, and pregnant

---

[1] Oxford, 1905 (four volumes).
[2] This, we may remember, was the case with Plutarch; cf. p. 162. As for Lucian, see A Slip of the Tongue: Fowler, II, 34.

dialogues. Whoever has been able to read Greek has generally found them both entertaining and stimulating. At least two of our enduring literary traditions have proceeded from them: Shakspere's Timon of Athens is remotely derived from Lucian's Timon, or the Misanthropist,[1] and Swift's Gulliver from Lucian's True History.[2] Any student of his times should know him well. But the fact that he wrote only in Greek kept him a sealed book in Western Europe for hundreds of years; and in Greek literature he can never have quite such dignity as marked it when from Homer to Theocritus it was not only the primal but the only expression of the spirit later to be European.

Among the translations in the Loeb Classical Library, Doctor Brock's version of Galen's treatise on the Natural Faculties stands out as at once clear and readable. His introduction gives a compactly summarised account of Galen's position in the history of medicine. This evidently takes us pretty far afield. The name of Galen has always remained traditional. Precisely what he wrote is not generally remembered, nor is the fact —incidentally not indexed in Bury's edition of Gibbon—that he lived during the Age of the Antonines and is said to have been consulted by Marcus Aurelius. That no Latin work nor any considerable work of pure literature distracts from him now such cursory eyes as ours, throws light or shadow, as you will, on the condition of European literature when the Second Century came to an end. The great literature of Rome was also a thing of the past.

[1] Fowler, I, 31.   [2] Fowler, II, 136.

CHAPTER V

THE ROMAN TRADITION

Though by the year 200, classical Latin literature, like Greek before it, was already classic,
there was no cessation of writings in the Latin
language. As the official language of the Roman
Empire, this was used and more or less understood for centuries throughout the civilised world.
Except for the prevalence of French since the reign
of Louis XIV, it has never been even remotely approached as a vehicle of communication among
Europeans whose native languages were different.
Until something like modern times, it stayed everywhere the standard language of law, of learning,
and of serious literature. The Divine Comedy of
Dante, written after 1300, is the first great and
enduring European poem ever composed in any
modern tongue. Even in the Nineteenth Century,
any educated European could be assumed able to
decipher a Latin letter. And to this day, as
everybody knows, Latin remains the world-wide
language of the ancestral Catholic Church. In
one sense, therefore, it has never died.

Its history as a still living language, however,
differs from that of Greek. There has never
been a time since the days of Homer when Greek
was not a language in which living men habitually thought and talked, and they do so still;
there has hardly been a time for more than a
thousand years when Latin was not, even among

those who knew it best, a foreign language learned at school, just as it is now. In this sense, Latin has long ceased to be humanly idiomatic. There is some reason, too, for believing that classical literary Latin was never humanly idiomatic at all. The classical Greek writers, believing everybody but Greeks barbarian, had before them only the simple problem of expressing what they had to say in the language which to them was native. When Romans attempted to make literature they were aware that admirable literature already existed in Greek. Their problem was to rival this in a language held by the Greeks comparatively barbarous. What is more, for all its sententiousness, it really was a far less flexible and sensitive means of communication. To improve it, at least from times before Cicero, they laboriously tried to make it as like Greek as they could. The more nearly they succeeded, the less it resembled the thoughtless dialect of their daily life.

At its best, accordingly, literary Latin was elegantly artificial; and all the while men were using with careless freedom such colloquial Latin as occasionally appears in the fragments of Petronius. One sometimes wonders whether the monkish Latin of the Middle Ages may not be about as like the every-day talk of imperial Rome as the speeches and essays of Cicero are, or the studied classics of the Augustans and the Flavians. Beyond question, this barbarous Latin of the times between antiquity and modernity served two purposes: as we have already seen, it was a useful international language; and whoever could easily use it had learned in the process to read currently not only classical Latin literature but also the numberless important works composed in Latin long after ancient Rome was dead and gone. To take a single random example of these, the Principia of Isaac Newton, which in 1687 set forth the doctrine of gravitation, was written in Latin as a matter of course. One curious result of the disuse of Latin since the Eighteenth Century has been futile effort to invent completely artificial languages, like Esperanto, for accepted international use; and one reason why worthy people persevere in such effort ingenuously revealed itself a few years ago. An ardent French advocate of Esperanto, setting forth its merits to an American friend, was nowise disturbed by the suggestion that a simpler plan would be to revive the old international language, current Latin, which had long served its purpose and already had a priceless literature. To this apparently wise plan, he said, there is an insuperable objection: no doubt Latin has proved admirable both for international communication and for literary purposes—"*mais, monsieur, c'est la langue de l'Eglise*" ("but, sir, it is the language of the Church"). All who deplore the influence of Christianity, should therefore do all they can to suppress Latin. At present the tendency of popular education appears to be in their favour. The prospects of Esperanto nevertheless look hardly auroral; and as long as the Church persists, Latin will considerably survive.

Evidently, at the same time, this modern phase of Latin has in common with almost everything written since the Second Century a feature which marks it as different from Latin literature and tradition before that period. We need hardly remind ourselves that even more than when we were touching on the traditions of Greece[1] we have left unnoticed much that would demand the attention of serious students, nor that we shall have to neglect more still, as we proceed to later times. All we can attempt is to call clearly to mind, century by century, what now seem the chief things added by each Century to European tradition. Thus regarded, we found that up to the Second Century before Christ European tradition, so far as it came to literary expression, was only Greek. To this Greek tradition the next four hundred years added that of imperial Rome, different, nearer to us in other aspects than mere time, assuming the primal traditions of Greece and unwittingly interposing itself between them and the future, but still—so far as we have yet considered it—purely European. Thus, in such perspective as ours, the traditions of classical Rome group themselves with those of Greece, clearly distinct from any later. For classical antiquity was pagan, and later Europe has been Christian, and Christianity—whatever else—is not of purely European origin.

Hereafter, Christian tradition becomes for our purposes increasingly important. Before long it had so blended the other than European traditions of the Jews with the traditions of Greece and of Rome that European tradition has never since been quite free from Asiatic. Our next business is evidently to consider Christianity. Before doing so we have only to define our impression of the condition in which it found the antique traditions of Europe.

[1] *Cf.* p. 153.

In the first place, as we have already reminded ourselves again and again, the secondary traditions of Rome, assuming and appropriating the primal traditions of Greece, had not supplanted these but had so mingled with them that only the critical scholarship of recent times has restored them in anything like their original lustre to the general knowledge of Europe. Even still we are carelessly apt to think of Greece not as it was, but rather as it looked for centuries on centuries through the interposed veil of Rome. Secondly, the Romans, nowhere near the Greeks in intelligence or in artistic perception, were decidedly their superiors in common-sense. Their language has never been surpassed for sententious wisdom; nor their conduct for practical administrative and military organisation. In the third place, although they adapted and modified the primal types of literary expression originated by the Greeks, they added to them nothing more important than the stinging ends of Martial's epigrams or the formal satire which culminated in Juvenal. But, finally, their genius for government had fully developed, after centuries of legal and political experience, the colossal ideal of Roman Empire—of a world kept at peace by the righteous power of an all-embracing sovereignty. This ideal, no doubt, has never been fully realised nor often long approached. But we of the Twentieth Century need only watch how men are trying to establish a League of Nations to be sure that, in altered form, this ideal is living still. The genius of Greece tended to diversity; that of Rome to unity; and we of America cherish no ideal more clearly than our national ideal of Union.

One great tradition, the while, neither Rome nor Greece had ever originated. What most clearly groups them as purely European is that, like all subsequent Europe, they never brought into being an enduringly potent religion.